DATE DUE			

Computer Simulation
in
Management Science

Computer Simulation in Management Science

Michael Pidd

Department of Operational Research
University of Lancaster

JOHN WILEY & SONS

Chichester · New York · Brisbane · Toronto · Singapore

Library of Congress Cataloging in Publication Data:

Pidd, Michael.
Computer simulation in management science.

Includes index.
1. Management science — Mathematical models.
2. Management science — Data processing. I. Title.
T57.62.F5 1984 658.4′0352 83-14489

ISBN 0 471 90281 0

British Library Cataloguing in Publication Data:

Pidd, Michael
Computer simulation in management science.
1. Management games — Data processing
I. Title
658.4′0352 HD30.26

ISBN 0 471 90281 0

Typeset by Activity, Salisbury, Wiltshire and printed by The Pitman Press, Bath, Avon.

For Sally,
whose affection is no simulation

Contents

PART II: DISCRETE EVENT SIMULATION

Preface

This book concentrates on the topics of simulation, model building,, and programming. I hope that it will aid analysts and students who wish to produce working computer simulations.

There are 3 sections.

SECTION I (Chapters 1 & 2): FUNDAMENTALS OF COMPUTER SIMULATION IN MANAGEMENT SCIENCE

This is a general introduction to the simulation methods commonly employed in management science. It is non-technical and requires no skill in computer programming. As well as introducing the rest of the book for specialist readers, it will give MBA and undergraduate business students a useful over-view of the subject.

SECTION II (Chapters 3 to 8): DISCRETE EVENT SIMULATION

Chapters 3–5 are devoted to model building for discrete event simulation. Chapter 3 introduces commonly used terminology and presents activity cycle diagrams. Chapters 4 and 5 describe the event, activity, process and three-phase approach to discrete event modelling. Particular emphasis is placed on the three-phase approach first suggested by Tocher. Examples of three-phase programs in BASIC are provided. Chapter 6 reviews the main simulation software available. Chapters 7 and 8 are concerned with the statistical aspects of the subject.

SECTION III (Chapters 9–11): SYSTEM DYNAMICS

Chapter 9 discusses the principles of modelling the type of feedback systems found in organizations. Chapter 10 describes the system dynamics approach and Chapter 11 presents 2 successful case studies.

Left to their own devices, most people who can program a computer can produce some sort of simulation. However, their approach is usually *ad hoc* and takes far longer than they imagined at the start. In most cases, the model is over-complicated and the program has grown into something with no obvious structure. This makes it very difficult to be sure that the simulation results are valid. This is particularly true of discrete simulations. It may also be impossible to enhance the programs if that later becomes necessary. By following the principles described here, the novice should be able to produce well-structured programs which produce valid simulations.

I have displayed most of the examples as flow diagrams because my experience suggests that novices find these easy to follow. Most of the programs are written in a standard, but very restricted, dialect of BASIC. This may not be the ideal language for simulation, but it is widely available and is easy to learn. Any readers unfamiliar with BASIC but knowing FORTRAN, ALGOL or Pascal ought to have no difficulty in following the examples. To follow Chapters 7 and 8, the reader should be familiar with elementary probability and statistics.

In discussing continuous simulation methods, I have chosen to concentrate on systems dynamics as developed by Forrester. It could be argued that management scientists ought to use rather more sophisticated methods. However, for a variety of reasons, practitioners do not make much use of the continuous simulation packages of the type favoured by engineers. Despite its limitations, system dynamics does find some use in practice. Hence its inclusion.

The book should be of use to four groups of readers. As a whole it should be of use to management science students and practitioners who need a detailed knowledge of the topics. It should also be valuable to business students who need an appreciation of the main methods in use. Finally, it will be of value to computer science students who need to be able to produce software simulations.

I am grateful to a number of my colleagues at Lancaster. Brian Parker carried out the work described in Chapter 11 and also provided useful criticisms of the rest of Section III. Stephen Taylor patiently reviewed Chapters 7 and 8. Mike Simpson who unfortunately died suddenly in July, encouraged me to get down to the job of writing, having recognized that I am easily diverted. Margaret Threlfall escaped the task of typing up most of my hieroglyphics, because I chose to use a simple word processor. However, she coped extremely well with the mathematics which my word processor could not handle. I am also grateful to the anonymous reviewers used by John Wiley & Sons.

PART I

FUNDAMENTALS OF COMPUTER SIMULATION IN MANAGEMENT SCIENCE

Chapter 1

The computer simulation approach

1.1 MODELS, EXPERIMENTS AND COMPUTERS

Management scientists are not easily separated from their computers and with good reason. Since the 1960s, computers have become smaller, cheaper, more powerful and easier to use by non-specialists. In particular, the development of powerful and cheap portable machines has opened up wide areas of work for the management scientist. Modern computers allow the analyst to explore the whole range of feasible options in a decision problem. These options could be explored without a computer but the process would be very slow and the problem may well change significantly before a satisfactory solution is produced. With a computer large amounts of data can be quickly processed and presented as a report. This is extremely valuable to the management scientist.

One way in which a management scientist uses a computer is to simulate some system or other. This is generally done when it is impossible or inconvenient to find some other way of tackling the problem. In such simulations, a computer is used because of its speed in mimicking a system over a period of time. Again, most of these simulations could (in theory at least) be performed without a computer. But in most organizations, important problems have to be solved quickly. Hence the use of computer simulation in management science.

Computer simulation methods have developed since the early 1960s and may well be the most commonly used of all the analytical tools of management science. The basic principles are simple enough. The analyst builds a model of the system of interest, writes computer programs which embody the model and uses a computer to imitate the system's behaviour when subject to a variety of operating policies. Thus, the most desirable policy may be selected.

For example, a biscuit company may wish to increase the throughput at a distribution depot. Suppose that the biscuits arrive at the depot on large articulated trucks, are unloaded and transferred onto storage racks by fork trucks. When required, the biscuits are removed from the racks and loaded onto small delivery vans for despatch to particular retail customers. To increase the throughput, a number of options might present themselves to the management. They could:

— increase the number of loading or unloading bays;
— increase the number of fork trucks;
— use new systems for handling the goods;
etc.

It would be possible to experiment on the real depot by varying some of these factors but such trials would be expensive and time consuming.

The simulation approach to this problem involves the development of a model of the depot. The model is simply an unambiguous statement of the way in which the various components of the system (for example, trucks and lorries) interact to produce the behaviour of the system. Once the model has been translated into a computer program the high speed of the computer allows a simulation of, say, six months in a few moments. The simulation could also be repeated with the various factors at different levels to see the effect of more loading bays, for example. In this way, the programmed model is used as the basis for experimentation. By doing so, many more options can be examined than would be possible in the real depot — and any disruption is avoided; hence the attraction of computer simulation methods.

To summarize, in a computer simulation we use the power of a computer to carry out experiments on a model of the system of interest. In most cases, such simulations could be done by hand — but few would wish to do so. Now that microcomputers offer significant computer power for a minimal cost, a computer simulation approach seems to make even more sense in management science.

1.2 MODELS IN MANAGEMENT SCIENCE

Models of various types are often used in management science. They are representations of the system of interest and are used to investigate possible improvements in the real system or to discover the effect of different policies on that system. This is not the place for a detailed exposition of modelling; for this the reader should consult Rivett (1972), White (1975) or Ackoff and Sasieni (1968). However some mention of the topic is necessary.

The simplest type of model employed in management is probably a scale model, possibly of a building. By using scale models it is possible to plan sensible layouts of warehouses, factories, offices, etc. In a scale model, physical properties are simply changed in scale and the relationship of the model to the full-scale system is usually obvious. However, such simple scale models do have significant disadvantages.

First, a scale model is concrete in form and highly specific. No one would contemplate using the same scale model for a chemical factory and a school — the two require distinctly different buildings. More subtly, to experiment with a scale model always requires physical alteration of the model. This can be tiresome and expensive.

Second, scale models are static. That is, they cannot show how the various factors interact dynamically. For example, suppose that a warehouse is being designed. One issue that must be considered is the relationship between the internal capacity of the building and the number of loading or unloading bays provided for vehicles. Though it is easy to design a warehouse which always has enough internal space — simply make it too big — this is clearly a waste of money. Given that both the demand for the products and the production level will vary, the art is to design a building which balances the cost of shortages with the cost of over-capacity. Such a balance will vary over time, particularly for seasonal products. No scale model could consider this.

Management scientists tend to employ mathematical and logical models rather than scale models. These represent the important factors of a system by a series of equations which may sometimes be solved to produce an optimal solution. Many of the commonly employed techniques described in management science textbooks are of this form. For example, mathematical programming, game theory etc. For computer simulation, logical models are usually required — though in the case of system dynamics (see Chapters 9–11) these are expressed in a mathematical form. The simplest way of thinking about logical models is to consider flow diagrams of various kinds. Industrial engineers often employ flow process charts in method study (Hicks, 1977) to display the various processes through which products pass in their manufacture and assembly. That is, the charts display the logic of the production process. Such a chart might show that a car body needs to be thoroughly degreased before any painting can begin. Instead of drawing a chart it is possible to represent the logic as a set of instructions. If these directions are clear and unambiguous, then they could be used to show someone how to do the job.

Any sequence of unambiguous instructions can form the basis of a computer program. Hence programs can be written which embody the logical processes which make up the system of interest. Whilst many programming languages are not designed to ease this task of logical expression, there are simulation programming languages such as SIMSCRIPT (Markowitz *et al.*, 1963) and ECSL (Clementson, 1982) which do so. Once the model is programmed, it may be easily modified, for example to introduce more loading bays in a warehouse model, by editing the program.

Flow diagrams as such do have their uses in computer simulation. In particular, they are often used in the early stages of a computer simulation project. One type of flow diagram will be introduced in Chapter 3.

1.3 SIMULATION AS EXPERIMENTATION

Computer simulation involves experimentation on a computer-based model of some system. The model is used as a vehicle for experimentation, often in a 'trial and error' way to demonstrate the likely effects of various policies. Thus,

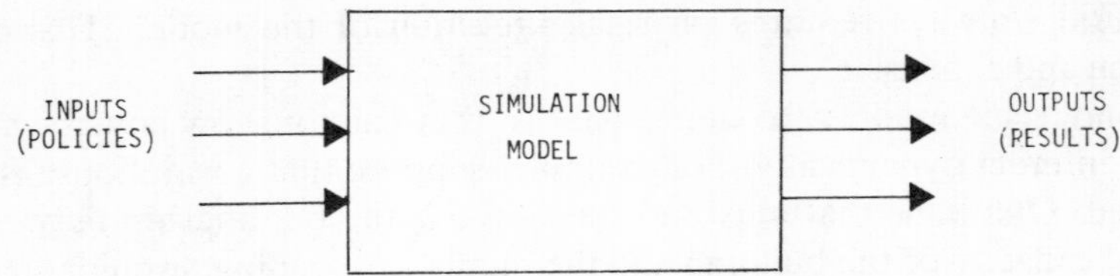

Figure 1.1 Simulation as experimentation

those which produce the best results in the model would be implemented in the real system. Figure 1.1 shows the basic idea.

Sometimes these experiments may be quite sophisticated, involving the use of statistical design techniques. Such sophistication is necessary if there is a set of different effects which may be produced in the results by several interacting policies. At the other extreme, the experimentation may be very simple, taking the form of 'what if?' questions. Thus, if the simulation model represents the financial flows in an organization over the next 12 months, typical questions might be:

'What if interest rates rise by 3%?'
'What if the market grows by 5% this year?'

To answer these questions, the simulation is carried out with the appropriate variables of the program set to these values.

An example of a more sophisticated approach can be found in the study described by McCurdy (1977). This was carried out for a motor manufacturer who wished to design a three-storey paintshop for a completely new car. Ideally, such a new paintshop would be all on the same level, but a shortage of land meant that three storeys were necessary. The floors of the paintshop were to be connected by automatic lifts in which the bodies would be carried. The nature of the processes meant that some of them had to be kept physically separate. For example, some of the preparation processes could not be sited next to the ovens because volatile solvents were to be used. Thus, as shown in Figure 1.2, the ground floor was to be two storage areas, one for the unpainted bodies arriving from the bodyshop and the other for painted bodies which had been through the paintshop. These painted bodies would later be required in the assembly area and it was important that they should arrive there in the correct colour sequence. The first floor was to contain all the processes necessary for preparing and painting the bodies and the second floor would house all the ovens through which the bodies passed after each coat of paint.

This outline design meant that each body would undergo a great many vertical and horizontal transfers. Indeed each body would require 14 transfers between floors via the automatic lifts. As most people know from their own experience, lifts do break down sometimes. This, combined with the possibility of stoppages in the main process, meant that some buffer storage would be needed — otherwise a breakdown or stoppage anywhere would bring the paintshop to an immediate halt. However, monocoque car bodies take up a

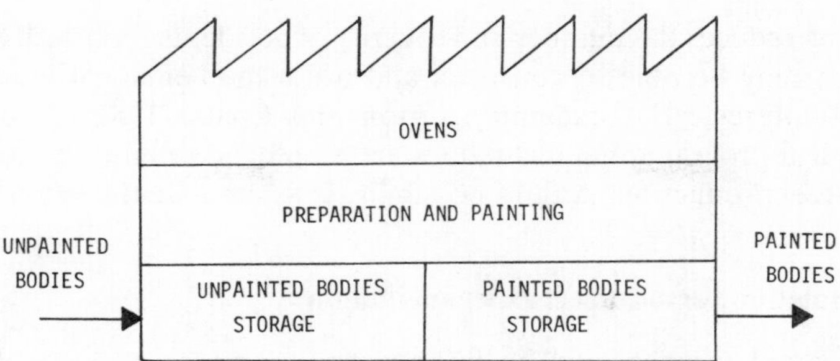

Figure 1.2 The three-storey paintshop

great deal of space and can only be stacked on racking. Thus the provision of storage space would be expensive and a limited budget meant that some sort of trade-off between output levels and in-process storage space was inevitable.

In order to provide this storage, various layouts were possible and therefore several versions of the simulation model were produced — each one representing a possible configuration. These models were then subject to inputs in the form of equipment failure rates, arrival rates of car bodies, size and location of buffer storage, track speeds, etc. In this way the possible dynamic operation of the various layouts was simulated over the equivalent of many real shifts. Great care was taken to ensure that these experiments revealed which of the various factors has caused the changes observed in the simulation. Thus it was possible to determine the sensitivity of output levels to the various configurations and to different assumptions about reliability and track speeds. From this, a design was developed which met the production targets whilst avoiding excessive expenditure on idle facilities. In particular, the designers were aware of the way in which each configuration would behave under extreme conditions.

1.4 WHY SIMULATE?

Certainly, computer simulation is no panacea. Realistic simulations may require long computer programs of some complexity. There are special purpose simulation languages and packaged systems available to ease this task, but it is still rarely simple. Consequently, producing useful results from a computer simulation can turn out to be a surprisingly time-consuming process. In one way, therefore, computer simulation should be regarded as a last resort — to be used if all else fails. However, there are certain advantages in employing a simulation approach in management science and it may be the only way of tackling some problems.

Assuming that a management scientist does not wish to make an instant 'seat of the pants' judgement of a particular problem, various modes of approach are possible. Firstly, it may be possible to conduct experiments directly on the real system. For example, the police may experiment with mock radar speed traps to see if this reduces the number and severity of accidents reported. Secondly, the analyst may be able to construct and use a mathematical model of the system of interest. For example, Sutton and Coats (1981) describe how mathematical programming techniques are employed to minimize the cost of stainless steel production. A third possibility is to simulate the system.

1.4.1 Simulation versus direct experimentation

Then why simulate when it will be time consuming and there may be alternative approaches? Considered against real experimentation, simulation has the following advantages.

Cost: Though simulation can be time consuming and therefore expensive in terms of skilled manpower, real experiments may also turn out to be expensive — particularly if something goes wrong!
Time: Admittedly it takes a significant amount of time to produce working computer programs for simulation models. However, once these are written then an attractive opportunity presents itself. Namely it is possible to simulate weeks, months or even years in seconds of computer time. Hence a whole range of policies may be properly compared.
Replication: Unfortunately, the real world is rarely kind enough to allow precise replication of an experiment. One of the skills employed by physical scientists is the design of experiments which are repeatable by other scientists. This is rarely possible in management science. It seems unlikely that an organization's competitors will sit idly by as a whole variety of pricing policies are attempted in a bid to find the best. It is even less likely that a military adversary will allow a replay of a battle. Simulations are precisely repeatable.
Safety: One of the objectives of a simulation study may be to estimate the effect of extreme conditions and to do this in real life may be dangerous or even illegal. An airport authority may take some persuading to allow a doubling of the flights per day even if they do wish to know the capacity of the airport. Simulated aircraft cause little damage when they run out of fuel in the simulated sky.

1.4.2 Simulation versus mathematical modelling

What then of the other possibility of building and using a mathematical model of the system? Here too there are problems. Firstly, most mathematical models cannot satisfactorily cope with dynamic or transient effects. For example, the steady state behaviour of the paintshop was of less concern to the motor manufacturer than the operation of the system after breakdowns. Secondly, though it is debatable (see Chapter 7) whether this is a good thing, it is possible to sample from non-standard probability distributions in a simulation model. However, queueing theory models permit only certain distributions and therefore cannot cope with many types of problem.

Computer simulation then may well be regarded as the last resort. Despite this, it is surprising how often such an approach is needed.

1.5 KEY PHASES IN COMPUTER SIMULATION

Assuming, and this is a big assumption, that the analyst and client have agreed which specific problems should be tackled, then the analyst may decide that it is sensible to follow a simulation approach. But how to proceed? Obviously, no two simulation projects will be identical but some generalization can be made. In particular, the simulation work of such a project can be viewed as having three phases:

— modelling
— programming
— experimentation

Because simulation is an experimental approach, modelling and programming can be regarded as preliminaries to the real business of simulation. That is, experimentation.

These three phases may be difficult to separate precisely in practice. It is difficult to program properly without an adequate model and experimentation is impossible without some working programs — nevertheless some overlap will occur. For instance, it would be foolish to ignore the programming implications of particular types of model. In this regard, Chapters 4 and 5 make clear the links between modelling and programming approaches. On another tack, it is inefficient to write programs in which it is difficult to reset the values of important variables for experimentation. Again, experience suggests that experimentation often leads to changes in the model and the program. Thus these three phases are intimately linked and this should not be ignored. However, it is still well worth considering each in turn.

1.5.1 Simulation modelling.

Chapter 2 introduces some of the choices to be made in deciding what type of simulation model should be built. Some type of model is essential in computer simulation, the real system being mimicked by unfolding the model through time. Whatever the type of model employed, it must be valid if it is to be useful at all. This may seem obvious — and it should. However, most management science is carried out under severe time pressure and validation is one thing easily pushed to the back of the mind when time is short.

What is meant by validity in this context? Usually it means two things that are closely linked. Firstly there is 'black box' validity; that is, ignoring the detailed internal workings of the model, does its output accurately reflect that of the real system? Would the manager of the system accept that the results of the simulation are effectively the same as those produced by his system? In this sense, black box validity is concerned with the predictive power of the model.

Does it adequately predict how the system would behave under given conditions? This is obviously a tricky question, but it must be faced.

The issue of black box validity is complicated by the common fact that the simulation may be carried out because something is going wrong with the real system. Even worse, it may be a simulation of a system that does not yet exist and there is nothing with which the model may be directly compared. In the example of the motor manufacturer quoted earlier (Section 1.3), the bodyshop did not exist — nor did anything like it. In this case it is only possible to validate the parts of the model and their links, hoping that the end result is satisfactory. Thus the operational research team working on the simulation of the bodyshop were able to compare the performance of their simulated lifts with those used in other factories.

The second consideration is that of 'white box' validity. Do the components of the model represent known behaviour and/or any valid theory which exists? One example of this is the process used to describe the arrival of customers at a queue. If the queueing system actually exists, then data may be collected which describe the arrival times of successive customers. At this point known theory can be useful. For arrival processes, certain probability distributions are known to provide a good description of the range of possible values which the inter-arrival time may take. For instance, if there is no pattern to the arrival times then a negative exponential distribution may be appropriate — particularly if the number of potential customers is very large. Should there be no explanation of why the arrival pattern should be so random, then the suspicion is heightened. If analysis reveals that the mean and standard deviation of the inter-arrival times have very similar values then the case for accepting a negative exponential distribution is very strong indeed. This is likely to be a valid representation of the arrival process. In this case then, the arrival component of the model was verified by reference to the appropriate theory. This implies that the analyst needs to be fully conversant with the relevant theory. The same applies in the forms of simulation used in economic forecasting. Here, the aim is to develop models which show the effect of the various competing theories.

Returning to the body shop simulation, full validation was impossible but some white box validation was possible. Consider again the lifts, the same types were being used by another manufacturer in France. Hence the trip times and failure rates of the lifts were modelled on the experience of the French users. As mentioned earlier, the result was that the simulated lifts behaved much as those in France. A similar approach could be applied to other parts of the model. This type of approach is far from foolproof. For example, temperature differences may cause different failure rates in the lift motors on different sites. However, such an approach is much better than nothing.

As well as the technical issues discussed in subsequent chapters, the analyst must be satisfied that he knows the system well enough to be sure that the model is valid. Without this knowledge, no amount of sophisticated programming and statistical wizardry will prevent the inevitable disaster.

1.5.2 Programming the simulation model

The technical issues involved in program design and the choice of appropriate programming languages are discussed in Chapter 6. Whatever the choice of programming language there is a growing tendency for a highly disciplined and structured approach to be taken to the programming. This is particularly important in large or complex programs. If large sums of money hang on the outcome of a computer simulation, then a professional approach is clearly necessary.

The modelling approaches described in Chapters 4 and 5 lead to programs with defined structures. In particular, the three phase approach (Tocher 1963) leads to programs with well-defined subroutines or procedures of a manageable size. This is to be encouraged for two reasons. Firstly, all programs need to be verifed; that is, the programmer should make certain that the program accurately reflects the model, the model itself having been validated. This is easier if the program consists of modules which can be individually tested. Secondly, many simulation models grow in an evolutionary manner rather than following a precise design. This means that successive enhancements are made to the programs. This is rather easier to do in a well-structured program.

As for language choice, the main issue is whether to program in a specially designed simulation language of the type discussed in Chapter 6 or to use a more general purpose language like FORTRAN or Pascal. There are things to be said for and against both courses of action.

The creators and vendors of special purpose simulation languages will argue, quite correctly, that there is no point whatsoever in redesigning the wheel. Thousands of simulations have been programmed since the early 1960s and general principles have emerged from these experiences. It is clear that certain specific features must be provided in any simulation — for example, a time flow mechanism and sophisticated error messages. The latter are important because simulation programs are notoriously difficult to debug. In addition, the tasks of debugging and verification can be greatly eased if the syntax of the language employs simulation terminology and also allows the entities of the system to have meaningful names. For these sorts of reasons it may seem correct to argue that the sensible course is always to write simulation programs in a special purpose simulation language.

However, there is another point of view. It can often be more convenient to write in a general purpose language. One commonly cited reason is that the analyst may be a member of a group which already has a significant investment of time and expertise in the general purpose language. Thus there will be someone around to sort out the programs later if the analyst has moved on to another job, possibly in another organization. A second reason is that some of the special purpose simulation languages are suited for only some types of system and it may be easier to write better programs in the general purpose language. Often there is no need to write these programs from scratch as sets of simulation subroutines are available (see Section 6.5) on a commercial basis. These carry out many of the commonly occurring tasks of a simulation.

1.5.3 Experimentation

The final crunch in any simulation project is the interpretation of the results from the experiments carried out on the model. As indicated earlier, this can be a straightforward task but this is not always the case. There are no substitutes for properly designed experiments which allow the analyst to infer the causes of model behaviour. Correct interpretation of the results depends rather more on good experimental design than on the subtleties of statistical analysis.

It is sometimes the case in practice that simulation projects do not reach this final stage of detailed experimentation because the effort put into modelling and programming has enabled the analyst and client to identify the best courses of action. That is, the need to explicitly describe the system and to carefully consider the various options may make the problem solution startlingly clear. If so, this is all well and good.

Often the analyst is not so fortunate and some considerable effort must be devoted to proper experimentation. Some of the issues have been introduced in Section 1.3 and detailed considerations are given in Chapter 8. Problems particularly arise with simulations which include stochastic elements (see Section 2.3.2). In these cases, different runs of the same simulation produce different results. For example, the sampling procedures may mean that a different number of customers arrive at a queueing system on each run of the model. It is important that the analyst allows for this variability when interpreting the results. No such difficulties arise with deterministic simulation methods such as system dynamics (Chapter 9–11).

EXERCISES

1. Suppose that a public authority is considering various policies for checking whether goods vehicles are overweight as they arrive at ferry ports. Discuss whether it might be sensible to consider a simulation approach.

2. Around 1980, spread-sheet packages such as Visi–Calc became common on personal computers. Discuss what type of simulation these packages allow.

3. If you were the manager of a factory whose production operations were being simulated by a management scientist, why might you not be wholly convinced that the simulation model was valid even if the production rates output from the simulation were the same as those of your factory?

4. Why is careful experimentation of such importance in computer simulation? Give some examples.

5. Computers are becoming easier to use by non-specialists. Should managers be

encouraged to undertake computer simulations themselves or is there still a place for the specialist?

REFERENCES

Ackoff, R. L., & Sasieni, M. W. (1968) *Fundamentals of Operations Research*. Wiley, New York.

Clementson, A. T. (1982) *Extended Control and Simulation Language*. Cle. Com Ltd., Birmingham, U.K.

Hicks, P. E. (1977) *Introduction to Industrial Engineering and Management Science*. McGraw–Hill Kogakusha, Tokyo.

McCurdy, A. W. (1977) The design of engineering facilities at Rover Triumph, in Littlechild, S. C. (ed.) *O.R. for Managers* (1977), Philip Allan, Oxford.

Markowitz, H. M., Hausner, B., & Karr, H. W. (1963) *SIMSCRIPT: A Simulation Programming Language*. RAND corporation RM-3310-PR 1962. Prentice–Hall, Englewood Cliffs, New Jersey.

Rivett, B. H. P. (1972) *The Art of Model Building*. Wiley, Chichester.

Sutton, D. W., & Coats, P. A. (1981) On-line mixture calculation system for stainless steel production by BSC stainless: the least through cost mix system (LTCM). *Jnl. Opl. Res. Soc.* **32**(3), 165–172.

Tocher, K. D. (1963) *The Art of Simulation*. English Universities Press, London.

White, D. J. (1975) *Decision Methodology*. Wiley, Chichester.

Chapter 2

A variety of modelling approaches

2.1 GENERAL CONSIDERATIONS

Before producing a model and thus a computer program, the analyst must decide what will be the principal elements of that model. In doing so, two aspects should be born in mind. The first is the nature of the system being simulated—obviously the model needs to be a close fit, a good representation of the system. Needless to say, some modelling approaches are more suited to certain problems than to others. The second aspect is the nature of the study being carried out. That is, what are the objectives of the study, what is the point of the simulation, what results are expected? Considering both of these aspects will allow the analyst to decide what level of accuracy and detail is appropriate for the simulation. There is clearly little point in producing an extremely detailed simulation if only crude estimates are required. The practical decisions that need to be made concern the following, each of which will be considered in this chapter:

time handling;
stochastic or deterministic durations;
discrete or continuous change.

2.2 TIME HANDLING

One of the advantages of simulation is that the speed at which the experiment proceeds can be controlled. In management science it is usual to speed up the passage of time so as to simulate several weeks or months in a few minutes of computer time. The essence of a simulation is that the state changes of the system are modelled through time. Hence it is important to consider how time-flow might be handled within the simulation.

2.2.1 Time slicing

Perhaps the simplest way of controlling the flow of time in a simulation is to move it forward in equal time intervals. This approach is often described as 'time slicing' and involves updating and examining the model at regular intervals.

Thus, for a time slice of length dt, the model is updated at time (t + dt) for changes occurring in the interval (t to (t + dt)).

One obvious problem with this approach is that some decision must be taken about the length of the time slice before the simulation is carried out. For example, the activity levels within a supertanker terminal may necessitate a time slice of one hour, whereas for a civil airport the time slice may be more appropriately set to a half minute or less. Clearly if the time slice is too large then the behaviour of the model is much coarser than that of the real system because it is impossible to simulate some of the state changes that occur. If, on the other hand, the time slice is too small then the model is frequently examined unnecessarily (when no state changes are possible) and this leads to excessively long computer runs.

As a simple example (based on an example in Jones, 1975),* consider a workshop with just two machines, A and B. Suppose that the time taken to complete a job on these machines depends on the size of the job. Thus the job times are:

machine A: (batch size/50 + 1) days
machine B: (batch size/100 + 3) days.

Suppose too that the workship only takes on jobs which must be processed on both machines and that each job must pass first through machine A as a complete batch and then through machine B as a complete batch. That is, no batch may be started on either machine until the previous batch is completed on that machine. If the workshop expects to receive the four orders shown in Table 2.1, when will the final batch be complete? Thus, the expected job times (days) are as shown in Table 2.1. Simulating the workshop using a time slice of one day leads to the times shown in Table 2.4. Thus job 4 is complete at the end of day 32.

Following this table through; on day 1, job 1 arrives and its processing immediately begins on machine A. Nothing new happens on days 2, 3, or 4 until the end of day 5 when machine A has finished job 1. Thus on day 6, machine B starts work on job 1. On day 7 nothing happens. On day 8, job 2 arrives and machine A begins its processing. This is obviously a tedious and

JOB NUMBER	BATCH SIZE	DAY ORDER EXPECTED
1	200	1
2	400	8
3	100	14
4	200	18

Table 2.1

*This example is reproduced in revised form with permission from the Open University from *T341 Systems Modelling*: Unit 6 Simulation Modelling, copyright © 1975 The Open University Press.

JOB NUMBER	MACHINE A	MACHINE B
1	5	5
2	9	7
3	3	4
4	5	5

Table 2.2

inefficient way of simulating such a simple system, for there is little point in examining and attempting to update the model each day — on many days, nothing changes.

2.2.2 Next event technique

Because many systems include such slack periods of varying length it is often preferable to use a variable time increment. In this case, the model is only examined and updated when it is known that a state change is due. These state changes are usually called events and, because time is moved from event to event, the approach is called the next event technique.

Consider again the simple workshop. Table 2.4 shows the results of a next event simulation of this system. Notice that the table is much smaller than that required for a time slicing approach. The method focusses on the progress of each job as it passes through the workshop. The events are:

a job arrives;
machine A starts a job;
machine A finishes a job;
machine B starts a job;
machine B finishes a job.

Day	Jobs queueing for MA	for MB	Jobs in progress MA	MB	Day	Jobs queueing for MA	for MB	Jobs in progress MA	MB
1	—	—	1	—	17	—	—	3	2
2	—	—	1	—	18	4	—	3	2
3	—	—	1	—	19	4	—	3	2
4	—	—	1	—	20	—	3	4	2
5	—	—	1	—	21	—	3	4	2
6	—	—	—	1	22	—	3	4	2
7	—	—	—	1	23	—	3	4	2
8	—	—	2	1	24	—	—	4	3
9	—	—	2	1	25	—	4	—	3
10	—	—	2	1	26	—	4	—	3
11	—	—	2	—	27	—	4	—	3
12	—	—	2	—	28	—	—	—	4
13	—	—	2	—	29	—	—	—	4
14	3	—	2	—	30	—	—	—	4
15	3	—	2	—	31	—	—	—	4
16	3	—	2	—	32	—	—	—	4

Table 2.3 The workshop: a time-slicing simulation

Each of these events may occur a maximum of 4 times during the simulation, once for each job. In fact, as Table 2.4 shows, some of these coincide and the model need only be updated on 16 occasions. By way of contrast, Table 2.3 shows the inevitable 32 updates of a time slicing approach.

Job No.	Arrival date	MA		MB	
		Start	Finish	Start	Finish
1	1	1	5	6	10
2	8	8	16	17	23
3	14	17	19	24	27
4	18	20	24	28	32

Table 2.4 The workshop: a next event simulation

2.2.3 Time slicing or next event?

Thus, a next event technique has two advantages over a time slicing approach. The first is that the time increment automatically adjusts to periods of high and low activity, thus avoiding wasteful and unnecessary checking of the state of the model. The second is that it makes clear when significant events have occurred in the simulation. Against these, rather more information must be held to control the simulation and simulated time does not flow smoothly. Of course, there are some systems whose events do occur at regular intervals. For example, a superstore may check its stock levels at the same time each day and replenishments may similarly arrive at predictable times. In such cases it is quite adequate to update the model at regular intervals to allow for the intervening changes.

2.3 STOCHASTIC OR DETERMINISTIC?

A deterministic system is one whose behaviour is entirely predictable. Provided that the system is perfectly understood, then it is possible to predict precisely what will happen. A cycle of operations on an automatic machine may be deterministic in this sense. Each repeated identical cycle will take the same length of time unless the conditions influencing the cycle times are altered.

A stochastic system is one whose behaviour cannot be entirely predicted, though some statement may be made about how likely certain events are to occur. For example, a lecturer may give the same lecture to several sets of students but the duration of the lecture may vary from occasion to occasion. Statistical statements may be made about the duration of the lecture, for example that it is normally distributed with a mean of 50 minutes and a standard deviation of 3 minutes. Thus it is highly likely that the duration of the lecture will exceed 44 minutes. However, it is impossible to precisely state how long a particular delivery of the lecture will last unless the lecturer's behaviour can be completely controlled — and that of the class too!

In some senses, the distinction between stochastic and deterministic systems is artificial. It is more a statement of the amount of knowledge about a system or the amount of control over that system exercised by an observer. However, it is important to notice that both stochastic and deterministic simulations are possible.

2.3.1 Deterministic simulation

Any simulation which contains no stochastic elements is usually called deterministic. A simple example was the four-job simulation of the workshop described in Section 2.2. As a rather more illuminating example, consider a factory which manufactures a single product. Raw material is bought from external suppliers and held in stock until required. When production is complete, finished goods are held in a warehouse pending delivery to customers. In order to simulate this system, it is useful to define the following variables.

$R(t)$ = raw material stocks (units)
$F(t)$ = finished goods stocks (units)
$B(t)$ = order backlog (units)
$T(t)$ = target stock level for finished goods (units)
All defined at the start of week t.

$X(t,t+1)$ = weekly orders received from customers
$M(t,t+1)$ = raw material supplied per week
$P(t,t+1)$ = production per week
$D(t,t+1)$ = amount despatched to customers per week
All defined over the week t to $t+1$. (i.e. during week t).

The operation of the factory and its warehouse can be expressed as a series of equations, each one representing some aspect of the company's policy.

(1) Order backlog

The amount of outstanding orders.

$$B(t+1) = B(t) + X(t,t+1) - D(t,t+1) \tag{1}$$

i.e. the backlog at the start of next week will be the backlog at the start of this week plus the difference between the order rate and the despatch rate in the intervening week.

(2) Target warehouse stock

Suppose that the company wishes to maintain 5 weeks stock of finished goods.

Thus the target stock level is 5 times the average of the last 4 weeks orders.

$$T(t+1) = (5/4)*(X(t,t+1) + X(t-1,t) + X(t-2,t-1) + X(t-3,t-2)) \quad (2)$$

(3) Raw material stock

$$R(t+1) = R(t) + M(t,t+1) - P(t,t+1) \quad (3)$$

i.e. the stock at the start of next week will be the stock at the start of this week plus the difference between the material supplied and the amount produced in the intervening week.

(4) Finished goods stock

$$F(t+1) = F(t) + P(t,t+1) - D(t,t+1) \quad (4)$$

i.e. the stock at the start of next week will be the stock at the start of this week plus the difference between the production rate and the despatch rate over the intervening week.

(5) Despatch rate

$$\begin{aligned} D(t,t+1) &= B(t) \quad \text{if } B(t) < F(t) \\ &= F(t) \quad \text{otherwise} \end{aligned} \quad (5)$$

i.e. the amount despatched during the week will be either the order backlog or the finished goods in stock at the start of the week, whichever is the smaller.

Suppose that, in its wisdom, the management of the company has decreed the following policies for the weekly production and material supply rates.

(6) Material supply rate

$$M(t,t+1) = P(t-1,t) \quad (6)$$

i.e. enough material will be ordered to replace that consumed by last week's production.

(7) Production rate

$$P(t,t+1) = T(t) - F(t) + D(t,t+1) \quad (7)$$

provided that

$$\begin{aligned} P(t,t+1) &= 0 \quad \text{if the result is negative} \\ &= R(t) \quad \text{if the result exceeds } R(t) \end{aligned}$$

i.e. the production rate will be that required to take the warehouse stock to the target stock level, allowing for despatches expected this week.

Thus, the model so far is as follows.

$$B(t+1) = B(t) + X(t,t+1) - D(t,t+1) \quad (1)$$

$$T(t+1) = (5/4)*(X(t,t+1) + X(t-1,t) + X(t-2,t-1) + X(t-3,t-2)) \quad (2)$$

$$R(t+1) = R(t) + M(t,t+1) - P(t,t+1) \quad (3)$$

$$F(t+1) = F(t) + P(t,t+1) - D(t,t+1) \quad (4)$$

$$\begin{aligned} D(t,t+1) &= B(t) \quad \text{if} \quad B(t) < F(t) \\ &= F(t) \text{ otherwise} \end{aligned} \quad (5)$$

$$M(t,t+1) = P(t-1,t) \quad (6)$$

$$\begin{aligned} P(t,t+1) &= T(t) - F(t) + D(t,t+1) \quad \text{if} \quad 0 < P(t,t+1) < R(t) \\ &= R(t) \quad \text{if} \quad P(t,t+1) > R(t) \\ &= 0 \quad \text{if} \quad P(t,t+1) < 0 \end{aligned} \quad (7)$$

Given initial values for these variables, it is possible to simulate how the system would respond to the order rate.

Suppose that initially all is calm, and that the system has operated as follows for the last 5 weeks:

despatch rate = 50/week
production rate = 50/week
material supply rate = 50/week
order backlog = 50
target warehouse stock = 250
finished goods stock = 250
raw material stocks = 150
order rate = 50/week

Suppose too that this behaviour continues for the first week of the simulation, but that during the next week orders double due to a sales promotion. During the third week orders drop to zero as all demand was satisfied the previous week. For the fourth and succeeding weeks, demand returns to an order rate of 50/week. What happens elsewhere in the system?

To answer this question, it is straightforward to carry out a deterministic time-slicing simulation using the following method.

(1) Compute the values of equations (1)–(4); i.e. the start of week t.
(2) Compute the values of equations (5)–(7); i.e. the new values of the rates during the following week.
(3) Move simulated time to the start of the next week.
(4) Repeat steps (1)–(3) until finished.

Table 2.5 shows the effect of such a simulation for 10 weeks and Figure 2.1 is a graph of the order rate and production rate over that period.

It is clear that all is not well! The policies espoused for the material supply rate (equation (6)) and the production rate (equation (7)) cause the production rate to overshoot dramatically. This overshoot is followed by an equally disastrous over-compensation which brings the production rate down to zero for two weeks. An equally dramatic effect is seen in the material supply rate.

Week	Order rate $X(t,t+1)$	Backlog $B(t)$	Finished stocks Target $T(t)$	Finished stocks Actual $F(t)$	Raw stocks $R(t)$	Material supply rate $M(t,t+1)$	Production rate $P(t,t+1)$	Despatch rate $D(t,t+1)$
1	50	50	250	250	150	50	50	50
2	100	100	313	250	150	50	50	50
3	0	0	250	313	33	50	163	100
4	50	50	250	313	200	163	0	0
5	50	50	250	263	200	0	0	50
6	50	50	188	250	163	0	38	50
7	50	50	250	200	200	38	0	50
8	50	50	250	250	100	0	100	50
9	50	50	250	250	150	100	50	50
10	50	50	250	250	150	50	50	50

Table 2.5 The factory: a deterministic time-slicing simulation

By week 9, things are back under control — until the next change in demand rate!

There must be a better way of operating such a system and simulation allows us to check whether this is the case, If the management, as is likely, regards such fluctuations in production as dangerous then one of their objectives might be to smooth out their responses to changes in the order rate. Imagine that a management scientist suggests the following policies.

(6a) Material supply rate

$$M(t,t+1) = 50*(T(t)/F(t)) \qquad \text{(6a)}$$

i.e. the material supply rate will be based on the ratio of the target warehouse stock and the actual finished goods in stock — both at the start of the week. This ratio is multiplied by 50, the typical weekly order rate.

(7a) Production rate

$$P(t,t+1) = R(t)/3 \qquad \text{(7a)}$$

i.e. the production rate will be that required to deplete the raw material stocks by one third.

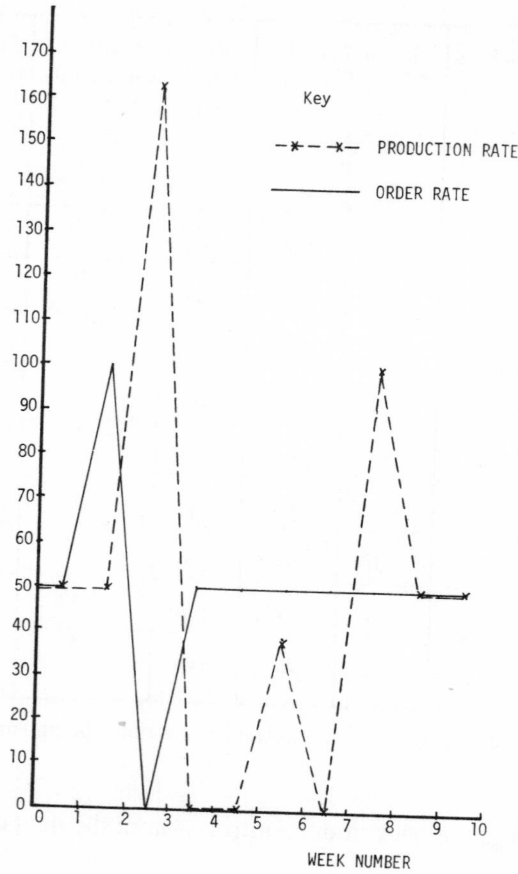

Figure 2.1 The factory: dynamic response

The revised model can be used to simulate the performance of the system under the new policies. Table 2.6 shows the results of a 10-week run and Figure 2.2 is a graph of the order rate and production rate over that period.

This time, things look much better. The production rates do vary, but now by a much smaller amount.

2.3.2 Stochastic simulation

Many systems behave stochastically and must therefore be simulated by a model with stochastic elements. This means that probability distributions are used in such stochastic simulation models. As the simulation proceeds, samples are taken from these distributions so as to provide the stochastic behaviour. As an example, consider the following replacement problem.

A multi-user computer system includes two disk units which, being mechanical, are prone to failure. If a disk unit fails in service, users lose their

Week	Order rate $X(t,t+1)$	Backlog $B(t)$	Finished stocks Target $T(t)$	Finished stocks Actual $F(t)$	Raw stocks $R(t)$	Material supply rate $M(t,t+1)$	Production rate $P(t,t+1)$	Despatch rate $D(t,t+1)$
1	50	50	250	250	150	50	50	50
2	100	100	313	250	150	50	50	50
3	0	0	250	200	163	63	50	100
4	50	50	250	254	171	63	54	0
5	50	50	250	261	163	49	57	50
6	50	50	188	265	157	48	54	50
7	50	50	250	268	140	35	52	50
8	50	50	250	264	140	47	47	50
9	50	50	250	261	141	47	47	50
10	50	50	250	258	142	48	47	50

Table 2.6 The factory: a revised simulation

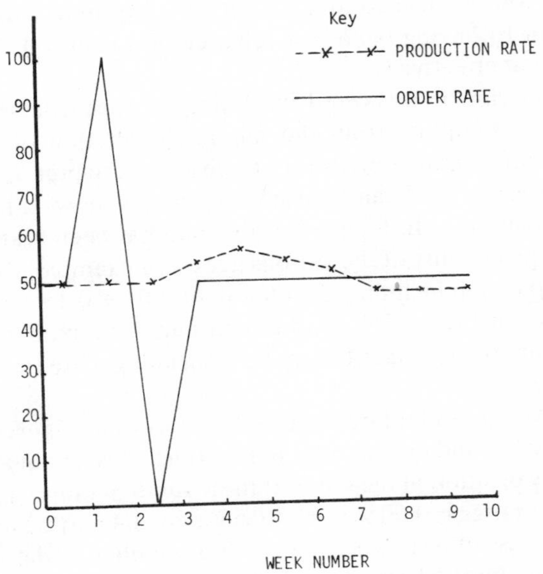

Figure 2.2 The factory: revised dynamic response

files (and their tempers) which need to be restored. Restoration is achieved by copying on to the disk back-up copies of the files held on magnetic tapes. This restoration is inconvenient and so a new operating policy is being considered. At the moment, the disk units are repaired and restored as and when they fail. The proposal is to introduce a joint repair system. Table 2.7 below shows the probability of a disk unit failing in the days following its last repair. That is, 5% of the units are expected to fail 1 day after repair or maintenance, 15% after 2 days, etc.

Days since repair or maintenance	Probability of failure
1	0.05
2	0.15
3	0.20
4	0.30
5	0.20
6	0.10
>6	0

Table 2.7 Probability of disk failure

Under the current policy, it costs $50/disk to repair and restore a failed unit. The joint repair system would operate as follows. When either unit fails, the failed unit is repaired and restored at a cost of $50 per unit. If operational, the other unit will be cleaned at a cost of $25. Cleaning a disk places it in a state equivalent to having been just repaired and restored. Is the new joint repair system cost effective?

This question can be answered by a simple stochastic simulation which involves random sampling from the failure distribution of the disks given earlier. Details of sampling methods are given in Chapter 7, but for present purposes a simple method can be used. Figure 2.3 shows a histogram of the disk failure distribution. In Figure 2.4, the data has been rearranged to show the cumulative probability of the various lives. For example, the probability of a disk lasting up to and including 3 days is 0.40(0.05 + 0.15 + 0.20). Using the cumulative form of Figure 2.4 and random number tables, random samples can be taken from the life distribution by associating a life (in days) with each random number.

An extract from a random number table is shown in Figure 2.5, the values range from 00 to 99, and any number in that range has an equal probability of appearing at any position in the table. If these random numbers are divided by 100, so that their range is 0.00 to 0.99, then Figure 2.4 may be used to generate random samples as follows. The first random number in the table is 27 (i.e. 0.27); if this is marked on the vertical axis of Figure 2.5, then the corresponding point on the horizontal axis is 3 days. That is, 3 days is the life

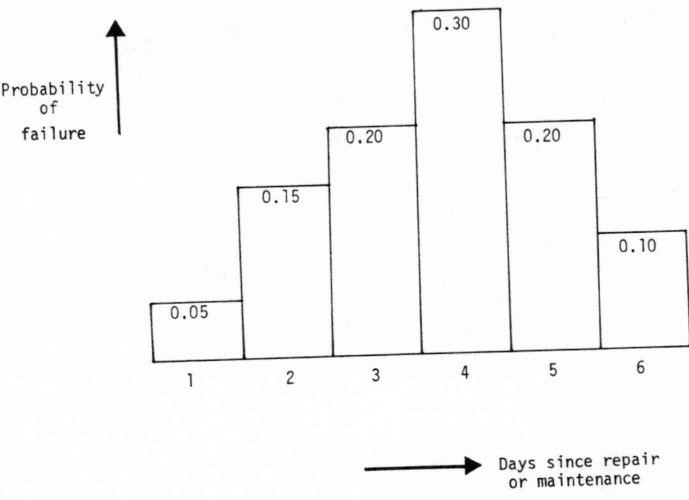

Figure 2.3 Histogram of failure probabilities

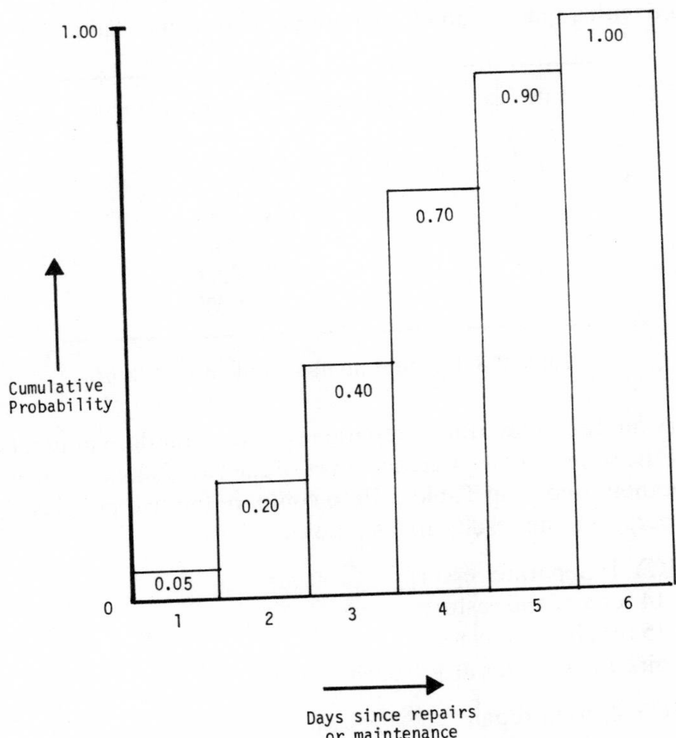

Figure 2.4 Histogram of cumulative failure probabilities

27	62	36	30	57	78	22	02	89	22
04	97	43	30	45	12	03	87	16	50
92	26	00	82	58	10	78	44	55	05
21	50	49	83	49	39	25	81	03	99
77	71	43	06	90	09	04	97	07	64
40	39	69	42	63	80	07	85	65	70
60	57	42	97	29	92	84	54	66	91
34	10	78	81	97	99	08	19	15	63
35	37	13	56	88	09	36	40	07	55
04	24	69	52	44	14	61	59	31	50
24	26	29	31	57	17	38	44	03	29
26	63	00	44	64	09	93	15	52	35
91	37	65	32	84	37	80	94	48	46
23	52	10	77	27	40	34	13	73	53
55	89	99	78	50	11	43	43	54	16

Figure 2.5 Some random numbers

associated with the random number 0.27. In general, each life may be associated with a range of random numbers as shown in Table 2.8.

Life (days	Associated random numbers
1	0.00–0.04
2	0.05–0.19
3	0.20–0.39
4	0.40–0.69
5	0.70–0.89
6	0.90–0.99

Table 2.8 Random numbers linked to disk life

To carry out the simulation, a separate stream of random numbers is used to represent the sequence of successive lives of the two disk units as in Table 2.9. These are then used as in Table 2.10 to compare the two policies. Thus, after 50 days operation, the results are as follows.

(a) POLICY 1: Separate repair
unit A: 14 repairs and restores
unit B: 15 repairs and restores
i.e. 29 repairs and restores at \$50 each = \$1450.

(b) POLICY 2: Joint repair
Carried out on 17 occasions. Of these, 9 involved both units in a repair and restore; 8 involved a single repair and restore with a clean up of the other disk.

	Unit A Random number	Life	Unit B Random number	Life
1	0.27	3	0.24	3
2	0.62	4	0.26	3
3	0.36	3	0.29	3
4	0.30	3	0.31	3
5	0.57	4	0.57	4
6	0.04	1	0.26	3
7	0.97	6	0.63	4
8	0.43	4	0.00	1
9	0.30	3	0.44	4
10	0.45	4	0.64	4
11	0.92	6	0.91	6
12	0.26	3	0.37	3
13	0.00	1	0.65	4
14	0.82	5	0.32	3
15	0.58	4	0.84	5
16	0.21	3	0.23	3
17	0.50	4	0.52	4
18	0.49	4	0.10	2
19	0.83	5	0.77	5
20	0.49	4	0.27	3

Table 2.9 A next event simulation of two disk units

i.e. 26 repairs and restores at $50 each = $1300
and 8 clean ups at $25 each = $ 200
TOTAL COST = $1500.

Thus on the basis of a single simulation, the new policy costs $50 more over a 50 day period. However it would be wrong to assume that a separate repair policy is therefore more cost effective. If a different set of random numbers had been used, the result could have been different for both policies and the new policy might appear cheaper. In stochastic simulations, it is important to realize that the results are dependent on the samples taken. Hence it is usual to make several simulation runs each with a distinct sampling pattern before drawing any conclusions. Chapter 8 gives details.

The sampling methods employed in stochastic simulations are well developed and documented. Commonly used methods are given in Chapter 7 and most simulation software systems have appropriate subroutines or procedures ready for use. Thus distribution sampling should not be a problem in model building. More likely, controlling the sequence of events is the major

	Policy 1: Separate repair	
	Cumulative lives	
	Unit A	Unit B
1	3	3
2	7	6
3	10	9
4	13	12
5	17	16
6	18	19
7	24	23
8	28	24
9	31	28
10	35	32
11	41	38
12	44	41
13	45	45
14	50	48
15		53

	Policy 2: Joint repair	
	Minimum joint life	Cumulative joint life
1	3	3
2	3	6
3	3	9
4	3	12
5	4	16
6	1	17
7	4	21
8	1	22
9	3	25
10	4	29
11	6	35
12	3	38
13	1	39
14	3	42
15	4	46
16	3	49
17	4	53

Table 2.10 The replacement policies compared

problem in model building. The interaction of the entities is responsible for the sequence of events, and in the above example these are trivial. But for complex systems a sensible structure is needed. Various common approaches are described in Chapters 3, 4 and 5.

2.4 DISCRETE OR CONTINUOUS CHANGE?

In the job-shop simulation, it was convenient to regard the system as moving from state to state through time. The concern with individual batches was whether their machining was complete or not, rather than with the rate at which the machining was proceeding. The variables which are included in a simulation model can be thought of as changing value in four ways:

(1) Continuously at any point of time. Thus, the values are changing smoothly and not discretely and the values taken are accessible at any time point within the simulation.
(2) Continuously but only at discrete time points. In this mode, the values again change smoothly but can only be accessed at predetermined times.
(3) Discretely at any point of time. In these simulations, state changes are easily identifiable but can occur at any point of time.

(4) Discretely and only at discrete points of time. The state changes can only occur at specified points of time.

Historically, computer simulation applications have tended to divide into those employing change and those which allow the variables to continuously change value.

2.4.1 Discrete change

Consider an underground railway in which trains move from station to station, picking up and depositing passengers at each. Viewed from the perspective of discrete change there are a number of obvious system events. For example:

train stops at a station,
doors now open,
doors now closed,
train starts to leave station.

Thus to simulate this system using a discrete model, the time taken to travel between stations or to open the doors would either be known deterministically or could be sampled from some appropriate distribution. Thus, for example, when the train starts to leave a station its arrival at the next station could be scheduled by referring to this 'known' journey time. In a discrete simulation the variables are only of interest as and when they point to a change in the state of the system. Chapters 3–8 are devoted to the exposition of methods suitable for discrete simulation.

2.4.2 Continuous change

If the underground railway were to be simulated via a model which allowed continuous change, then the variables would be continuously changing their values as the simulation proceeds. Consider, for example, the train as it travels between stations. If the locomotive is electrically powered, its speed will increase smoothly from rest until it reaches an appropriate cruising rate. The speed does not change by discrete amounts. Thus, if the results of the simulation are to include the state of the system in relation to the continuous variable 'speed', then a continuous change model is needed. These continuous changes could be represented by differential equations which would, in theory, allow the variables to be computed at any point of time.

In considering continuous change models it must be recognized that digital computers operate only with discrete quantities. Hence changes cannot actually be occurring continuously within a 'continuous' simulation. In system dynamics (see Chapters 9–11), the continuity is achieved by allowing the variables to be inspected or changed at a multitude of fixed points in simulated time.

Continuous simulation 'proper' is not covered in detail in this book because management scientists seem to be more often concerned with systems that can satisfactorily be simulated discretely. More often continuous simulations are the concern of economists in modelling the behaviour of economic systems via sets of differential equations, or the concern of engineers designing equipment. Early continuous simulations were mainly carried out using analogue computers. Though these have some appeal for those with an interest in electrical hardware, they tend to be tedious to reprogram and of limited accuracy. Therefore analogue–digital simulators, such as CSMP (1970), were developed. Early versions of these simulators employed the block diagram terminology of analogue computers, a description of the block diagram being the 'program' from which digital computers could be programmed to simulate analogue computers. Later versions allow systems to be directly represented as sets of differential equations which are integrated numerically.

2.4.3 Mixed discrete/continuous change

More recently, the vendors of simulation software systems have realized that the separation of discrete and continuous simulation is somewhat artificial. Consequently, a number of simulation software systems now allow the user to program discrete, continuous or mixed models. The best known of the genre is GASP IV (1974) and competitive products appear from time to time.

EXERCISES

1. Using the revised deterministic model of Section 2.3.1, show the effect of putting

$$M(t,t+1) = A(t) * T(t)/F(t)$$

where $A(t)$ is the average of the last 4 weeks orders.

2. Carry out 3 more simulations of the disk failure problem described in Section 2.3.2. Now what would you recommend to the management?

3. Write computer programs to carry out both simulations of the simple job shop described in Section 2.2.

4. Discuss why analogue computers are rarely used in management science, when many systems do change continuously.

REFERENCES

IBM Corporation (1970) *Introduction to 1130 Systems Modelling Program II (CSMP II)*. GH20-0848-1. White Plains, New York.

Jones, L. (1975) *Simulation Modelling*. Unit 6, course T341, Systems Modelling. Open University Press, Milton Keynes, UK.

Pritsker, A. A. B. (1974) *The GASP IV Simulation Language*. Wiley, New York.

PART II

DISCRETE EVENT SIMULATION

Chapter 3

Discrete event modelling

3.1 FUNDAMENTALS

As the name suggests, a discrete event simulation is one which employs a next event technique (Section 2.2) to control the behaviour of the model. Many applications of discrete event simulation involve queueing systems of one kind or another. The queueing structure may be obvious as in a queue of jobs waiting to be processed on a batch computer or in a stack of aircraft waiting for landing space at an airport. In other cases, the queueing structure may be less obvious as in the deployment of fire appliances in a large city. In this case, the customers are the fires needing attention and the servers are the fire-fighters together with their associated equipment.

As another example, consider again the car body paint shop described in Chapter 1. The bodies were to pass through a series of processes such as spray booths, ovens and rectification areas. They were to be moved from area to area on lifts, conveyors and other transfer machines until, satisfactorily painted, they reached the painted-body store. In some cases, for example immediately after a vertical transfer in a lift, the bodies were not to be processed straight away but were to enter a temporary storage area to wait with other bodies. Because of this part-finished stock, a lift breakdown would not immediately bring the succeeding process to a halt. That is, the stocks are used to de-couple two processes. This stock can be thought of as a queue and, in the simplest case, the queue would operate with a first in first out (FIFO) discipline. The car bodies are waiting for the next process.

Quite a variety of systems can be regarded as having a queueing structure and as such they lend themselves well to discrete event simulation. The purpose of this chapter is to introduce some general terminology that may be used to build models suitable for discrete event simulation. A particular modelling device, the activity cycle diagram, is then introduced as a way of developing the structure of a model.

3.2 TERMINOLOGY

Some of the terminology employed in discrete event simulation is highly varied. Different writers occasionally use the same term to mean different things and this can lead to some confusion. The terminology defined here is fairly standard and is deliberately quite limited to try to minimize confusion. It is divided into two parts. The first set provides labels for the objects which constitute a system to be simulated. The second set defines the operations in which these objects engage over time.

3.2.1 Objects of the system

(1) *Entities*. These are the elements of the system being simulated and can be individually identified and processed. Examples may be machines in a factory, jobs waiting to be processed, vehicles, people or anything else that changes state as the simulation proceeds. The system is thus regarded as a set of related entities that co-operate to produce some result. In a managed system this co-operation is controlled and co-ordinated. The interactions of the entities produce the distinctive behaviour of the system.

Entities that remain in the system throughout the simulation are regarded as *permanent*. Examples may be spray booths in the paint shop or communications equipment in a telecommunications network. Others only pass through the system and cease to be individually of interest once they have left it. These are called *temporary* entities. Examples may be the car bodies in the paint shop or individual messages in a telecommunications network.

From a different perspective, some entities are processed by others. Those that are processed can be regarded as *passive*, whereas the processors can be regarded as *active*. In the above examples, the temporary entities are all passive but this need not be the case.

(2) *Classes*. Entities are individually identifiable but grouped into classes of like entities. This obviously makes it easier to refer to all or several of the same type of entity. Hence, car bodies and spray booths may constitute two distinct classes of entity in a simulation model.

(3) *Attributes*. Each entity may possess one or more attributes which convey extra information about the entity. There are useful for a variety of purposes. For example, it may be important to subdivide a class — so the car manufacturer may wish to distinguish between the various different coloured car bodies in order to sequence the final assembly operations. Hence colour would be an attribute of the car bodies. Another use for attributes would be to control the behaviour of the entity. For example, an attribute of this type may be the payload of an aircraft, and this may affect the flying speed and thus the journey time of passengers. A third way of using attributes may be to control queue discipline. A job arriving in a workshop may be allocated some priority level depending on its profitability. This priority attribute may be used to select jobs for processing when there is a choice.

(4) *Sets*. Though permanently organized into classes, during the simulation the entities change state and these states may be represented as sets. For example, during a simulation of the paint shop there will be bodies which are temporarily members of the set awaiting rectification of faulty paintwork. After this rectification they could be transferred to the set of bodies waiting, say, for a spray booth. The current membership of the sets of the system can be used as an indication of the state of the system at a particular point in time.

In some cases, a number of the sets can be thought of as queues in which the entities wait for something to happen. These queues have a specified queue discipline, FIFO being the most common.

At this point it should be obvious that some of the above terminology is redundant. The set of which an entity is currently a member could be regarded as an attribute of the entity and its value changed as the entity moved from set to set. Despite this redundancy, some commercial simulation software systems find it useful to maintain a distinction between attributes and set membership.

3.2.2 Operations of the entities

As the simulation proceeds, the entities co-operate and thence change state. Some terminology is thus needed to describe these operations and also to describe the flow of time in the simulation.

(1) *Event*. This is an instant of time at which a significant state change occurs in the system. Such as when an entity enters or leaves a set, or some operation begins. Note that it is up to the analyst to define whether an event is significant or not in the context of the objectives of the simulation. In the paint shop, the start or completion of an operation such as rectification may be regarded as an event.
(2) *Activity*. Entities move from set to set because of the operations in which they engage. Thus the operations and procedures which are initiated at each event are known as activities. The activities are what transform the state of the entities. Thus the activity 'rectification' transforms a body from the state 'awaiting rectification' to the state 'waiting for spray'.
(3) *Process*. Sometimes it is useful to group together a sequence of events in the chronological order in which they will occur. Such a sequence is known as a process and is often used to represent all or part of the life of temporary entities. For example, a car body arrives, is degreased, hot-dipped, primed, etc.
(4) *Simulation clock*. This is the point reached by simulated time in a simulation. Hence in a simulation where the time unit is minutes, the test

'is clock = 240?'

might be used to test whether a lunch break is due. If so, appropriate activity could then be initiated in the simulation.

3.3 ACTIVITY CYCLE DIAGRAMS

In a discrete event simulation the various entities interact through simulated time and these interactions can be described in the terms introduced in Section 3.2. In order to build a model suitable for discrete event simulation, it is necessary to

identify the important classes of entity;
consider the activities in which they engage;
link these activities together.

From the skeleton, the fine detail of the model can be built up.

Whilst considering the topic of simulation modelling, it is as well to bear in mind the 'principle of parsimony'. This requires the analyst to begin model building with the well-understood and obvious elements of the system of interest. Once these are properly modelled and validated, then the more complicated and less well-understood elements can be added later. In most modelling there is an overwhelming temptation to dive straight into the complicated features. This temptation is to be resisted.

Activity cycle diagrams are one way of modelling the interactions of the entities and are particularly useful for systems with a strong queueing structure. They were popularized by Hills (1971) and are normally associated with the activity based approach described in Section 4.3. One example of this is HOCUS (see Section 6.7.1) which is a simulation software system built around the activity cycle diagram concept. However, Matthewson (1974) points out that they are just as useful for other modelling approaches such as event-based methods (Section 4.2) or process based methods (Section 4.4) and hence would seem to be of general value. In most cases they cannot include the full complexity of a system being simulated, but they do provide a skeleton which can be enhanced later.

Activity cycle diagrams make use of only 2 symbols and these are shown in Figure 3.1. The diagram itself is a map which shows the life history of each class of entity and displays graphically their interactions. Each class of entity is

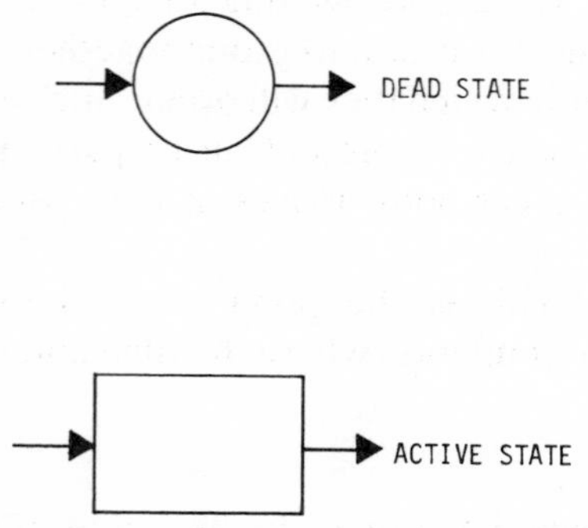

Figure 3.1 Symbols for activity cycle diagrams

considered to have a life cycle which consists of a series of states. The entities move from state to state as their life proceeds.

An *active state* usually involves the co-operation of different classes of entity. The duration of an active state can always be determined in advance — usually by taking a sample from an appropriate probability distribution if the simulation model is stochastic. The sampling methods are described in Chapter 7. In a queueing system, a service is one such active state because it involves the co-operation of a server and a customer. An appropriate distribution for the service time would provide a way of determining the duration of the active state.

On the other hand, a *dead state* involves no co-operation between different classes of entity and is generally a state in which the entity waits for something to happen. Dead states are often thought of as sets or queues (see the descriptions of HOCUS and CAPS/ECSL in Chapter 6). Therefore, the length of time that an entity spends in a dead state cannot be determined in advance. It depends on the duration of the immediately preceding and succeeding live states. For example, in the simulation of the paint shop, the time spent by a car body in the dead state 'waiting for rectification work' depends on when its painting was finished and also on when resources are available to carry out the rectification.

Drawing an activity cycle diagram involves listing the states through which each class of entity passes, and normally these are drawn as alternate dead and active states. The complete diagram consists of a combination of all the individual cycles.

3.3.1 Example 1: a simple job shop

Consider a simple engineering job shop which consists of several identical machines. Each machine is able to process any job and there is a ready supply of jobs with no prospect of any shortages. Jobs are allocated to the first available machine. The time taken to complete a job is variable but independent of the particular machine being used. The machine shop is staffed by a single operative who has to perform two tasks:

(1) reset machines between jobs if the cutting edges are still OK;
(2) retool those machines whose cutting edges are too worn to be reset.

Thus there are two classes of entity:

the operative;
the machines.

(1) The operative

He is responsible for the two tasks RETOOL and RESET as described above. In addition he may be unavailable whilst attending to personal needs. Obviously, a real job-shop would be much more complicated — however, this example is aimed solely at introducing the concepts of activity cycle diagrams. With this information, the activity cycle for the operative is as shown in Figure 3.2.

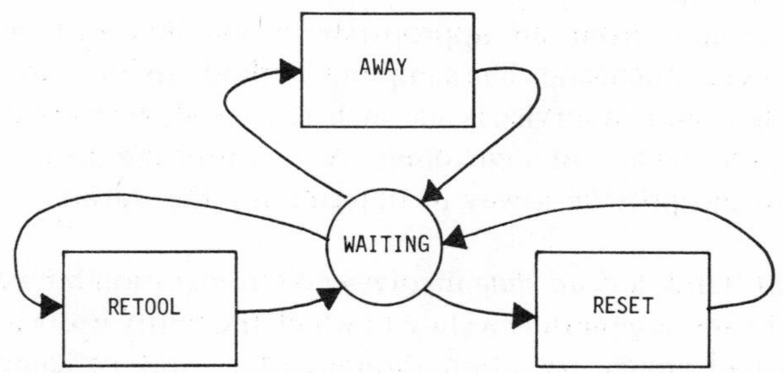

Figure 3.2 The operative's activity cycle

This shows three active states:

AWAY, RETOOL, RESET.

Obviously, RETOOL and RESET are carried out in co-operation with the machines (the other class of entity) and are therefore active states. Their duration could be obtained by sampling from appropriate probability distributions. The distributions themselves might be obtained by observing the actual times taken by the operative to carry out these tasks. AWAY is also an active state because a probability distribution could be performed to describe its duration and thus it meets one of the conditions for an active state.

When not in any of these active states, the operative is in the dead state WAITING and is available for work of some kind or is able to attend to his personal needs. In practice he may be in this dead state for quite some time or he may merely pass instantaneously through this state between two active states.

Notice, therefore, that the diagram consists of alternate active and dead states. That is, the operative must pass through a dead state when moving between active states.

(2) The machines

These have three active states:

RETOOL, RESET, RUNNING.

The latter active state represents the time when the machine is satisfactorily processing a job. Hence the activity cycle for the machines is as in Figure 3.3.

Following the convention for activity cycle diagrams, the active states have been separated by three dead states. After a machine stops RUNNING (that is, a job is complete) it moves into the dead state STOPPED. From STOPPED it may move to

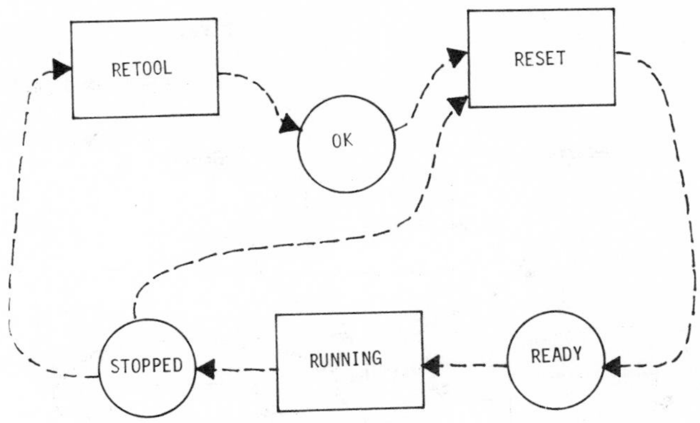

Figure 3.3 The machines' activity cycle

RESET: if its cutting edges are serviceable, or to
RETOOL: if the cutting edges are too worn.

During a simulation, an attribute may be used to decide whether a machine moves to RESET or RETOOL on each occasion.

After RETOOL, a machine is OK (another dead state) and is then RESET. Now the machine is READY (another dead state) following which it is RUNNING again. In real life, the dead states OK and READY may not exist, as the operative may move smoothly between the three active states. OK and READY are included here for two reasons. Firstly to maintain the convention of alternate active and dead states. Secondly, they would allow the model to be enhanced so as to consider, say, two operatives, one of whom is responsible for RETOOL and the other is responsible for RESET.

The two cycles may now be combined into the complete activity cycle diagram shown in Figure 3.4. Note that the dead states are unique to each class of entity. Only the operative can be WAITING and only the machines can be OK, STOPPED or RUNNING. On the other hand, at least two of the active states involve co-operation between the two classes of entity.

Activity cycle diagrams provide a graphical way of describing the interactions which must be built into the skeleton of the simulation model; that is, they show the logic of the system. Thus, they allow precise specification of the conditions that must hold before state changes can occur. For example, before RETOOL can begin there must be at least one machine STOPPED and in need of a retool and the operative must be available (i.e. WAITING) to do the work. The next example will show in more detail how these diagrams may be used as the basis of a simulation model — this time of an explicit queueing system.

3.3.2 Example 2: the harassed booking clerk

A theatre employs a booking clerk during the day-time. The clerk is employed to sell tickets and to answer any enquiries which may arise. Seat bookings are

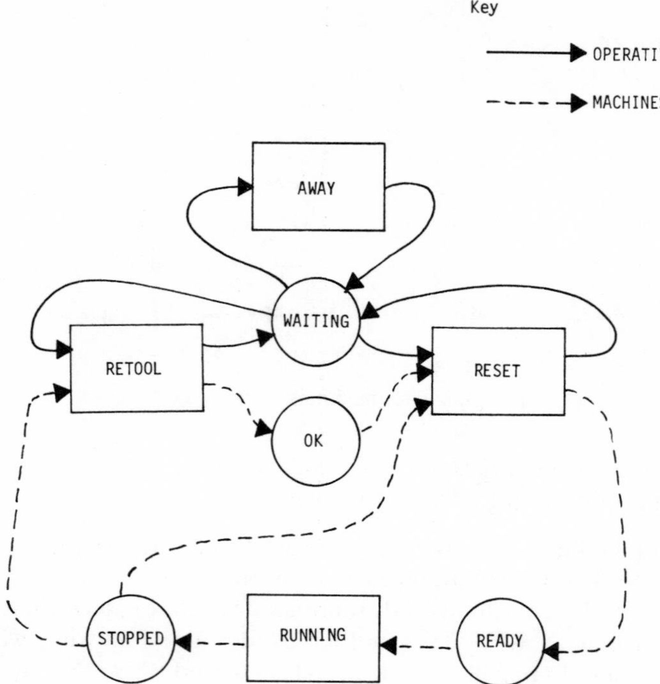

Figure 3.4 The job-shop activity cycle diagram

accepted only if the customer turns up in person at the theatre and pays for the tickets. Enquiries can come either from someone there in person or from someone phoning the theatre. The clerk is instructed to give priority to personal customers — after all, they may hand over some cash. Thus if the phone rings just as a customer arrives in person, then the personal enquirer is served first. Thanks to a sophisticated phone system, incoming calls can queue on a FIFO basis until answered. Phone callers never ring off in frustration.

There are three classes of entity;

(1) a single booking clerk;
(2) personal enquirers;
(3) phone callers.

We will consider each of these in turn.

(1) The booking clerk

The booking clerk clearly has two active states.

SERVICE: serving personal enquirers. Either selling tickets, answering questions or both.

TALK: speaking to phone callers.

When not engaged in these active states, the booking clerk is in a dead state IDLE. Thus the activity cycle for the clerk is as shown in Figure 3.5. As before, the clerk goes through a sequence of alternate active and dead states. On occasions, the clerk will spend zero time in the dead state between two active states.

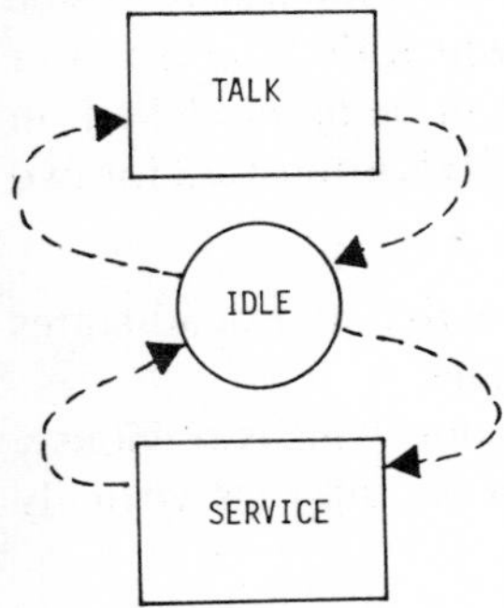

Figure 3.5 The booking clerk's activity cycle diagram

(2) Personal enquirers

These are initially OUTSIDE the theatre. They then ARRIVE, QUEUE for service and then SERVICE begins. After the clerk has completed their service, they leave the theatre and are once again OUTSIDE.

Firstly consider the state SERVICE. This is a co-operative state which requires an enquirer and the clerk if it is to occur. There is therefore no doubt that this is an active state according to the earlier definitions. Secondly consider the state QUEUE. As its name suggests, this is the state in which the enquirers wait until they are at the head of the queue and the booking clerk is able to serve them. Thus, as it is not a co-operative state and its duration clearly depends on the duration of the previous customer's service — it is a dead state.

This means that ARRIVAL is an active state, though why this should be so is probably not clear. To understand this, it may be helpful to imagine a machine which somehow transfers personal enquirers one at a time from OUTSIDE the theatres into the QUEUE. It returns for the next enquirer once it has safely placed an enquirer into the QUEUE. This arrival machine takes a finite time to execute this transfer and the enquirers are considered to be in the ARRIVAL state during that time. Hence, the duration of the ARRIVAL state becomes the interval between successive arrivals. In this way, the arrival process may be modelled as an active state provided that the inter-arrival time is determinable. Two obvious ways of doing this would be to use a timetable of arrivals or to take samples from some appropriate probability distribution.

If the inter-arrival times are taken as samples from some probability distribution then the arrivals are usually controlled by a bootstrapping process. This works as follows.

If enquirer N arrives at time T, then take a sample from the distribution of inter-arrival times and use the sample as the interval t between customers N and $N + 1$. Thus customer $N + 1$ arrives at time $T + t$.

Clearly this process must be initiated by a prior determination of the arrival time of the first enquirer. However, once that is done, the method allows successive arrivals to be modelled as active states.

Finally consider the dead state OUTSIDE. This represents the world outside the theatre from which the enquirers emerge and to which they return after SERVICE. It constitutes the environment of the system being modelled; in effect, the arrivals are quasi-exogeneous events. OUTSIDE is inserted for two reasons.

(1) To give the personal enquirers the sequence of active and dead states required by the conventions of activity cycle diagrams.
(2) Because it is normal for all cycles to be closed loops. This is obviously artificial in one sense as the number of potential enquirers is virtually infinite.

Figure 3.6 shows the resulting activity cycle.

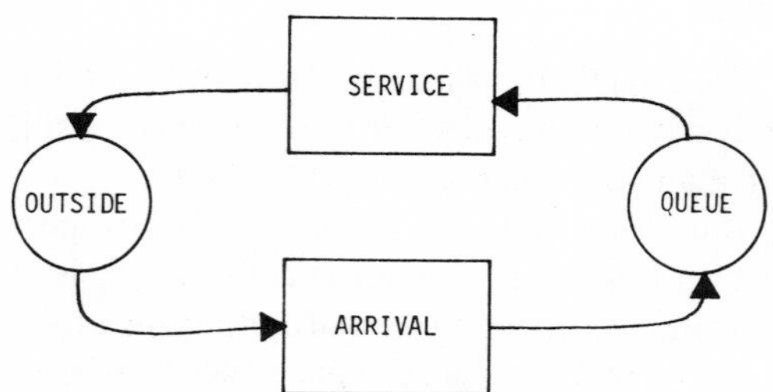

Figure 3.6 The personal enquirers' activity cycle diagram

(3) Phone callers

This cycle parallels that of the personal enquirers. This time the arriving 'customers' are phone calls to the theatre which are allowed to queue until the phone is answered. The interval between successive calls is modelled by the active state CALL and the active service state is TALK. The activity cycle is shown in Figure 3.7 and shows that dead states WAIT and ELSEWHERE separate the two active states. As before, ELSEWHERE represents the environment of the theatre from which phone calls emerge.

The three cycles may now be combined to form the activity cycle diagram shown in Figure 3.8.

3.3.3 Example 3: the delivery depot

A delivery depot serves two functions. Firstly goods are received from the factory on large lorries and are held in stock. Secondly, goods are delivered to

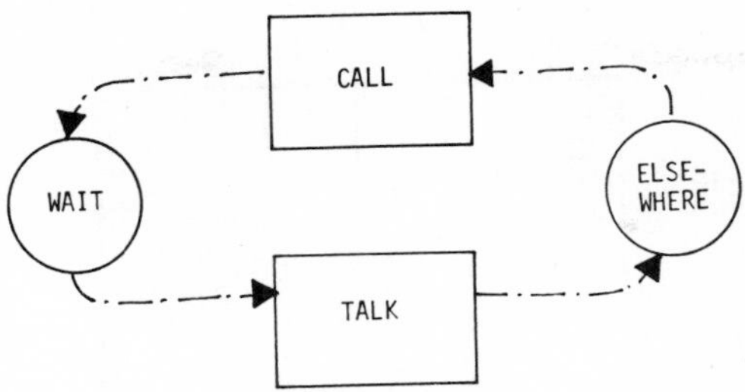

Figure 3.7 The phone enquirers' activity cycle diagram

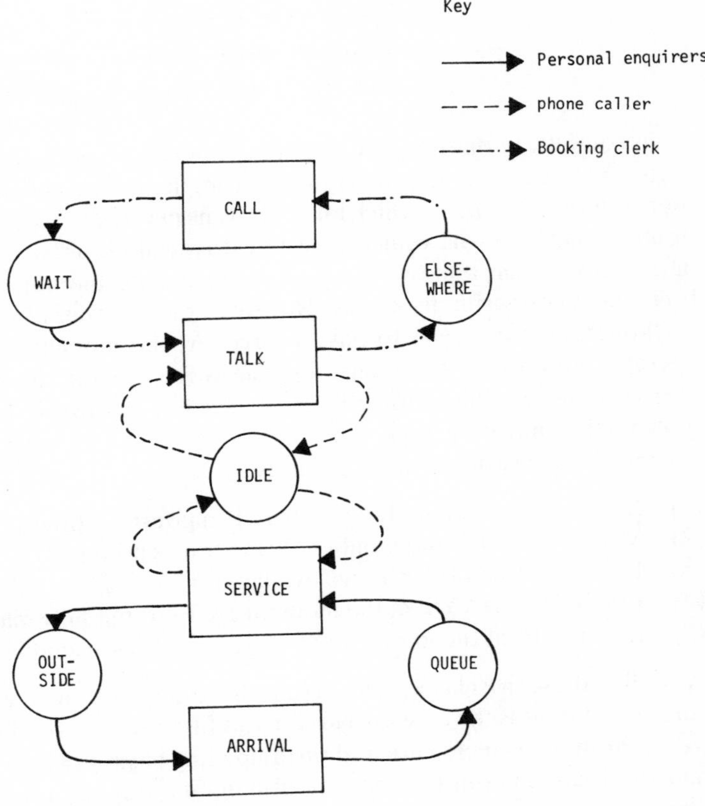

Figure 3.8 The theatre activity cycle diagram

customers by small vans which collect their loads from the stock held at the depot. At the moment, the depot has two unloading bays for the lorries and four loading bays for the vans. The same labour force is used for loading and unloading, either operation requiring a gang of two men. There are ten men available at the moment. The owners of the depot wish to know how many loading bays are needed to meet current demand.

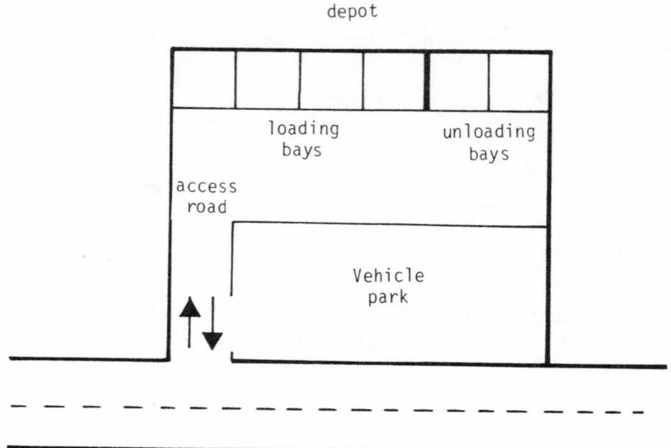

Figure 3.9 The delivery depot: site plan

To complicate matters, the depot is on a rather awkward site as shown in Figure 3.9. Access to the site is gained from the main road and at the entrance there is a vehicle park in which lorries or vans may wait. To get to either loading or unloading bays, the vehicles must be driven along a narrow access road. Its narrowness means that two lorries cannot pass one another — even if they are travelling in opposite directions. However, there is room for two vans to pass — though not for a van to pass a lorry. At the moment, the site manager operates with a rule which ensures that lorries leaving the site have priority over any other vehicles on this road. Second priority is to lorries moving towards the unloading bays.

Consider the various classes of entity.

(1) LORRIES: an unlimited number. Temporary entities;
(2) VANS: an unlimited number. Temporary entities;
(3) UNLOADING BAYS: two available;
(4) LOADING BAYS: at the moment are four, but how many are needed?
(5) LABOUR: at the moment there are five gangs available.

As well as these five classes, there is another limited resource which needs to be considered, that is the access road. Lorries fill the entire road when they move to and from the vehicle park and the unloading bays. In effect, vans need only half the road. Therefore, one way of handling this resource constraint is to divide the road into two and this gives the remaining classes as follows.

(6) ROAD IN: only 1 available.
(7) ROAD OUT: only 1 available.

We consider each of these classes in turn.

(1) Lorries

These come from OUTSIDE, which is a dead state, and ARRIVE at the site.

From this active state they join a QUEUE of vehicles — another dead state. From this they MOVE to the loading bays, another active state. This particular active state requires the co-operation of other classes of entity. For the lorry to MOVE both the ROAD IN and the ROAD OUT must be free. Also, there must be an unloading bay available and ready to take the lorry. Once in the bay, the lorry will enter the active state UNLOAD provided a labour gang is available to do the job. If not, the lorry must WAIT in the bay. This is a dead state. Once unloaded, the lorry is EMPTY — a dead state in which it must remain until the roads are both free, thus allowing it to LEAVE for OUTSIDE again.

(2) Vans

These have a very similar cycle to the lorries, though the states obviously have different names. The principal difference is that ENTER needs only the ROAD IN and EXIT requires only the ROAD OUT.

(3) Unloading bays

If treated as entities, these are engaged from the time a lorry begins to MOVE from the lorry park and until it finishes its LEAVE state. An easier way is to simply introduce a variable into the simulation. Call this variable UNBAY and set it initially to 2. For a lorry to MOVE, both road in and road out must be open and UNBAY must be greater than zero. As soon as the lorry begins to move, the value of UNBAY is reduced by 1. Its value is increased by 1 at the end of the lorry's LEAVE state.

(4) Loading bays

As with the loading bays, these are best represented by a simple variable, this time called BAY. This is set initially to 4 (or whatever number is being simulated), reduced by 1 at the start of ENTER, and increased by 1 at the end of EXIT. It must be greater than 0 for the active state ENTER to begin.

(5) Labour

This class may also be represented by a variable, this time called MEN and set initially to 10. For either of the active states UNLOAD or LOAD to begin, MEN must be greater than or equal to 2. As either of these states begins, MEN is reduced by 2 and, at their completion, men is increased by 2.

(6) and (7) Road in and road out

These entities may also be represented by variables. For lorries to MOVE or LEAVE, then both ROADIN and ROADOUT should equal 1. For vans to

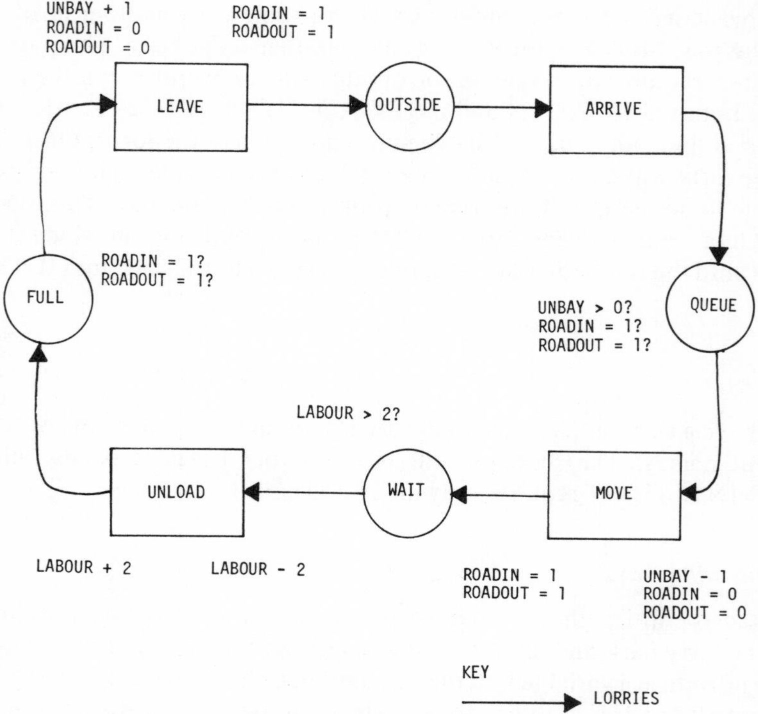

Figure 3.10 The lorries' activity cycle

ENTER, ROADIN should equal 1. For vans to EXIT, ROADOUT should equal 1.

The complete diagram is shown in Figures 3.10 and 3.11. The variables mentioned above are marked at the appropriate places. Notice that the two principal classes of entity, LORRIES and VANS, are linked only by variables. The diagram cannot, however, show the full complexity of the system. For example, it may be possible for vehicles to travel in 'convoy' down the roads.

3.3.4 Using the activity cycle diagram

As described so far, activity cycle diagrams are simply a way of showing the interactions between the various classes of entity involved in the system. It would be possible to consider these interactions by the use of lists, but most poeple find some sort of flow diagram helpful at the early stages of simulation modelling. In drawing these diagrams, the analyst is also forced to consider the events which occur as the system changes state. Initially it is useful to imagine that events occur at the beginning and end of activities. Thus, using the theatre booking clerk as an example, the following changes of state are evident.

SERVICE BEGINS	SERVICE ENDS
ARRIVAL BEGINS	ARRIVAL ENDS

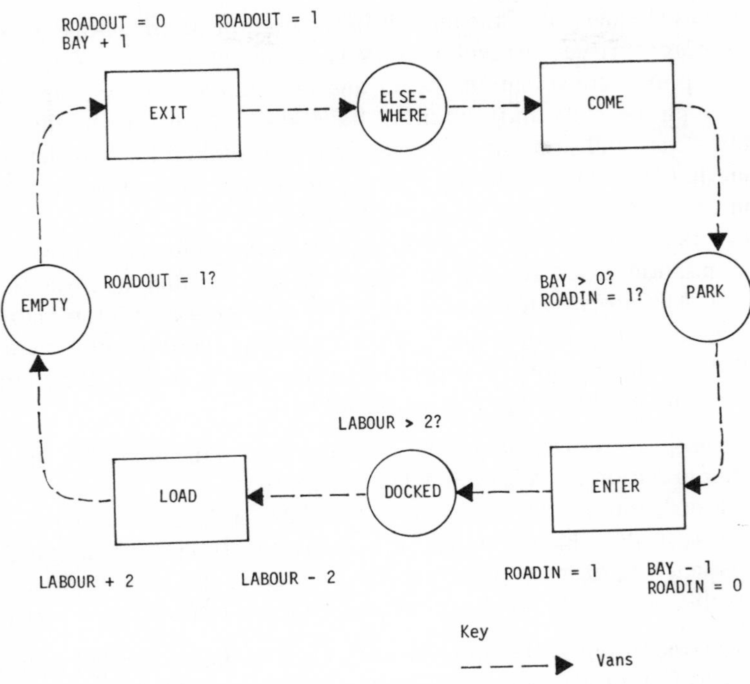

Figure 3.11 The vans' activity cycle

TALK BEGINS
CALL BEGINS

TALK ENDS
CALL ENDS.

For instance, when service begins the following changes occur.

- the booking clerk is no longer idle but engaged in service;
- the queue of waiting enquirers is reduced by 1.

Needless to say, the event will only take place if

- there is at least one enquirer in the queue;
- the clerk is free (i.e. idle).

Though eight events are listed above, some of them will always coincide. Consider the active state ARRIVAL which has two associated events ARRIVAL BEGINS and ARRIVAL ENDS. Section 3.3.2 pointed out that arrival processes may easily be modelled by a bootstrapping process and this means that two events will always coincide. That is, the ARRIVAL ENDS event for enquirer N occurs at the same time as ARRIVAL BEGINS for enquirer $N + 1$. Hence, the two can be combined into a single ARRIVAL event. Identical logic allows CALL BEGINS and CALL ENDS to be combined into CALL. In this way, the list of events is reduced from 8 to 6.

In a discrete event simulation the simulated time (simulation clock) is moved forward from event to event. At each event, state changes occur and these constitute the behaviour of the model. In the example of the harassed booking clerk, enquirers arrive at irregular intervals, the telephone rings, service begins and ends, phone conversations begin and end and so on. As this happens, queues of phone calls and enquirers build up and run down, the clerk is sometimes busy and sometimes idle, and money is taken for seat tickets. The problem that faces anyone trying to simulate such a system from scratch is to find some way of controlling the state changes.

A difficulty is that on some occasions, several operations may be due at the same simulation clock time. That is, there are parallel operations to be simulated. An unfortunate characteristic of most digital computers is that they operate serially and not in parallel. That is, parallel events cannot be made to occur at the same real time. This problem is handled by making the simulation program perform a two-stage process as follows:

(1) The program moves the simulation to the time of the next state change(s). The simulation clock is then held at that time.
(2) Any operations now due at that time are performed in some sort of priority order. For example, the harassed booking clerk must serve personal enquirers in preference to answering the phone. Once all the possible operations are complete, the program returns to the first stage.

Thus serial operations in the program are used to simulate parallel processes.

Various different ways of modelling the operations of the system exist and four methods are described in Chapters 4 and 5. All have in common the fact that the operations are broken down into a set of basic building blocks. The nature of the blocks varies between the four methods, but in all cases each block becomes a segment of computer program. The job of sorting out priorities and of sequencing the operations therefore becomes one of ensuring that the segments of program are executed in the right order. In this way, the question of 'who' does 'what' and 'when' is easily managed.

EXERCISES

1. Draw an activity cycle diagram for the following system. A barber's shop employs two barbers each of which has his own barber's chair. Both barbers work between the hours of 9.00 am to 5.00 pm and both take a 60 minute lunch break at 12.00 noon. Customers arrive at random at the shop and are served by the first available barber. If neither is free then the customers sit in the waiting area in one of the five chairs provided and read the appropriate literature. There being no shortage of barbers, customers who arrive and find the waiting area full do not remain to wait for a seat. The length of time taken to cut a customer's hair varies randomly.

2. What revisions would you need to make to the activity cycle diagram produced for Exercise 1 if each customer had a preferred barber?

3. Draw an activity cycle diagram for the following system. Trucks laden with feed grain for export arrive at a dock. At the entrance to the dock, each load of grain is sampled and if the quality is unacceptable, the truck leaves immediately still laden. Time taken to

sample a load varies randomly, as does the size of a load. Accepted loads are driven to one of three conveyors which transfer the grain to a suitable silo, of which five are available. The silos have a finite capacity and if no space is available, the trucks must wait. Periodically, ships arrive at the docks and receive grain from the silos, no ship taking grain from more than a single silo.

4. Modify the diagram drawn for Exercise 3 so that no trucks are accepted into the port if all three conveyors are in use or if all the silos are full.

5. What events would you need to consider if you were to simulate the system described in Exercise 3?

6. Consider a 'T' junction at which all normal turns are permitted. What system events would you need to consider if you were to simulate this system?

REFERENCES

Hills, P. R. (1971) *HOCUS*. P.E. Group, Egham, Surrey.
Matthewson, S. C. (1974) Simulation program generators. *Simulation* **23**(6), 181–189.

Chapter 4

Event, activity and process approaches to modelling

4.1 GENERAL IDEAS

If a novice were asked to write a program to simulate a system of interacting entities, it seems likely that he would proceed as follows. First he would identify the various classes of entity which interact within the system and then he would set down the life history of typical entities within each class. This, of course, is remarkably similar to the use of activity cycle diagrams as described in Chapter 3. However, once this stage is passed, the naïve analyst faces a difficult question. How should a program be written which embodies all of the interactions of the entities? Is there a better way than simply tracing out the life history of each entity in turn? The short answer to the second question is 'yes'. There are at least four widely used approaches to modelling for discrete simulation, and this chapter deals with three of them. These are

the event approach;
the activity approach;
the process interaction approach.

The fourth, 'the three phase approach' (Tocher, 1963) is described in some detail in Chapter 5. Each of these modelling/programming approaches embodies a distinctive world view.

The first advice to a novice simulation analyst is thus to avoid the temptation to just sit down and write the program. It is much better to consciously follow one of the approaches described here and in the next chapter. For reasons to be discussed later, it is the author's contention that the three phase method is preferable to the others.

4.1.1 A three level hierarchy

All four methods have in common the fact that they produce programs with a three level hierarchical structure (Fishman, 1973). This is as follows:

Level 1: executive (control program);
Level 2: operations;
Level 3: detailed routines.

At the highest level, there is the control program or EXECUTIVE. This is responsible for sequencing the operations which occur as the simulation proceeds; that is, it controls level 2. Hence the executive includes routines to identify when the next event is due and to ensure that the correct operations occur at that time. If the program is being written using a collection of subroutines (Section 6.5) such as GASP IV (Pritsker, 1974) or a statement description language (Section 6.6) such as ECSL (Clementson, 1982) then the executive will be hidden from the programmer. In such cases, the programmer need not know the detailed programming of the executive as long as its general principles are understood. If the program is to be written from scratch in a general purpose language, such as FORTRAN, then knowledge of the detail is clearly crucial. This chapter and the next set out to describe the principles of four different styles of executive.

The second level of a simulation program is the set of statements describing the operations that make up the model. These are the explicit instructions to the computer about the interactions of the entities. This level constitutes the simulation program 'proper' and is the major concern of the analyst in model building.

Each of the four main approaches imposes its own structure on level 2 of the program. Each requires the analyst to divide the operations of the system into its own basic building blocks. These are event routines in the case of the event approach, activities in the activity approach and processes in the process interaction approach. In the program, each of these building blocks ideally occupies its own program segment and the execution of the segments is controlled by the executive. Any interaction between the segments is also controlled by the executive.

The third level is the set of routines used by the second level to model the detail of the system of interest. It consists of routines for taking random samples, for producing reports, for collecting statistics, etc. and others for checking errors. The analyst writes the second level to call these whenever they are needed.

4.2 THE EVENT APPROACH

This is embodied in the commonly used language SIMSCRIPT (Markowitz *et al.*, 1963) and is probably more common in the USA than in Europe. The second level, or simulation program 'proper' is made up of a set of EVENT ROUTINES, each of which describes the operations in which entities engage when the system changes state. An event routine is defined as the set of actions that may follow from a state change in the system.

Consider for example, a single server queueing system. If customers arrive randomly, join the queue and are served on a first in first out (FIFO) basis, then there are two state changes in the system:

(1) arrival of a new customer;
(2) end of a service, i.e. departure of a customer.

If an event based approach is being followed, each of these events requires an event routine in the simulation. If it is not important to distinguish between individual customers, then the arrival event routine is as shown as a flow diagram in Figure 4.1. The event routine for the end of service is shown as a flow diagram in Figure 4.2.

The inter-arrival times and service times are generated by using level 3 sampling routines. The events themselves are scheduled by interfacing with the executive.

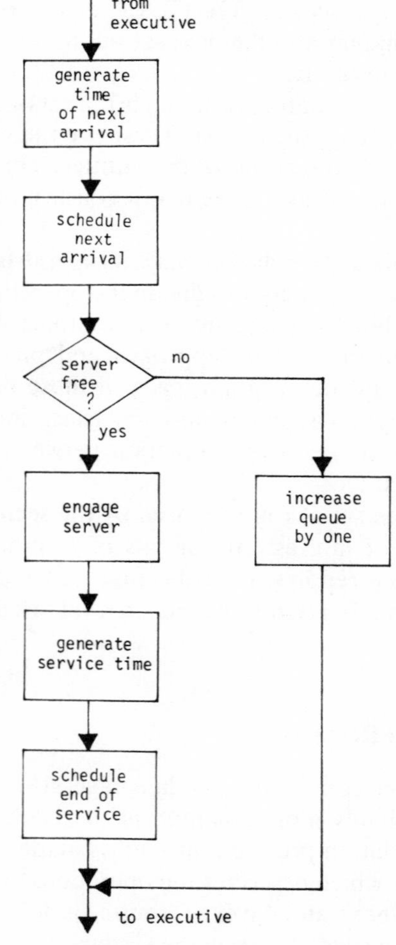

Figure 4.1 Simple queue: arrival event routine

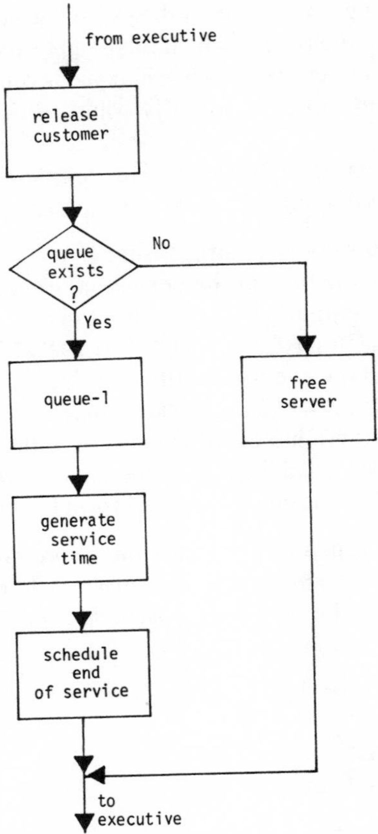

Figure 4.2 Simple queue: end of service event routine

4.2.1 An event based executive

In order to control the operation of a simulation, an event based executive must perform the following tasks:

(1) TIME SCAN: determining when the next event is due to occur and moving simulation clock time to then;
(2) EVENT IDENTIFICATION: correctly identifying which events are due at that time;
(3) EVENT EXECUTION: executing properly those events identified as due now.

A simple event based executive would manage these tasks by the use of an EVENT LIST, which can be thought of as a diary into which future event notices are written. Event notices are added to and removed from this list as the simulation proceeds. For example, in the simple queueing system, an arrival might cause an event notice for the end of a service to be added to the event list.

At the very least, each event notice on the event list should contain two pieces of information. Firstly, the time at which this event is due to occur and secondly something to identify the event. It is often also convenient to include an extra record with each event notice to identify which entities are involved in this event.

As the simulation proceeds, the executive completes a continual two phase cycle until the simulation is complete. The two phases are as follows:

(1) TIME SCAN. This involves three tasks:
  (a) determining the time of the next event by scanning the event list;
  (b) moving the simulation clock to that time;
  (c) producing a CURRENT EVENTS LIST which consists of the event notices of all the events identified as due now;
(2) EVENT EXECUTION. This ensures that each event on the current events list is executed. No event may occur without instruction from the executive, thus all logical links are controlled by the executive. After the event is executed, its notice is removed from the current events list.

This two phase cycle is repeated until the simulation is over. See Figure 4.3.

Needless to say, if the simulation is complex, then many events will be scheduled for the future, thus producing a sizable event list. Hence designers of

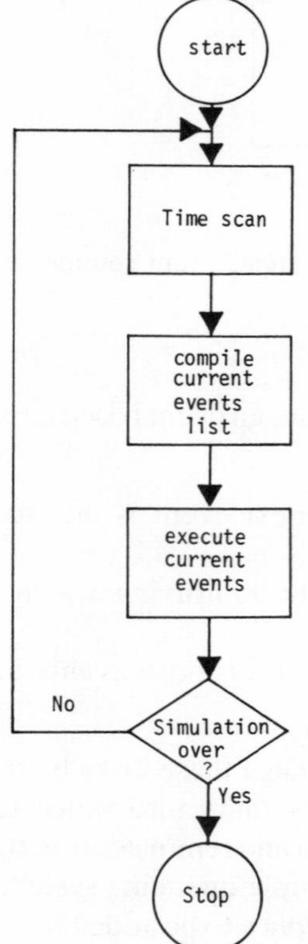

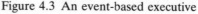

Figure 4.3 An event-based executive

simulation executives need to be careful to use appropriate list processing techniques to minimize the amount of computer time consumed by the executive in scanning the event list and operating the current events list.

4.2.2 The harassed booking clerk — an event based model

Assuming the existence of at least a simple event based executive of the type described in Section 4.2.1, it is quite simple to produce an event based model of the problem introduced in Figure 3.8. This model is, in effect, a specification of level 2 of the program. For this example, there are four events to be considered and these are described below.

ARRIVAL OF NEXT PERSONAL ENQUIRER, who is immediately served if the clerk is free and no queue exists. Otherwise, the enquirer joins the queue (see Figure 4.4).
END OF PERSONAL SERVICE: the enquirer leaves the premises. The clerk serves the next enquirer if any are waiting in the queue. If none are waiting, the clerk talks to the first phone caller in the waiting line. Otherwise, the clerk becomes idle (see Figure 4.5).
ARRIVAL OF NEXT PHONE CALL: if the clerk is free and there are no enquirers or phone calls waiting, then a phone conversation with this caller begins. Otherwise, the call is added to the waiting line (see Figure 4.6).
END OF PHONE CONVERSATION: the caller rings off. The clerk serves the next personal enquirer if any are waiting. If none are waiting, the clerk talks to the next phone caller in the waiting line. Otherwise, the clerk becomes idle. Much of this event routine is the same as the END OF PERSONAL SERVICE routine (see Figure 4.7).

Each ‘arrival’ type event routine includes the scheduling of the next arrival by a bootstrapping procedure as discussed in Section 3.3.2.

Notice two things about these event routines. Firstly that it is important that the executive should give the lowest priority to the ARRIVAL OF NEXT PHONE CALL event. This is done by making sure that this event is processed last of all if it is scheduled to occur at the same time as any other event. This ensures that phone conversations will begin only if there are no personal enquirers waiting. Secondly, they do not treat all phone calls or all enquirers as alike.

As described so far, this event based model of the harassed booking clerk makes no provision for the collection of data about the performance of the system as the simulation proceeds. One convenient way of doing this is to simply collect data at regular intervals as the simulation proceeds. The easiest way to implement this is to add an extra event routine, DATA COLLECTION (Figure 4.8). Each time the DATA COLLECTION event occurs, the data are recorded and the next data collection event is scheduled. This allows, for example, the regular collection of data about the number of personal enquirers and the number of phone calls waiting to be served. This is far from being the

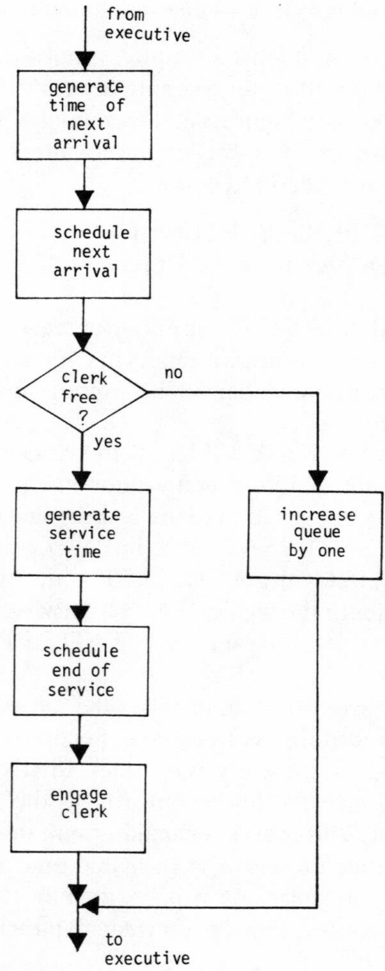

Figure 4.4 Arrival of personal enquirer event routine

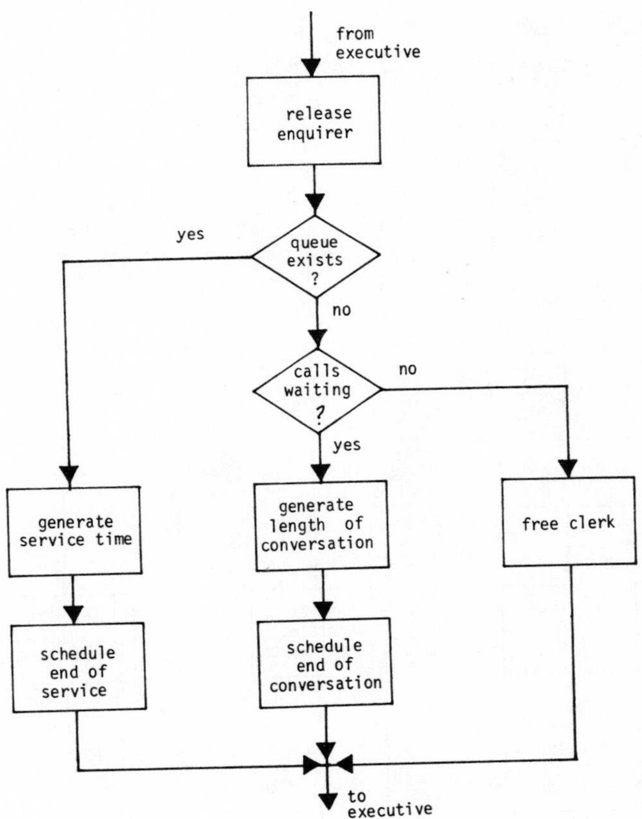

Figure 4.5 End of personal service event routine

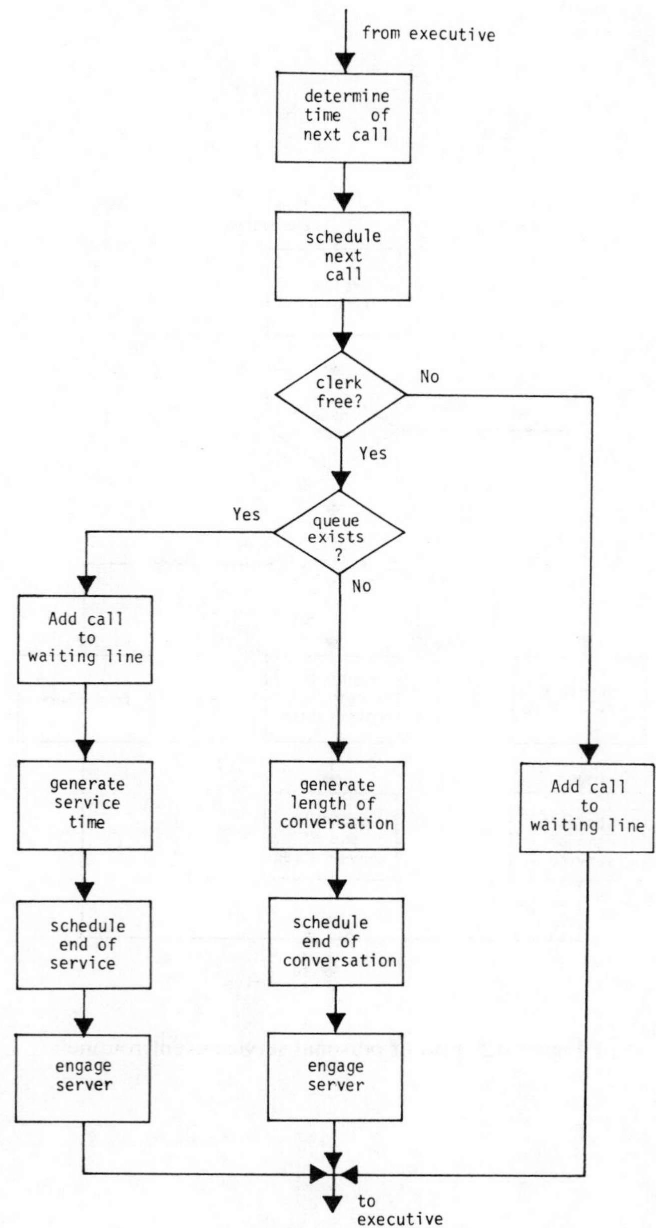

Figure 4.6 Arrival of next phone call event routine

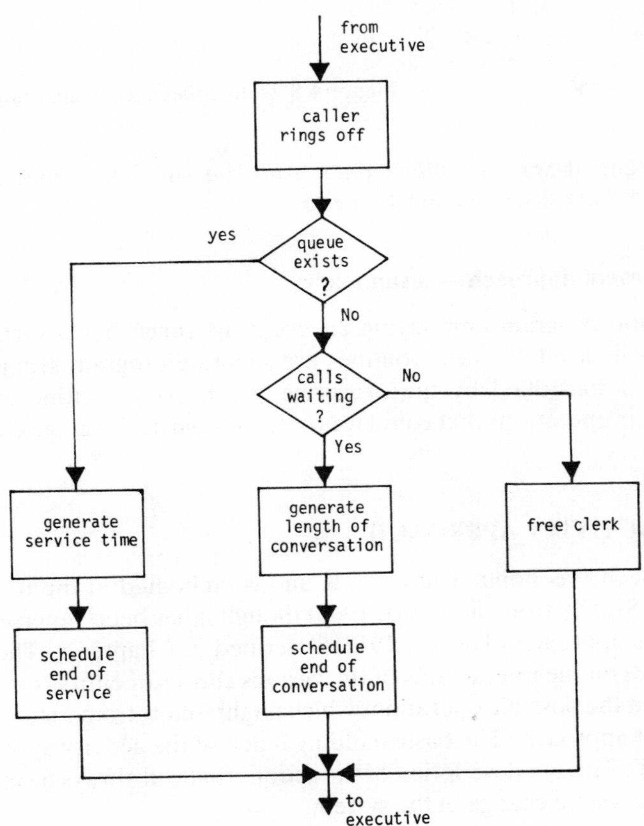

Figure 4.7 End of phone conversation event routine

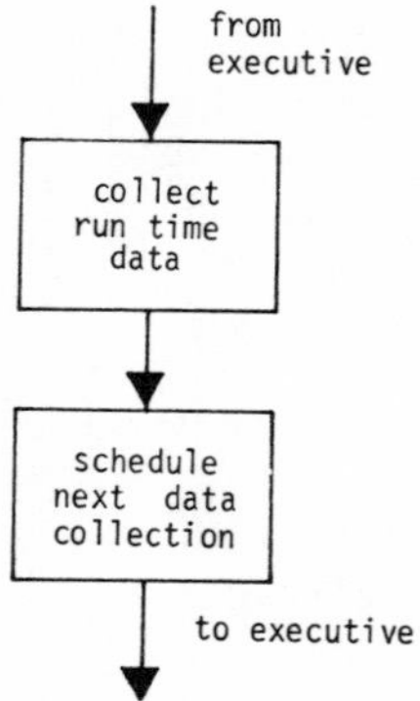

Figure 4.8 Data collection event routine

most convenient way to collect data from the simulation and other more efficient ways are discussed in Chapter 5.

4.2.3 The event approach — a summary

A simulation program embodying an event approach has a series of event routines as its level 2. These routines are separate program segments whose execution is controlled by the executive. Each event routine exhaustively describes the operations that could follow from a particular stage change in the system.

4.3 THE ACTIVITY APPROACH

This approach was popular in the UK and is embodied in the programming language CSL (Buxton and Laski, 1962) though it has been superseded by the three phase approach (Tocher, 1963) described in Chapter 5. The approach concentrates on the interactions of the various classes of entity, rather than on mapping out the possible operations which might follow from a state change, as in the event approach. The basic building block of the activity approach is the ACTIVITY. This is a description of the actions that will always be immediately triggered by a state change in the system.

As before, consider a single server queueing system. Though there are two event routines needed to simulate this system's operation (Section 4.2), these need to be represented by three activities. Thus, instead of the events CUSTOMER ARRIVAL and END OF SERVICE, there are the following three activities:

(1) ARRIVAL OF A NEW CUSTOMER;
(2) BEGIN A NEW SERVICE;
(3) END OF SERVICE.

That is, there are now three events — BEGIN A NEW SERVICE having been separated from the others. When coded as program segments, each of these activities will have the same two part structure:

TEST HEAD: the conditions which must be satisfied if the activity is to be executed.
ACTIONS: the operations which constitute the activity. Only performed if the tests are passed.

Level 2 of an activity based program thus consists of a set of independent segments each of which has this two part activity structure. Flow diagrams of the three activities are shown in Figures 4.9–4.11.

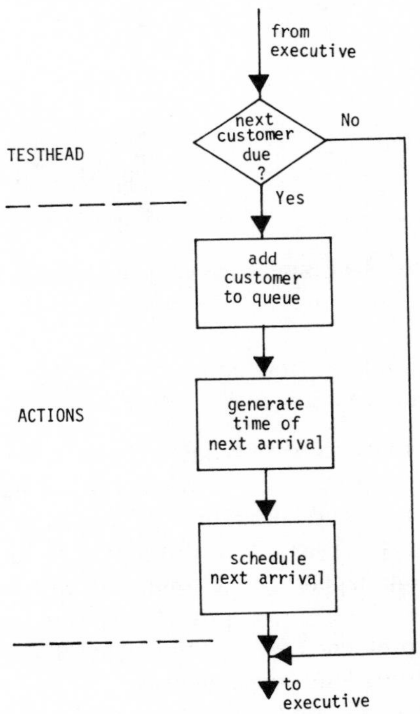

Figure 4.9 Simple queue: arrival activity

This simple example illustrates an important feature of the activity approach. Each activity should be considered as a segment of program waiting to be executed. The actions will be performed if, and only if, the tests are passed. Thus, the actions

engage server
remove customer at head of queue
generate service time
schedule end of service

will only be executed if

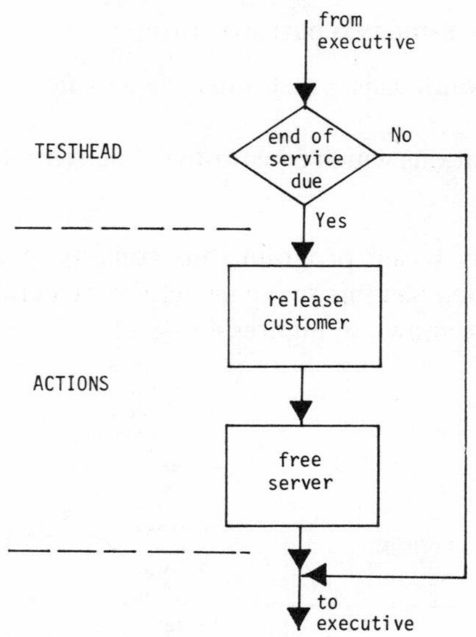

Figure 4.10 Simple queue: end service activity

(1) the server happens to be free; and
(2) there are customers waiting to be served.

At the end of each activity, control is passed back to the executive. If the tests are failed, then control is returned to the executive without performing the actions. As with event based simulations, the system moves from event to event. At each event, each activity is attempted in turn. The actions to be performed at each event depend on the conditions within the simulation at that event. Thus, whereas the event approach requires the analyst to state all possible outcomes from each event, the activity approach requires only identification of the immediate consequences.

Notice too that some apparent anomalies are caused by this approach. For example in the arrival activity, customers move straight into the queue. This happens whether or not the server is free and regardless of the number of waiting customers. In fact this is not an anomaly if the BEGIN SERVICE activity is scanned after ARRIVAL. Placing the customer in the queue satisfies one of the conditions for the BEGIN SERVICE activity and thus service will begin if the server is free. Hence the arriving customer will be delayed for zero time. This means that the order in which the activities are processed is crucial.

4.3.1 An activity based executive

In a simple activity based simulation, the executive has only one major task to perform. This is the TIME SCAN, which involves the identification of when

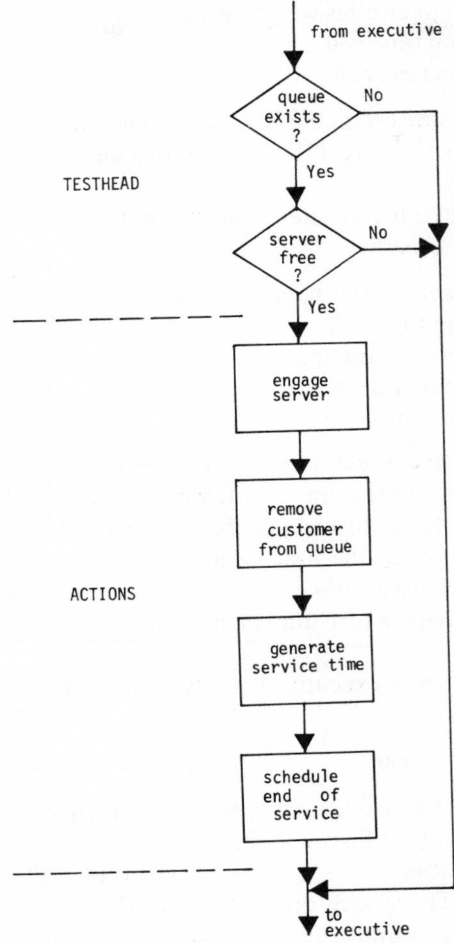

Figure 4.11 Simple queue: begin service activity

the next event is due. Whereas the event approach used a dynamic event list to achieve this diary effect, time cells are used in the activity approach. Time cells are attributes of the permanent entities and indicate when each entity is due to change state. This is done in one of two ways:

(1) *By setting the time cell to the time at which the entity is due to change state.*

For example, SERVER(TIME) = 509 indicates that a state change is due at time 509.

If the simulation clock (i.e. current simulation time) is greater than the value of the time cell, then this indicates that the entity is in an idle state waiting for something to happen, e.g. the server is waiting because there are no customers to serve. With this type of time cell, the time scan is implemented as follows:

```
FOR all permanent entities with time cell > clock
   FIND minimum time cell
clock = minimum time cell.
```

(2) *By setting the time cell to the interval until the state change.*

For example, if SERVER(TIME) = 10, this indicates that a state change is due in 10 time units.

A negative time cell indicates that the entity is idle. The time scan is implemented as follows:

```
FOR all permanent entities with time cell > 0
   FIND minimum time cell
clock = clock + minimum time cell
FOR all permanent entities
   time cell = time cell − clock.
```

In a simple executive, the time cells may be held as a list which is not ordered by value. During the time scan no attempt is made to identify which of the entities will cause the state change. No attempt is made to identify which activity is due next. After the time scan the clock is moved to the next event time and the executive makes repeated activity scans. These involve attempting each activity in turn until no more action is possible, i.e. until all sets of tests are failed.

Thus, an activity based executive has a two phase structure as follows:

(1) time scan;
(2) repeated activity scan.

At the completion of phase (2), the executive returns to phase (1), etc., until the simulation is over (see Figure 4.12).

As mentioned earlier, the sequence in which the activities appear in the program is crucial. Those with the highest priority must be attempted first in the activity scan. For example, in the single server queue, the activities should be scanned in the following order:

(1) END SERVICE;
(2) ARRIVAL;
(3) BEGIN SERVICE.

Thus, before a service can begin, the executive checks to see if any in-progress service can finish and to see if any other customer will arrive. In more complex simulations it is necessary to ensure that, after each time scan, repeated activity scans occur until no more action is possible at that time. The time cells themselves are updated during each activity. For example, the activity BEGIN SERVICE involves resetting the time cell of the server to the time at which the service will finish. Earlier, the apparent anomaly of new customers being fed into the queue was raised. This happens whether or not other customers are waiting. Provided that the arrival activity is scanned before the begin service activity, then the customer will in fact remain in the queue for zero time if there are no other customers in the queue and if the server is free.

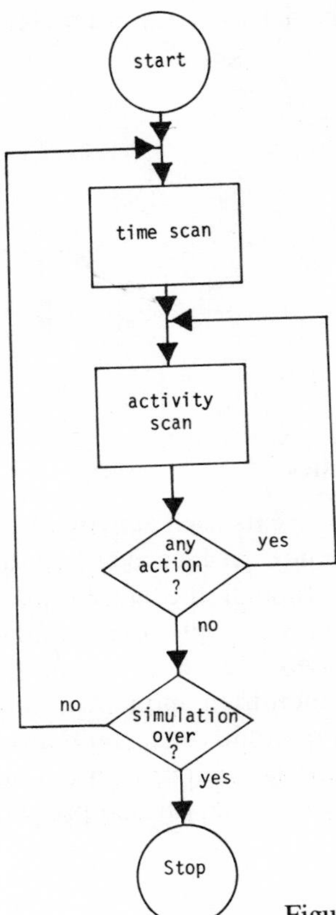

Figure 4.12 An activity based executive

4.3.2 The harassed booking clerk — an activity based approach

From the activity cycle diagram (Figure 3.8) there are four active states which lead to the four event routines described in Section 4.2.2. Considering each of these active states in turn leads to a list of appropriate activities:

(1) *Arrival of next personal enquirer*. This active state leads to a single activity in which successive arrivals are bootstrapped.

(2) *Service of a personal enquirer*. This leads to two activities:
   (i) begin service;
   (ii) end service.

(3) *Arrival of next phone call*. This too leads to a single activity in which successive arrivals are bootstrapped.

(4) *End of phone conversation*. This active state leads to two activities:
   (i) begin conversation
   (ii) end conversation.

As with the event based approach, the easiest way of collecting run-time statistics is to add an extra routine.

To preserve the logic of the system, the activities should be scanned in the following order.

end personal service;
arrival of personal enquirer;
end phone conversation;
arrival of phone call;
begin personal service;
begin phone conversation;
collect run statistics.

Flow diagrams are shown in Figures 4.13–4.19.

4.3.3 Activity versus event based approaches

Because the activity approach deliberately treats each activity as independent this can obviously lead to run-time inefficiency. At each event, the activity scan attempts each activity in turn — even though the conditions within the simulation may mean that only one activity is possible. On the other hand, an event based approach (Section 4.2) involves execution of only those events known to be possible, these having been identified and passed to the current events list. Hence an event based simulation should run faster than one which is activity based. Why then should the activity based approach have developed? The answer is that it is rather easier to write activity based programs for two

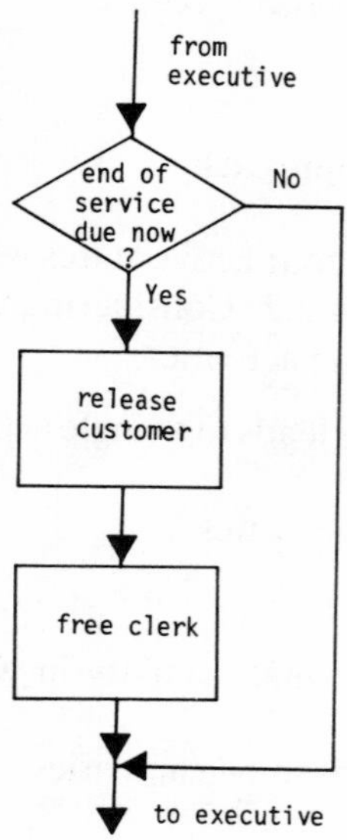

Figure 4.13 End of personal service activity

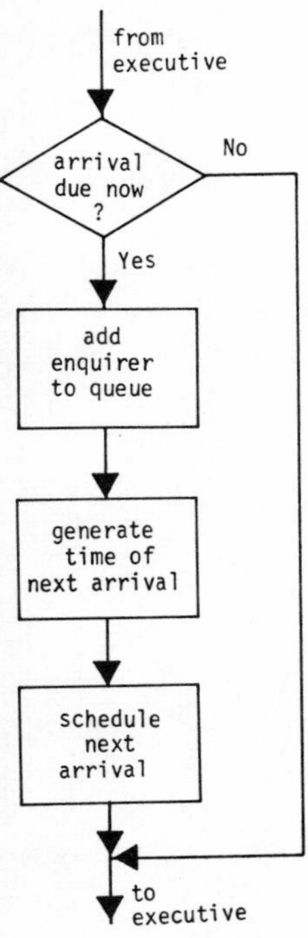

Figure 4.14 Arrival of personal enquirer activity

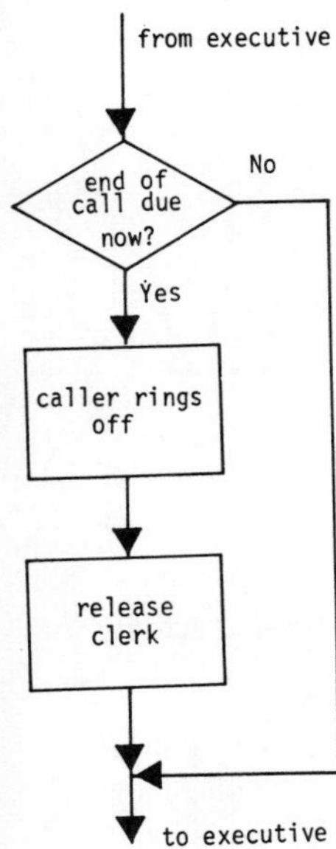

Figure 4.15 End of phone conversation activity

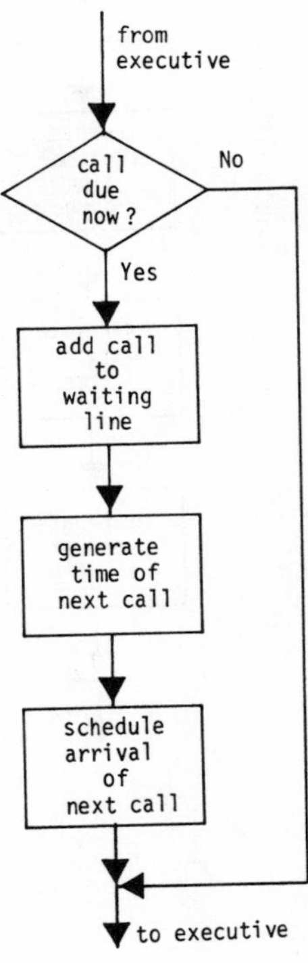

Figure 4.16 Arrival of phone call activity

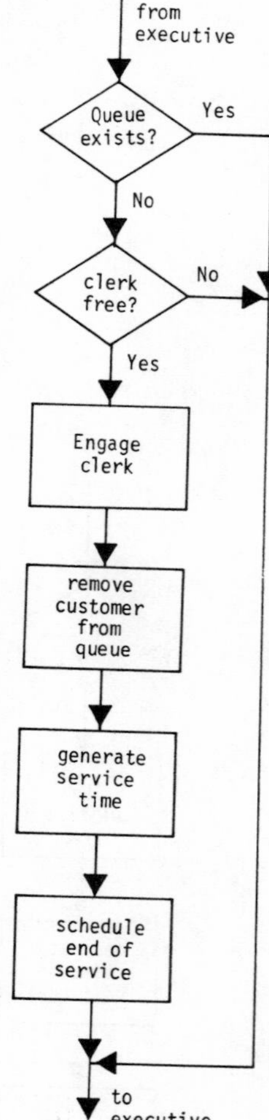

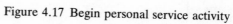

Figure 4.17 Begin personal service activity

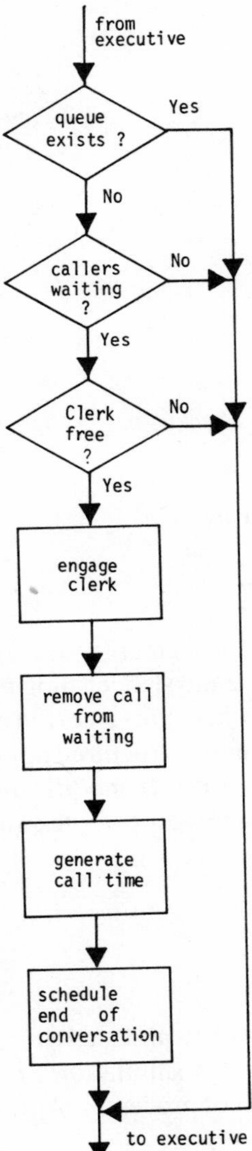

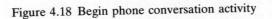

Figure 4.18 Begin phone conversation activity

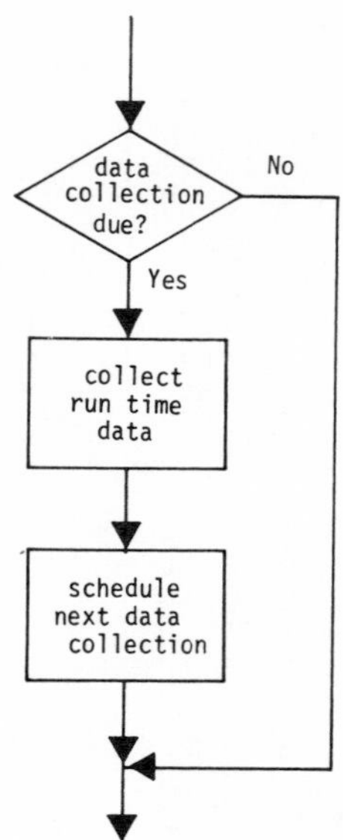

Figure 4.19 Data collection activity

reasons. Firstly, they tend to produce smaller program segments for activities than would be the case for events. Secondly, the analyst need not be too concerned about the sequence of activities at each event — this is sorted out by the executive in the activity scan. This allows a much more structured approach to the initial programming and also makes for much easier modification of existing models. This is particularly important in large and complex simulations.

4.4 THE PROCESS INTERACTION APPROACH

This is an attempt to combine features of both event and activity based approaches. Rather than making the second level of a simulation program consist of event routines or activities, it consists of a set of processes. As before, each of these is a separate segment of program.

A process is defined as the sequence of operations through which an entity passes during its life within the system. It is important to notice that each separate temporary entity (e.g. each customer) has its own process which stops and starts as the simulation proceeds. At its simplest, this approach is closest to that which a naïve analyst (Section 4.1) might try to follow. Two well-known process based simulation programming 'languages' are SIMULA (Hills, 1973) and GPSS (Greenberg, 1972). SIMULA is rather more versatile than GPSS in that GPSS only allows the user to model the processes of temporary entities (e.g. customers). SIMULA allows processes for temporary and permanent entities.

Consider again the single server queueing system. The customer process is as follows:

customer arrives;
waits until head of the queue;
moves into the service channel;
remains in the service channel until service is complete and finally leaves the system.

A flow diagram for this process is shown in Figure 4.20. The points marked * are re-activation points. The entity is held there in its process until re-activation occurs, due either to the end of a scheduled delay or to favourable conditions within the simulation.

Typically, a process interaction approach views each entity as moving through the various operations which constitute its process. Its progress continues until the entity is blocked or delayed for some reason. Generally two kinds of delay are considered.

(1) *Unconditional delays*, e.g. the service time. In these, the entity remains at the same point in its process until the pre-determined time has elapsed. In the simple queueing system, a customer remains in the service channel until the service is complete.

(2) *Conditional delays* (wait until), whose duration is dependent on the general state of the system. Hence the entity remains at that point in its process until conditions allow it to move. For example, the customer remains in the queue until the server is free and the customer is at the head of the queue.

The re-activation points indicate where the entity will move to when its current delay is complete. In the case of the single server queueing system, these are analogous to the events and activities of the other two approaches. Thus each customer may be re-activated when it arrives, when service begins and when service ends.

4.4.1 A process based executive

The simplest way to implement a process interaction executive is to employ two lists of records. Each record identifies the following:

(1) the entity concerned;
(2) its next re-activation point.

In GPSS (Greenberg, 1972) these two lists are known as the Future Events List and the Current Events Lists. The same terminology will be used here.

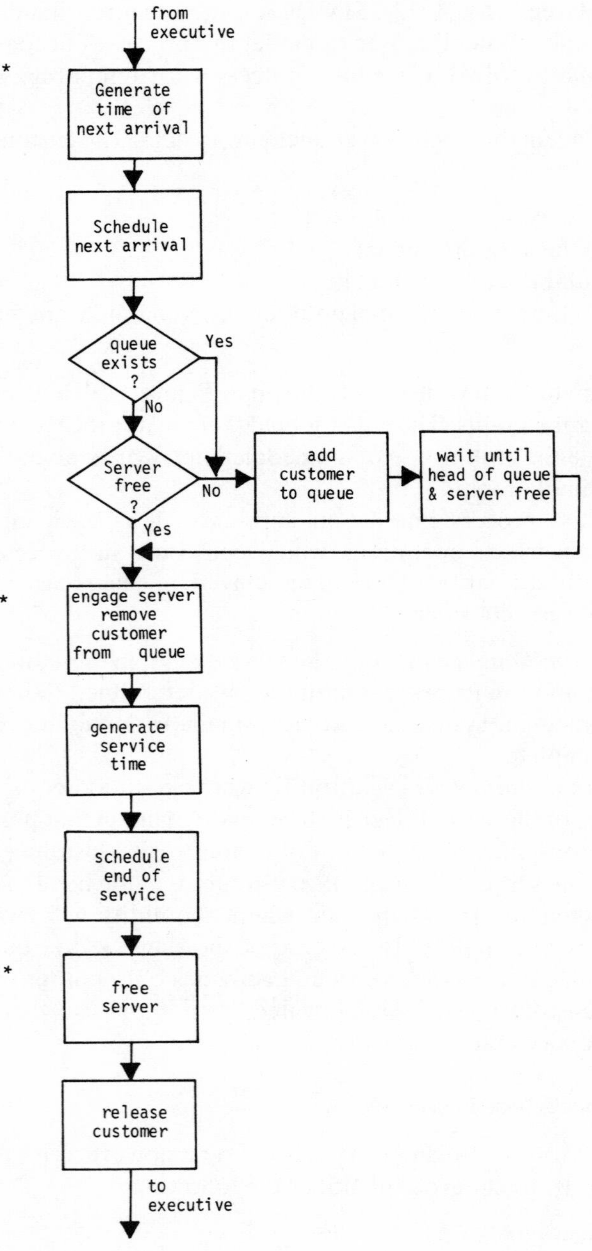

Figure 4.20 Simple queue: customer process

The Future Events List includes the records for those entities whose movement is delayed and whose re-activation time is known. For convenience, the re-activation time may be added to the record. In the single server queueing system, an arrival due some time in the future or a scheduled end of service would be entered on this list.

The Current Events List contains the records of two types of entity.

(1) Those whose movement is delayed and whose re-activation is scheduled for the current clock time in the simulation. For example an arrival may be due now.

(2) Those whose movement is delayed by conditions within the simulation. They will be re-activated when conditions are right. Hence a customer might be held on this list after arrival and until reaching the head of the queue.

As the simulation proceeds, the executive goes through the following cycle.

(1) FUTURE EVENTS SCAN. From the records on this list, pick out those entities with the earliest re-activation time. The simulation clock is then moved forward to that time.

(2) MOVE RECORDS of now current entities from the future events list to the current events list.

(3) CURRENT EVENTS SCAN. Attempt to move each entity on the current events list through its process from its re-activation point. If the entity moves, note where it is finally blocked. If the delay it now encounters is unconditional, file a new record for this entity on the future events list. The record should identify the re-activation point. If the delay will be conditional, file a new record on the current events list. In both cases remove the previous record from the current events list. If an entity completes its process, delete its record entirely. Repeat the current events scan until no entities move.

This is shown in Figure 4.21.

Associated with each entity there will generally be one or more attributes which may be used to determine whether movement is possible if the entity is on the current events list. For example, one attribute might record the position of a customer in the queue.

4.4.2 The harassed booking clerk — a process based approach

In this case there are two obvious types of process, one for each class of

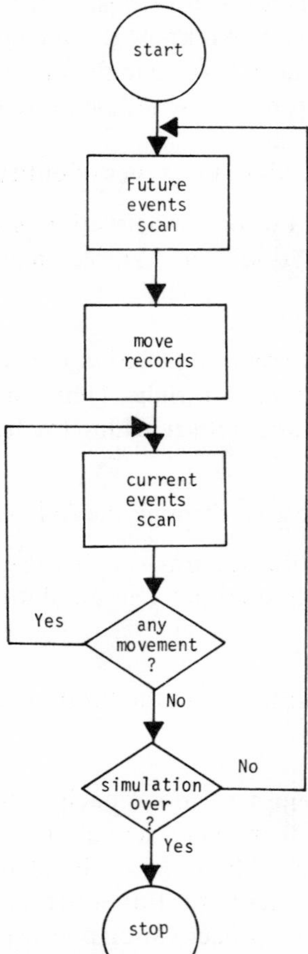

Figure 4.21 A process based executive

temporary entity. Thus each personal enquirer will have a process rather like that of the customers in the single server queueing system. The phone calls will have a similar process except that the fact that personal enquirers have priority must be included. As before, each of the processes will have three re-activation points. The process for personal enquirers is similar to that shown in Figure 4.20. In this case, 'customers' are renamed 'personal enquirers' and the 'server' is the 'clerk'. The phone callers' process is shown in Figure 4.22.

The points marked with a cross (+) are conditional re-activation points and are re-activated direct from the current events list. The points marked with an asterisk (*) are conditional re-activation points which are re-activated by transferring the event from the future events list to the current events list. The events themselves are scheduled in the immediately preceding section of program.

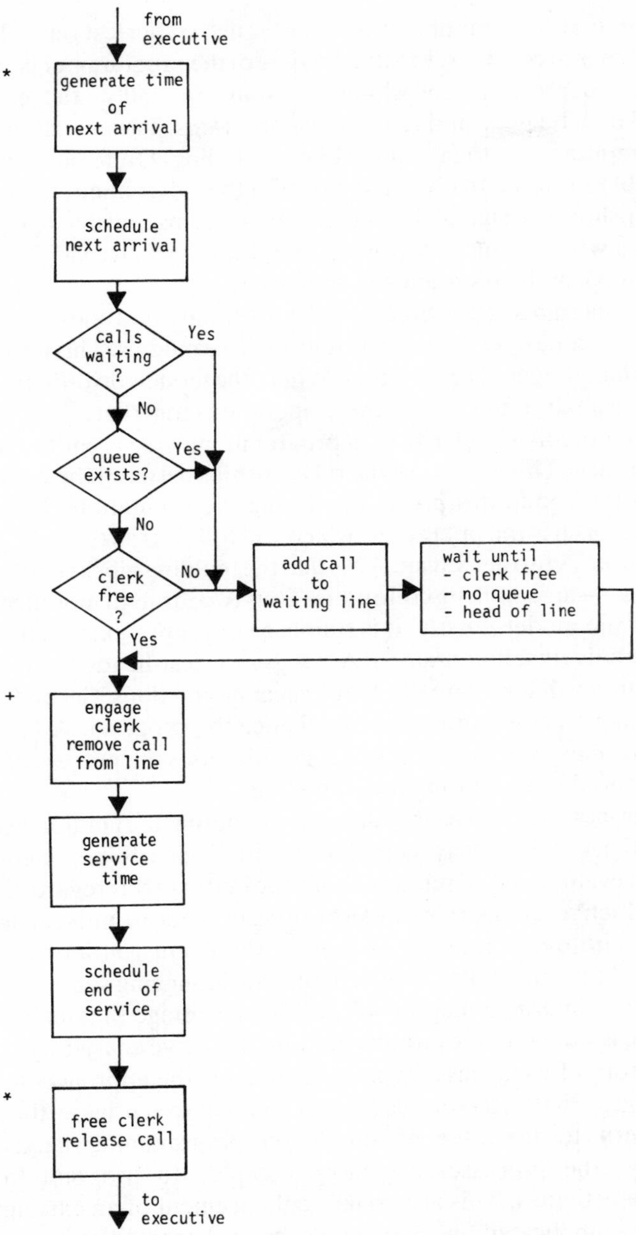

Figure 4.22 The phone callers' process

4.5 A COMPARISON OF THESE APPROACHES

In deciding which of these various approaches is best, it should be remembered that the aim of any method used should be to aid the production of a valid, working simulation at minimum cost and/or in the shortest time. There are two costs and times to consider. Firstly, the time of the programmer or analyst who is attempting to produce a working program. Secondly, the computer time consumed in debugging and running the programs. The current trend is for the cost of computer time to fall and to keep on falling. Quite powerful computers are available for a relatively small cost. On the other hand, the cost of skilled manpower shows no sign of dropping. Thus it seems sensible to concentrate on approaches which reduce the time to produce working, valid simulations by easing the task of the programmer or analyst.

The flow diagrams of the three versions of the harassed booking clerk example show that the same operations appear in all three models. This is to be expected, as all are simulating the same system. Where the models do differ is in the degree to which the analyst must string these operations together.

It is undoubtedly simpler from a programming viewpoint to use an activity based approach. This is because the relationships between the activities is taken care of by the conditions prevailing during the simulation. The focus of the activity approach is the operations which will follow from specific conditions in the simulation. A further advantage is that the building blocks of the approach—the activities—are small, discrete units. Thus two forms of modification are easy to make to the model. Firstly, it is simple to introduce extra activities because these are relatively self-contained. As long as the test-heads are well formulated the simulation will take care of other logical interactions. Secondly, individual activities may be easily modified to enhance the program. A further point in favour of an activity approach is that it greatly eases the process of "top-down" design favoured in structuring programming.

However, not all is in favour of the activity approach. A major disadvantage is that the activity scan is always complete and this is clearly inefficient and a waste of time. An event based simulation should be better in this regard as there are no conditional activities to sort out by an event scan. The testing is carried out within an appropriate event routine. However, the event routines can get rather complex and this can make enhancement and debugging somewhat tortuous.

The process interaction approach has the advantage that its building block, the process, is similar to the intuitive notions of a naïve analyst trying to map out the life history of each class of entity. However, the approach does have two disadvantages. Firstly, it requires a rather complex executive—though that is of little concern to the user of simulation programming languages. More importantly, the processes are more complex to program than are the comparable activities. This also makes enhancement of an existing program a much more complicated business, unless careful consideration is given to this possibility when the programs are originally written. Whether a process based approach is particularly efficient to run very much depends on how the executive is implemented.

Given the high cost of skilled manpower and the relatively low cost of computer time, the activity approach is appealing in its simplicity. The next chapter discusses the three phase approach (Tocher, 1963) which retains the simple programming of the activity approach yet allows much more efficient execution of the program.

EXERCISES

1. Find out which discrete simulation languages are available on your computer and check whether they are event, activity or process based.

2. Using a general purpose language such as BASIC, program each of the three executives mentioned in this chapter. Try to use the same blocks of program in each executive.

3. Devise ways of collecting statistics from the simulations other than the simple way suggested in this chapter.

4. Describe how you would modify the activities, events or processes of the harassed booking clerk problem if there were two clerks. Assume that both clerks attend to both types of customer.

5. Describe what modifications would be needed to your answer to Exercise 4 if one clerk answered the phone and the other attended to personal enquirers.

6. What events, activities and processes would be needed to simulate the barbers' shop described in the Exercises at the end of Chapter 3?

7. What events, activities and processes would be needed to simulate the grain dock described in the Exercises at the end of Chapter 3?

8. Using an executive developed for Exercise 2, write a program to simulate the simple queueing system.

9. Using an executive developed for Exercise 2, write a program to simulate the harassed booking clerk problem.

10. Modify your program for the harassed booking clerk problem to allow for two clerks.

REFERENCES

Buxton, J. N., & Laski, J. G. (1962) Control and simulation language. *The Computer Journal*, **5**, 1962.

Clementson, A. T. (1982) *Extended Control and Simulation Language*. Cle. Com Ltd, Birmingham, UK.

Fishman, G. S. (1973) *Concepts and Methods of Discrete Event Digital Simulation*. Wiley, New York.

Greenberg, S. (1972) *GPSS primer*. Wiley, New York.

Hills, P. R. (1973) *An Introduction to Simulation Using SIMULA*. NCC Publication 5-Ss. Norwegian computing centre, Oslo.

Markowitz, H. M., Hausner, B., & Karr, H. W. (1963) *SIMSCRIPT: A Simulation Programming Language*. RAND Corporation RM-3310-pr 1962. Prentice–Hall, Englewood Cliffs, New Jersey.

Pritsker, A. A. B. (1974) *The GASP IV Simulation Language*. Wiley, New York.

Tocher, K. D. (1963) *The Art of Simulation*. English Universities Press, London.

Chapter 5

The three phase approach

5.1 'B' AND 'C' ACTIVITIES

The three phase approach was first described by Tocher (1963) and succeeds in combining the simplicity of the activity approach (Section 4.3) with the efficient execution of the event based approach to discrete event simulation (Section 4.2). As with the activity approach, the basic building block is the activity — this time there are two types of activity.

'B' ACTIVITIES: (bound or book-keeping activities) which are executed directly by the executive program whenever their scheduled time is reached.

'C' ACTIVITIES: (conditional or co-operative activities) whose execution depends on either

the co-operation of different classes of entity; or

the satisfaction of specific conditions within the simulation.

The 'B' activities are simply those operations and actions that occur immediately after a scheduled system event. 'C' activities are the remaining operations whose start is dependent upon whatever conditions prevail during the simulation. Each of these 'B' and 'C' activities is programmed as an independent program routine or procedure, as in the simple activity approach (Section 4.3).

Consider again the simple single server queueing system in which customers arrive at random intervals for service; wait until served; are served, their service time also being random; and then leave the system. Thus there are two events which can reliably be scheduled.

(1) CUSTOMER ARRIVAL: Assuming that arrivals are bootstrapped, then the nth customer will arrive when the inter-arrival time between customer $n - 1$ and customer n has elapsed. No other conditions exist and thus this activity is bound to occur then. Therefore, this is a 'B' activity.
(2) END OF SERVICE: This will occur when the service time has elapsed, the service time being determined from some sample at the start of the service. Thus, the activity which follows (releasing the customer and

freeing the server) is bound to occur whatever the other conditions in the simulation. Therefore, this is also a 'B' activity.

Finally, the third activity is

(3) BEGIN SERVICE: This can occur only if two conditions are met. Firstly there should be at least one customer waiting to be served. Secondly, that server should be free to serve. Thus, the activity is conditional and co-operative — indicating that it can safely be regarded as a 'C' activity. Hence, to simulate this system, two 'B' activities and a single 'C' activity are needed.

If flow diagrams were to be drawn for each of these activities, they would be virtually the same as those shown in Figures 4.9–4.11. The only differences is that the two 'B' activities would have no test heads and would therefore consist of only a set of actions.

5.2 A THREE PHASE EXECUTIVE

The three phases to be performed are usually expressed as A, B, and C to make them more memorable. The executive cycles through the phases as the simulation proceeds.

A PHASE (time scan): determine when the next event is due and decide which 'B' activities are then due to occur. Move simulation clock time to the time of the next event.

B PHASE (B calls): execute only those 'B' activities identified in the 'A' phase as being due now.

C PHASE (C scan): attempt each of the 'C' activities in turn and execute those whose conditions are satisfied. Repeat the 'C' scan until no more activity is possible.

An outline flow diagram for such an executive is shown in Figure 5.1.

A simple way of implementing a three phase executive is to assign a three part record to each entity. The first part is the time cell which indicates the simulation time at which this entity is next due to change state. The second part indicates which 'B' activity is due to occur at that state change. If the entity is waiting to take part in a 'C' activity, then some indication is given that the next activity is undetermined. The third part indicates the activity in which the entity was last engaged. See Figure 5.2.

During the time scan, the executive examines those entities for which a 'B' activity is scheduled. From the records of these entities it finds the minimum time cell. It then makes a list of all entities which have this minimum time cell. This indicates the entities which will be involved in the next event. After moving the simulation clock forward to the next event, the executive starts those 'B' activities known to be due now. This is done by linking the list of 'due now' entities to their records. When this 'B' phase is complete, the executive enters the 'C' phase as in a conventional activity scan (Section 4.3).

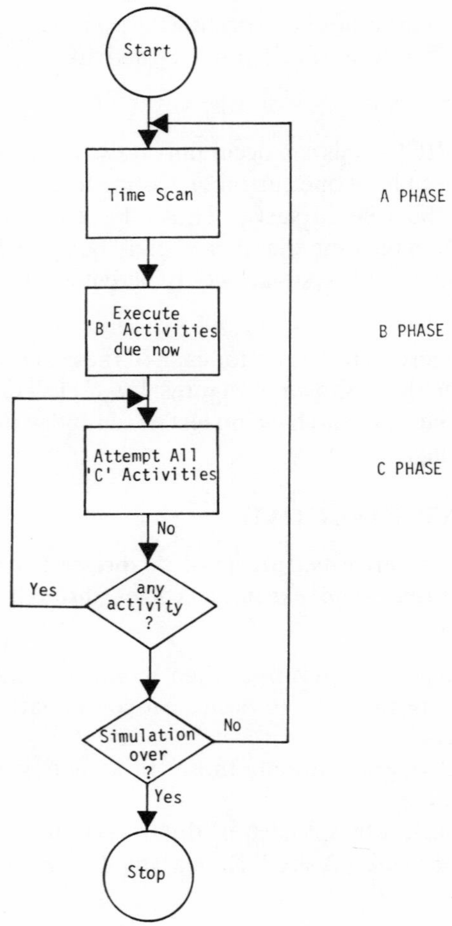

Figure 5.1 A three phase executive

From the standpoint of the three phase structure, an event based model has no separate 'C' activities, all action being directly controlled by the executive. Hence there are no tests at the head of the event blocks shown in Section 4.2. On the other hand, an activity based model has no 'B' activities. In the proper activity model, all the activities have test heads. The process interaction approach appears as a rather roundabout way of producing linked 'B' and 'C' activities.

time cell	next 'B' activity	previous activity

Figure 5.2 The three part BASIM record

5.3 BASIM: A THREE PHASE EXECUTIVE

In order to indicate in more detail how a simple three phase executive can work, this section describes one written in BASIC. It is based on one produced by John Crookes of the University of Lancaster. The version presented here is written in BASIC simply because the language is extremely widely known. The dialect used here is very simple, making it possible to implement BASIM on virtually any computer which supports BASIC. It is extremely simple to rewrite the executive in languages such as FORTRAN or Pascal; anyone with difficulties is invited to contact the author. A complete listing of BASIM is given in Figure 5.3 and BASIM is used in Sections 5.4ff as the basis for a three phase simulation of the harassed booking clerk example. By making fairly small modifications to BASIM it is simple to run programs with event, activity or process interaction based structures.

5.3.1 An overview of BASIM.

At the heart of BASIM is a two dimensional array *M* with dimensions *M9* by *R9* + 3, where:

M9 is the number of entities of all classes in the model
and *R9* is the maximum number of attributes per entity.

The *M* array is organized as follows.

Rows 1 to *M9*: each entity is permanently assigned a unique row of the array.

Column 1: this contains the TIME CELLS, indicating when each entity is next due to change state.

Column 2: this indicates the next activity due to be undertaken by each entity as it changes state. A positive value indicates a particular 'B' activity and a minus 1 (−1) indicates that some 'C' activity is expected next.

Column 3: this shows the activity in which each entity was last engaged. A positive value indicates a particular 'B' activity and a negative value indicates a specific 'C' activity.

Columns 4ff: these each contain values of the attributes of each entity.

Hence the array is as shown in Figure 5.4.

The BASIM program (Figure 5.3) is organized as follows.

Lines 10–130: establish the size of the simulation in terms of
M9 — the total number of entities
B9 — the number of 'B' activities
C9 — the number of 'C' activities
R9 — the number of attributes per entity.

Lines 140,150: send control to the initialization section (lines 5000 to 5999) in which the programmer should set up the initial values of all variables to be used in the program.

Lines 160–330: perform the time scan, described in detail in Section 5.3.3.

```
LIST 10,1050

10  REM  3 PHASE EXECUTIVE
20  PRINT
30  PRINT "BASIM: A 3 PHASE EXECUTIVE"
40  PRINT "*************************"
50  PRINT
60  PRINT
70  PRINT "HOW MANY OF THE FOLLOWING ARE THERE?"
80  PRINT
90  INPUT "    ENTITIES           :";M9
100  INPUT "    B ACTIVITIES       :";B9
110  INPUT "    C ACTIVITIES       :";C9
120  INPUT "    ATTRIBUTES/ENTITY :";R9
130  DIM M(M9,R9 + 3),M1(M9),P(3)
140  REM   TO INITIALISATION
150  GOSUB 5000
160  REM   ----------- TIME SCAN --------------
170 X9 = 999999
180 Y9 = 1
190  FOR I9 = 1 TO M9
200  IF M(I9,2) < 0 THEN 290
210  IF M(I9,1) < X9 THEN 260
220  IF M(I9,1) <  > X9 THEN 290
230 M1(Y9) = I9
240 Y9 = Y9 + 1
250  GOTO 290
260 X9 = M(I9,1)
270 M1(1) = I9
280 Y9 = 2
290  NEXT I9
300  IF X9 <  > 999999 THEN CO = X9
310  PRINT
320  PRINT
330  PRINT "CLOCK= ";CO
340  REM  -------- B CALLS --------------------
350 V9 = 1
360  FOR I9 = 1 TO Y9 - 1
370 MO = M1(I9)
380 Z9 = M(MO,2)
390 M(MO,2) =  - 1
400  ON Z9 GOSUB 10000,11000,12000,13000,14000,15000,16000,17000,18000,19000
410  NEXT I9
420  REM  -------- C SCAN --------------------
430 V9 =  - 1
440 Q9 = 0
450  FOR I9 = 1 TO M9
460 C1(I9) = M(I9,1)
470  NEXT I9
480  FOR Z9 = 1 TO C9
490  ON Z9 GOSUB 50000,51000,52000,53000,54000,55000,56000,57000,58000,59000
500  NEXT Z9
510  IF Q9 = 1 THEN 440
520  IF CO < T9 THEN 170
530  REM   TO FINALISATION
540  GOSUB 9000
550  STOP
1000  REM  -------- SCHEDULE AN ACTIVITY -----
1010 M(P(1),1) = CO + P(3)
1020 M(P(1),2) = P(2)
1030 M(P(1),3) = Z9 * V9
1040  IF V9 =  - 1 THEN Q9 = 1
1050  RETURN
```

Figure 5.3 The BASIM three phase executive

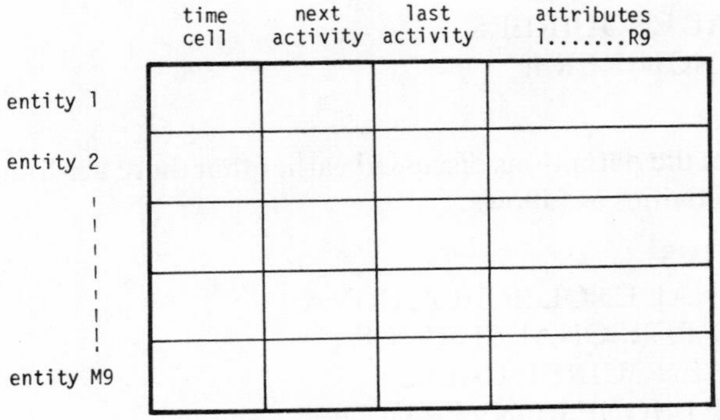

	time cell	next activity	last activity	attributes 1.......R9
entity 1				
entity 2				
⋮				
entity M9				

Figure 5.4 The BASIM 'M' array

These lines also establish which 'B' activities are due at the next event. (In effect they produce a current activity list.)

Lines 340–410: execute the correct 'B' activities (see Section 5.3.3).

Lines 420–510: perform the C scan and force repeat scans until no more activity occurs.

Lines 520,530: transfer control to the finalization section (lines 9000–9999), if the simulation clock time (*C0*) exceeds the simulation duration (*T9*).

Lines 1000–1050: schedule future activities and are called from the activity blocks.

Lines 5000–5999: the initialization section.

Lines 9000–9999: the finalization section.

5.3.2 Activities in BASIM

The activities are placed in two separate groups. The 'B' activities occupying lines 10000–49999. Activity B1 should begin on line 10000, activity B2 on line 11000, activity B3 on line 12000, and so on. As shown here BASIM accommodates up to ten 'B' activities but this is easily changed.

The 'C' activities occupy lines 50000–99999. Activity C1 should begin on line 50000, activity C2 on line 51000, etc. Again it is simple to adapt BASIM to cope with any reasonable number of 'C' activities.

5.3.3 The BASIM time scan

This can best be illustrated by an example. Consider the harassed booking clerk introduced in Section 3.3.2. In the activity cycle diagram of Figure 3.8 there are three classes of entity:

PERSONAL ENQUIRERS;
PHONE ENQUIRERS;
CLERK.

It is clear from the definitions discussed earlier that there are four 'B' activities and two 'C' activities as follows:

'B' ACTIVITIES
(1) PERSONAL ENQUIRER ARRIVAL
(2) END OF PERSONAL SERVICE
(3) PHONE ENQUIRER CALLS
(4) END OF PHONE CONVERSATION

'C' ACTIVITIES
(1) BEGIN PERSONAL SERVICE
(2) BEGIN PHONE CONVERSATION.

Notice that the clerk is instructed to serve personal enquirers rather than phone callers if there is a choice. Therefore BEGIN PERSONAL SERVICE has a higher priority than BEGIN PERSONAL SERVICE. Thus, BEGIN PHONE CONVERSATION appears lower in the list of 'C' activities.

As mentioned in Section 3.2 it is often more convenient to consider arrival machines as entities in this type of simulation. In this case there will be separate arrival machines for the two types of enquirer. Thus the simulation model will have the following entities.

(1) PERSONAL ENQUIRER ARRIVAL MACHINE
(2) PHONE ENQUIRER ARRIVAL MACHINE
(3) CLERK.

Consequently, if there are no attributes to consider, the *M* array has dimensions of (3 × 3) and the time scan will operate as follows.

Suppose that the *M* array is as shown in Figure 5.5 at some stage in the simulation.

The A phase

Time (*C0*) is at 47 and all activity is complete for that time. Lines 160–330 of BASIM perform the following A PHASE.

	time cell	next activity	last activity
(1) Personal enquirer	53	1	1
(2) Phone enquirer	54	3	3
(3) Clerk	51	2	-1

CØ = 47
Q = Ø
W = 2

Figure 5.5 The 'M' array before the 'A' phase

(1) Pick out the minimum time cell ($M(I9,1)$) amongst those whose next activity ($M(I9,2)$) is a 'B'. Thus, ignore those entities for which $M(I9,2) = -1$. When the time scan is complete, assign this minimum value ($X9$) to the simulation clock ($C0$).

(2) Whilst picking out this minimum value, assign the numbers of the 'due now' entities to a push-down stack $M9()$. Thus, when the time scan is complete, the vector $M9()$ identifies those entities responsible for the next state change. The variable $Y9$ is used to count the number of entities in the stack, the final number being $Y9 - 1$.

In the example of Figure 5.5, all three entities are waiting for a 'B' activity, entity 3 (the clerk) has the minimum time cell (=51) and is due to engage in activity B2 (END PERSONAL SERVICE) at that time. The M array is unchanged at the end of the A phase, but $C0$ had been reset to 51.

The B phase

Lines 340–410 perform the B phase as follows.
Examine each entity in the push-down stack and

(1) Assign its number to the variable $M0$.
(2) Assign its next activity (a 'B') to the variable $Z9$.
(3) Set its new next activity (i.e. to follow this 'B') to be a 'C' by putting $M(M0,2) = -1$. If this default state is not required, it can be over-written in the appropriate activity block.
(4) Branch to the subroutine of the appropriate 'B' activity.

In this case

$$M0 = 3$$
$$Z9 = 2$$

sending the program to activity *B2*, END PERSONAL SERVICE. After the 'B' phase, the clerk is freed and ready for either a personal or phone service. Thus, the M array is now as shown in Figure 5.6.

The C phase

Lines 420–510 ensure that BASIM attempts each 'C' activity in turn and

	time cell	next activity	last activity
(1) Personal enquirer	53	1	1
(2) Phone enquirer	54	3	3
(3) Clerk	51	-1	2

CØ = 51
Ø = Ø
W = 2

Figure 5.6 The 'M' array after the 'B' phase

leaves the last activity of each entity correctly set. In this example:
activity C1 (BEGIN PERSONAL SERVICE) is impossible since $Q = 0$.
But, activity C2 (BEGIN PHONE SERVICE) may start since $W > 0$
and $M(3,2) = -1$, i.e. the clerk is free.

If this activity were to lead to a phone conservation whose duration is sampled to be 5 minutes, then
$M(3,1)$ is reset to 56
$M(3,2)$ is reset to 4 (i.e. activity B4 — END PHONE CONVERSATION)
$M(3,3)$ is reset to -2 (i.e. activity C2 — BEGIN PHONE SERVICE)
and W is reset to 1.

That is, the next activity for this clerk is the end of a phone conversation at time 56.

Hence the M array is as shown in Figure 5.7 after the C phase.

	time cell	next activity	last activity
(1) personal enquirer	53	1	1
(2) phone enquirer	54	3	3
(3) clerk	60	4	-2

CØ = 51
Q = Ø
W = 1

Figure 5.7 The 'M' array after the 'C' phase

5.3.4 Scheduling future activities in BASIM.

This is done by using the subroutine beginning at line 1000. This employs three pointers; $P(1)$, $P(2)$, and $P(3)$. To schedule a future activity, the programmer must reset the values of these pointers in the appropriate activity block and then GOSUB 1000. Values are assigned to the pointers as follows:

$P(1)$ = the entity whose activity is being scheduled;
$P(2)$ = the next activity for this entity;
$P(3)$ = the time interval to elapse before the activity is due.

Lines 1000–1040 revise the M array appropriately.

5.4 THE HARASSED BOOKING CLERK: BASIM VERSION

As mentioned in Section 5.3.2, there are four 'B' activities and two 'C' activities. In order to regularly collect data about the performance of the simulation, an extra 'B' activity could be added to execute the data collection. This requires an extra entity, an imaginary observer, whose activity will be scheduled. There are now four entities. BASIM allows the activities to begin on the following lines of the program.

10000 REM B1: PERSONAL ENQUIRER ARRIVES

```
11000 REM B2: END OF PERSONAL SERVICE
12000 REM B3: PHONE ENQUIRER CALLS
13000 REM B4: END OF PHONE CONVERSATION
14000 REM B5: COLLECT RUN STATISTICS
50000 REM C1: BEGIN PERSONAL SERVICE
51000 REM C2: BEGIN PHONE CONVERSATION
```

In addition, the simulation will be initialized in lines 5000–5999 and final output will be produced by lines 9000–9999.

A complete listing of the activities is shown in Figure 5.8 and full descriptions follow. The program is completed by adding BASIM (lines 10–1050).

5.4.1 B1: Personal enquirer arrives

Occupies lines 10000–10999 and operates as follows:

10010: counts the enquirers as they arrive;
10020: adds the latest enquirer to the queue;
10030–10060: schedule the next arrival, sampling from a negative exponential distribution with a mean of 12 minutes (see Section 7.5.1 for details);
10070: prints out run-time information for debugging;
10999: returns to the B calls in the executive.

5.4.2 B2: End of personal service

Occupies lines 11000–11999 and operates as follows:

11010: counts the number of personal enquirers successfully served;
11020: prints out run-time information for debugging;
11999: returns to the B calls in the executive;

5.4.3 B3: Phone enquirer calls

Occupies lines 12000–12999 and is very similar to activity B1.

5.4.4 B4: End of phone conversation

Occupies lines 13000–13999 and is very similar to activity B2.

5.4.5 B5: Collect run statistics

Occupies lines 14000–14999 and operates as follows:

14000–14040: reset the next occurence of this activity to 20 minutes hence;
14050–14070: record the length of the two queues;

```
10000  REM     ---- B1: PERSONAL ENQUIRER ARRIVES--
10010 P = P + 1
10020 Q = Q + 1
10030 P(1) = 1
10040 P(2) = 1
10050 P(3) =  - 12 *  LOG ( RND (6))
10060  GOSUB 1000
10070  PRINT "PERSONAL ENQUIRER NO. ";P;" ARRIVES, QUEUE= ";Q
10999  RETURN
11000  REM   ---- B2: END OF PERSONAL SERVICE ---
11010 N1 = N1 + 1
11020  PRINT "END OF PERSONAL SERVICE NO. ";N1
11999  RETURN
12000  REM   ------- B3: PHONE ENQUIRER CALLS ----
12010 C = C + 1
12020 W = W + 1
12030 P(1) = 2
12040 P(2) = 3
12050 P(3) =  - 10 *  LOG ( RND (6))
12060  GOSUB 1000
12070  PRINT "PHONE CALL NO. ";C;" ARRIVES, CALLERS= ";W
12999  RETURN
13000  REM   ------ B4: END OF PHONE CALL ---------
13010 N2 = N2 + 1
13020  PRINT "END OF PHONE CALL NO. ";N2
13999  RETURN
14000  REM     ----- B5: COLLECT RUN STATISTICS -----
14010 P(1) = 4
14020 P(2) = 5
14030 P(3) = 20
14040  GOSUB 1000
14050 R = R + 1
14060 Q1(R) = Q
14070 W1(R) = W
14080  PRINT "RECORDING, PERSONAL QUEUE= ";Q;" PHONE QUEUE= ";W
14999  RETURN
15000  REM  SPARE
16000  REM  SPARE
17000  REM  SPARE
18000  REM  SPARE
19000  REM  SPARE
50000  REM    ------- C1: BEGIN PERSONAL SERVICE --
50010  IF Q = 0 THEN 50999
50020  IF M(3,2) <  >  - 1 THEN 50999
50030 Q = Q - 1
50040 P(1) = 3
50050 P(2) = 2
50060 P(3) =  - 6 *  LOG ( RND (6))
50070  GOSUB 1000
50080  PRINT "PERSONAL SERVICE STARTS, CUSTOMER NO. ";N1 + 1
50999  RETURN
51000  REM   --- C2: BEGIN PHONE CONVERSATION ---
51010  IF W = 0 THEN 51999
51020  IF M(3,2) <  >  - 1 THEN 51999
51030 W = W - 1
51040 P(1) = 3
51050 P(2) = 4
51060 P(3) =  - 5 *  LOG ( RND (6))
51070  GOSUB 1000
51080  PRINT "PHONE SERVICE STARTS, CALLER NO. ";N2 + 1
51999  RETURN
]
```

Figure 5.8 BASIM activities: harassed booking clerk

Figure 5.8 continued.


```
LIST 5000,5999

5000  REM  ------- INITIALISATION-----------
5010  REM  SET SIMULATION DURATION
5020 T9 = 480
5030  REM  SET UP FIRST PERSONAL ENQUIRER
5040 P(1) = 1
5050 P(2) = 1
5060 P(3) = 2
5070  GOSUB 1000
5080  REM  SET UP FIRST PHONE CALL
5090 P(1) = 2
5100 P(2) = 3
5110 P(3) = 3
5120  GOSUB 1000
5130  REM  SETUP CLERK AS IDLE
5140 P(1) = 3
5150 P(2) =  - 1
5160 P(3) = 0
5170  GOSUB 1000
5180  REM  SET FIRST DATA COLLECTION
5190 P(1) = 4
5200 P(2) = 5
5210 P(3) = 20
5220  GOSUB 1000
5230  REM  INITIALISE OTHER VARIABLES
5240 Q = 0
5250 W = 0
5260 N1 = 0
5270 N2 = 0
5280 P = 0
5290 C = 0
5300  FOR I = 1 TO  INT (T9 / 20) + 1
5310 Q1(I) = 0
5320 W1(I) = 0
5330  NEXT I
5340  FOR I = 1 TO M9
5350 M1(I) = 0
5360  NEXT I
5999  RETURN

]

LIST 9000,9999

9000  REM  ------- FINALISATION -----------
9010  PRINT
9020  PRINT
9030  PRINT
9040  PRINT "HARASSED CLERK"
9050  PRINT "THREE PHASE SIMULATION"
9060  PRINT
9070  PRINT
9080  PRINT "SIMULATION OVER AFTER ";C0;" TIME UNITS"
9090  PRINT
9100  PRINT
9110  PRINT "TIME       PERSONAL QUEUE   PHONE QUEUE"
9120  PRINT
9130  FOR I = 1 TO  INT (T9 / 20)
9140  PRINT I * 20,Q1(I),W1(I)
9150  NEXT I
9160  PRINT
9170  PRINT
9180  PRINT N1;" PERSONAL ENQUIRERS & ";N2;" PHONE CALLERS SERVED"
9999  RETURN

]
```

14080: prints out run-time information for debugging;
14999: returns to the B calls in the executive.

5.4.6 C1: Begin personal service

Occupies lines 50000–50999 and operates as follows:

50010, 50020: the test head — if there are no enquirers in the queue or if the clerk is occupied, then go to 50999;
50030: reduces the queue length by one;
50040–50070: set up the end of personal service (B2) to occur at a time sampled from a negative exponential distribution with a mean of 6 minutes;
50080: prints out run-time information for debugging;
50999: returns to the C phase of the executive.

5.4.7 C2: Begin phone conversation

Occupies lines 51000–51999 and is very similar to activity C1.

5.4.8 Initialization

Occupies lines 5000–5370 and sets up the following initial values:

5010, 5020: simulation duration = 480 minutes;
5030–5070: first personal enquirer will arrive 2 minutes after the start of the simulation;
5080–5120: first phone caller will arrive 3 minutes after the start;
5130–5170: the clerk is initially idle;
5180–5220: the first data collection will occur 20 minutes after the start;
5230–5360: initialize other variables to zero;
5999: returns to the executive.

5.4.9 Finalization

Occupies lines 9000–9999 and prints out the queue lengths as they were sampled during the run. Also shows the number of successful services.

5.4.10 Running the program

Figure 5.9 shows the effect of running the program with the debugging print statements intact. Figure 5.10 shows a final printout after a run of 480 minutes.

5.5 MODIFYING THE HARASSED BOOKING CLERK PROGRAM

One of the beauties of activity type approaches is the ease with which programs may be successively enhanced. Thus it is possbile to develop a complex simulation by starting with a relatively simple program and adding the

```
RUN

BASIM: A 3 PHASE EXECUTIVE
**************************


HOW MANY OF THE FOLLOWING ARE THERE?

    ENTITIES           :4
    B ACTIVITIES       :5
    C ACTIVITIES       :2
    ATTRIBUTES/ENTITY  :0


CLOCK= 2
PERSONAL ENQUIRER NO. 1 ARRIVES, QUEUE= 1
PERSONAL SERVICE STARTS, CUSTOMER NO. 1


CLOCK= 3
PHONE CALL NO. 1 ARRIVES, CALLERS= 1


CLOCK= 3.15576433
PHONE CALL NO. 2 ARRIVES, CALLERS= 2


CLOCK= 7.45530554
END OF PERSONAL SERVICE NO. 1
PHONE SERVICE STARTS, CALLER NO. 1


CLOCK= 10.1953026
PERSONAL ENQUIRER NO. 2 ARRIVES, QUEUE= 1


CLOCK= 10.548313
END OF PHONE CALL NO. 1
PERSONAL SERVICE STARTS, CUSTOMER NO. 2


CLOCK= 12.785652
PERSONAL ENQUIRER NO. 3 ARRIVES, QUEUE= 1


CLOCK= 13.4031716
END OF PERSONAL SERVICE NO. 2
PERSONAL SERVICE STARTS, CUSTOMER NO. 3


CLOCK= 14.3200468
PERSONAL ENQUIRER NO. 4 ARRIVES, QUEUE= 1

BREAK IN 10070
]
```

Figure 5.9 BASIM run-time output

complications once the simple program is running satisfactorily. Being based on the activity structure, the three phase approach shares this advantage. To illustrate the point, consider the following modifications to the harassed booking clerk problem.

(1) The clerk already gives priority to personal enquirers because they may purchase tickets, thus providing cash for the theatre. Suppose that there is

```
HARASSED CLERK
THREE PHASE SIMULATION


SIMULATION OVER AFTER 480 TIME UNITS

TIME        PERSONAL QUEUE   PHONE QUEUE

20               2                1
40               0                1
60               5                3
80               3                4
100              3                8
120              1                9
140              0                14
160              0                12
180              0                9
200              2                10
220              0                8
240              0                7
260              0                8
280              4                7
300              4                11
320              5                13
340              3                13
360              0                17
380              0                17
400              0                16
420              1                16
440              0                18
460              0                18
480              0                18


54 PERSONAL ENQUIRERS & 37 PHONE CALLERS SERVED

BREAK IN 550
]
```

Figure 5.10 BASIM output: harassed booking clerk

a 50% chance that each personal enquirer will buy tickets for the show and that the histogram of Figure 5.11 shows how likely a purchaser is to buy 1–4 tickets. Consequently, it makes sense to keep track of the number of tickets sold. If tickets are sold, this increases the service time by 2 minutes.

(2) No waiting lines for incoming calls could possibly have an infinite capacity; in this case, suppose that the capacity is five calls. Calls which arrive when the line is full are turned away by the engaged tone.

(3) The phone enquirers will not wait forever for service. Suppose that any caller waiting more than 3 minutes for service rings off in frustration.

(4) Harassed though the booking clerk may be, a lunch is necessary at some stage. Suppose that the theatre booking office opens at 9.00 a.m. and the clerk takes a lunch break for an hour from 1.00 p.m. At 1.00 p.m. no more personal enquirers are admitted to the theatre and those already waiting are served. All waiting phone calls are disconnected and no more calls or personal enquirers are accepted until one hour later.

Figure 5.12 shows most of the enhanced program and the following sections

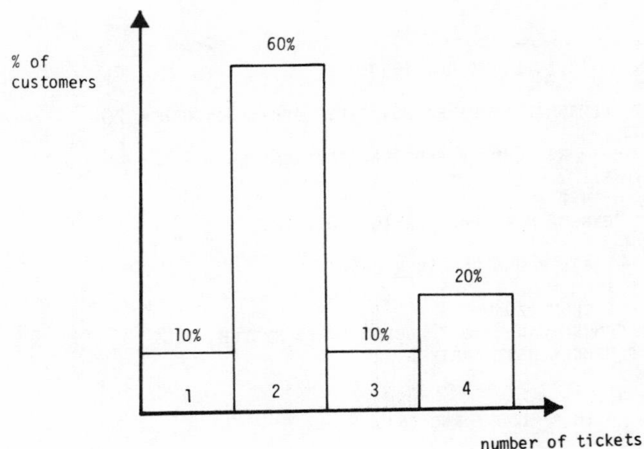

Figure 5.11 Histogram of probability of buying tickets

discuss how the modifications were made. Lines 10–1050 obviously remain unchanged.

5.5.1 Selling tickets

This modification is simply made by altering activity C1 (BEGIN PERSONAL SERVICE). If the test head is successfully passed, then an extra test, 'does the enquirer buy any tickets?' is encountered. In this case, the test is implemented by sampling a uniform random number on the interval 0 to 0.999999 (see Chapter 7). If the sampled value is less than 0.5, then the enquirer buys tickets. The histogram of Figure 5.11 is then sampled to provide the number purchased.

Hence the new activity is as shown in lines 50000–50999 as follows:

50010, 50020: test head;
50030: reduces the queue by one;
50040–50060: establishes the pointers for scheduling the end of service;
50070: sets the number of tickets bought to zero;
50090: tests whether the enquirer buys any tickets — GOTO 50230 if not;
50110: increases the service time by 2 minutes;
50120–50220: sample the number of tickets bought;
50230: keeps track of the total number of tickets sold;
50240: schedules the end of the service;
50250: prints out run-time information for debugging;
50999: returns to the C phase of the executive.

In addition, some new variables need to be initialized and the data collection activity (B5) needs to include the number of tickets sold. Similarly, the finalization section needs small alterations to the PRINT statements.

```
10000  REM     ---- B1: PERSONAL ENQUIRER ARRIVES--
10010 P = P + 1
10020 Q = Q + 1
10030 P(1) = 1
10040 P(2) = 1
10050 P(3) =  - 12 *  LOG ( RND (6))
10060  GOSUB 1000
10070  PRINT "PERSONAL ENQUIRER NO. ";P;" ARRIVES, QUEUE= ";Q
10080  RETURN
11000  REM    ---- B2: END OF PERSONAL SERVICE ---
11010 N1 = N1 + 1
11020 M(3,2) =  - 1
11030  PRINT "END OF PERSONAL SERVICE NO. ";N1
11999  RETURN
12000  REM  --- B3: PHONE ENQUIRER CALLS ---
12010 C = C + 1
12020  IF W < 5 THEN 12050
12030  PRINT "PHONE CALL ";C;" TURNED AWAY, SYSTEM FULL"
12040  REM  SCHEDULE NEXT ARRIVAL
12050 P(1) = 2
12060 P(2) = 3
12070 P(3) =  - 10 *  LOG ( RND (6))
12080  GOSUB 1000
12090  IF W = 5 THEN 12999
12100 W = W + 1
12110  REM  SCHEDULE POSSIBLE FRUSTRATION
12120 P(1) = 5 + W
12130 P(2) = 6
12140 P(3) = 3
12150  GOSUB 1000
12160  REM  NOTE WHICH CALL HAS ARRIVED
12170 M(P(1),4) = C
12180  PRINT "PHONE CALL NO. ";C;" ARRIVES, CALLERS= ";W
12999  RETURN
13000  REM    ------ B4: END OF PHONE CALL ---------
13010 N2 = N2 + 1
13020 M(3,2) =  - 1
13030  PRINT "END OF PHONE CALL NO. ";N2
13999  RETURN
14000  REM    ---- B5: COLLECT RUN STATISTICS ----
14010 P(1) = 4
14020 P(2) = 5
14030 P(3) = 20
14040  GOSUB 1000
14050 R = R + 1
14060 Q1(R) = Q
14070 W1(R) = W
14080 T1(R) = N7
14090 F1(R) = F
14100  PRINT "RECORDING, PERSONAL QUEUE= ";Q,", PHONE QUEUE= ";W;
14110  PRINT ", ";N7;" TICKETS SOLD & ";F;" RUSTRATED CALLERS GONE."
14999  RETURN

1

15000  REM    ---- B6: CALLER GIVES UP IN FRUSTRATION --
15010 W = W - 1
15020  PRINT "PHONE CALL NO. ";M(M0,4);" GIVES UP IN FRUSTRATION"
15030  FOR I = M0 TO 9
15040  FOR J = 1 TO 4
15050 M(I,J) = M(I + 1,J)
15060  NEXT J
15070  NEXT I
15080 M(10,4) = 0
15090 F = F + 1
15999  RETURN
```

```
16000  REM  ---- B7: START LUNCH BREAK
16010  REM  RESET ARRIVAL TIME OF NEXT PERSONAL ENQUIRER
16020 M(1,1) = M(1,1) + 60
16030  PRINT "**** DOOR CLOSED FOR LUNCH****"
16040  REM  CLEAR PHONE QUEUE
16050 W = 0
16060  FOR I = 6 TO 10
16070 M(I,4) = 0
16080 P(1) = I
16090 P(2) =  - 1
16100 P(3) = 0
16110  GOSUB 1000
16120  NEXT I
16130  REM  RESET ARRIVAL TIME OF NEXT PHONE CALL
16140 M(2,1) = M(2,1) + 60
16150  RETURN
16999  RETURN
17000  REM  SPARE
18000  REM  SPARE
19000  REM  SPARE


]
50000  REM   ------- C1: BEGIN PERSONAL SERVICE --
50010  IF Q = 0 THEN 50999
50020  IF M(3,2) < >  - 1 THEN 50999
50030 Q = Q - 1
50040 P(1) = 3
50050 P(2) = 2
50060 P(3) =  - 6 *  LOG ( RND (6))
50070 N8 = 0
50080  REM  DOES CUSTOMER PAY?
50090  IF  RND (6) >  = 0.5 THEN 50230
50100  REM  CUSTOMER PAYS, SAMPLE NO. OF TICKETS
50110 P(3) = P(3) + 2
50120 N9 =  RND (6)
50130  IF N9 > = 0.1 THEN 50160
50140 N8 = 1
50150  GOTO 50230
50160  IF N9 >  = 0.7 THEN 50190
50170 N8 = 2
50180  GOTO 50230
50190  IF N9 >  = 0.8 THEN 50220
50200 N8 = 3
50210  GOTO 50230
50220 N8 = 4
50230 N7 = N7 + N8
50240  GOSUB 1000
50250  PRINT "PERSONAL SERVICE STARTS, CUSTOMER NO. ";N1 + 1;" BUYING ";N8;" TICKETS"
50999  RETURN
51000  REM  ---- C2: BEGIN PHONE CONVERSATION ---
51010  IF W = 0 THEN 51999
51020  IF M(3,2) <  >  - 1 THEN 51999
51030 W = W - 1
51040 P(1) = 3
51050 P(2) = 4
51060 P(3) =  - 5 *  LOG ( RND (6))
51070  GOSUB 1000
51080 C1 = M(6,4)
51090  FOR I = 6 TO 9
51100  FOR J = 1 TO 4
51110 M(I,J) = M(I + 1,J)
51120  NEXT J
51130  NEXT I
51140 M(10,4) = 0
51150  PRINT "PHONE SERVICE NO. ";N2 + 1;" STARTS, CALLER NO. ";C1
51999  RETURN

]
```

Figure 5.12 BASIM program: enhanced booking clerk problem

5.5.2 Limited waiting line capacity

This modification is slightly more complicated than that of Section 5.5.1. A straightforward method involves the creation of five extra entities (numbers 6 to 10), one for each position in the waiting line. Thus alterations are required to two activities: PHONE ENQUIRER CALLS (B3) and BEGIN PHONE CONVERSATION (C2).

As phone calls arrive, activity B3 checks whether the line is full. If space is available, the call is accepted. If the phone is not answered in 3 minutes this requires a new B activity, CALLER GIVES UP IN FRUSTRATION (B6), which is scheduled in B3. Thus the revised and new activities are as follows.

B3: Phone enquirer calls

12010: counts the number of calls made;
12020: checks whether there are less than 5 calls already waiting — if so GOTO 12050;
12030: prints out run-time information for debugging;
12040–12080: schedules the next phone call;
12090: if the call is rejected ($W = 5$) GOTO 12190;
12100: adds the call to the waiting line;
12110–12150: schedule the potential frustration of a caller in 3 minutes time;
12170: notes, in the attribute of the waiting line slot, which call has just arrived and puts it into this slot;
12180: prints out run-time information for debugging;
12999: returns to the B phase of the executive.

B6: Caller gives up in frustration

15010: reduces the number of waiting callers by one;
15020: prints out run-time information for debugging;
15030–15080: move later waiting calls one slot up the line;
15090: keeps track of the number of frustated callers;
15999: returns to the B phase of the executive.

C2: Begin phone conversation

51010, 51020: test head;
51030: reduces the number of waiting callers by one;
51040–51170: schedule the end of the phone conversation;
51080: identifies which caller is being served;
51090–51140: moves each waiting call one slot up the waiting line;
51150: prints out run-time information for debugging;

51999: returns to the C phase of the executive.

Further modifications are also made to activity B6 (COLLECT RUN STATISTICS) as well as to the initialization and finalization sections.

5.5.3 Lunch break

The start of the lunch break is obviously a B activity and thus B7 (BEGIN LUNCH BREAK) is added. This is controlled by a new entity, number 5. When this activity is executed, the arrival times of the next personal enquirer and the next phone caller are put back by 60 minutes and the phone waiting line is cleared. Thus activity B7 is as follows:

16020: moves the arrival time of the next personal enquirer back 60 minutes;
16030: prints out run-time information for debugging;
16040–16120: clears the phone queue;
16140: moves the arrival time of the next phone caller back 60 minutes;
16999: returns to the B phase of the executive.

5.5.4 Some results

Figure 5.13 shows the results of a single simulation of the enhanced version of the harassed booking clerk problem. It is clear that the queue of personal enquirers is kept to manageable lengths. However, many phone callers ring off in frustration. Some action seems necessary — though it would be extremely foolish to act solely on the basis of this single, short simulation. Much more care is needed, as discussed in Chapter 9.

5.6 RECORDING STATISTICS DURING A RUN

5.6.1 Recording as time series.

This method was illustrated in the harassed booking clerk problem presented earlier. It involves the addition of an extra program segment (an activity or event) to ensure that the specified values are stored at regular intervals. Section 5.4.5 described a simple 'B' activity which serves this purpose for the three phase version of the problem. The recording interval is established in the initialization section of the program.

5.6.2 Variations in queue lengths

When queueing systems are simulated, the analyst is often interested in the queue lengths which occur. One measure of this is the average queue length over the entire simulation. However, even if this turns out to be acceptable, some customers may have to wait too long. To avoid this, performance criteria

```
HARASSED CLERK
THREE PHASE SIMULATION

SIMULATION OVER AFTER 480 TIME UNITS
```

TIME	PERSONAL QUEUE	PHONE QUEUE	TICKETS SOLD	CALLS LOST
20	1	0	0	1
40	2	0	2	3
60	2	0	4	4
80	3	0	10	4
100	2	0	12	6
120	4	0	15	8
140	1	0	17	9
160	0	0	19	10
180	0	0	19	10
200	0	0	19	10
220	0	0	21	10
240	0	0	21	10
260	0	0	21	11
280	0	0	21	13
300	0	0	21	13
320	0	0	21	13
340	0	0	21	13
360	0	0	21	16
380	1	0	25	16
400	3	0	25	17
420	0	1	31	22
440	0	0	36	25
460	2	0	38	27
480	1	1	43	32

```
46 PERSONAL ENQUIRERS & 18 PHONE CALLERS SERVED
```

Figure 5.13 Enhanced booking clerk results

are often expressed as in the following specification of a hospital outpatients department.

'The appointments system must allow
50% of patients to be seen within 15 minutes of the appointment,
90% of patients to be seen within 30 minutes of their appointment
all patients to be seen within 60 minutes of their appointment.'

Thus when simulating such systems it is much more useful to record the variations in queue lengths and waiting times.

A simple way of recording queue lengths is to add an extra program segment at the end of the activities or event routines. This recording block should be executed at every event time but *after* all events or activities are complete. As an example, consider the three phase version of the harassed booking clerk problem. Here, two queues form as personal enquirers and phone callers wait for service. The recording block is placed after the last proper 'C' activity. Thus it is treated as an extra 'C' activity to be executed at each event time. However, this new 'C' activity has no test-head. In effect, an extra phase for data collection has been added to the program.

Using the BASIM program shown in earlier sections, it might be written as follows:

```
52000  REM: UPDATE QUEUE LENGTH HISTOGRAMS
52010  C3 = C0 - C2
52020  Q2(Q) = Q2(Q) + C3
52030  W2(W) = W2(W) + C3
52040  C2 = C0
52999  RETURN
```

where *C0* = current simulation clock time,
C2 = time of previous event,
Q2() = array for histogram of personal enquirer queue lengths
and *W2*() = array for histogram of phone caller queue lengths.

Thus if there are three personal enquirers waiting, the time interval since the last event is added to *Q2*(3). In this way, the histograms are built up.

Now $Q2(1) + Q2(2) + \cdots + Q2(K) = T9$,
where *K* is the maximum queue length occurring and *T9* is the duration of the simulation. Hence dividing each element of *Q2*() and *W2*() by *T9* gives the relative frequencies of each queue length.

5.6.3 Variations in waiting times

To record this information there must be some way of storing the waiting time of each customer as long as they are in a queue. If each customer is already a separate entity, then this presents no problems. For instance, in the harassed booking clerk problem, phone calls wait in one of the five exchange lines. When a new call arrives and is accepted, its time cell is set to (*C0* + 3). That is, the caller will ring off in frustration if not spoken to within three minutes. This has two implications:

(1) The maximum waiting time is three minutes.
(2) If the caller is served before the three minutes elapse, then the waiting time is
$$(C0 - M(6,1) + 3) \text{ in activity } C2,$$
where $M(6,1)$ is the time cell of the call at the head of the queue.

To collect waiting times, a histogram should be established via an array in which the values of waiting times are stored.

Sometimes, as is the case with personal enquirers, the customers do not exist as entities. In this case, extra information needs to be collected. This is simply done by adding an array *Q4*(). Its dimension is the maximum conceivable queue length. As an enquirer arrives and is at position *K* in the queue, its arrival time is stored in *Q4*(*K*). As personal service occurs in activity *C*1, each customer's record is moved one position up the array *Q4*(). Thus the waiting time of the enquirer when served is (*C0* – *Q4*(1)). This data may be stored in a histogram.

Hence to record variations in waiting times there is no need to add extra activities or events.

5.7 ADDING GRAPHICAL DISPLAY

The recent development of computing has been characterized by three features. First, the cost of hardware has fallen dramatically since the introduction of solid state devices. Secondly, very large-scale integrated circuits have allowed the designers to pack more and more computing power into yet smaller boxes. Thirdly, software has tended to become more robust and more friendly towards the non-specialist user. One result of this development is that quite sophisticated graphic display facilities are available at a relatively low cost. Most microcomputers include high resolution graphics facilities which require only the equivalent of a domestic television as a display console. Not surprisingly, this has a major impact on computer simulation.

5.7.1 Graphics in simulation

There seem to be two related reasons for introducing graphic, and preferably coloured, display into discrete simulations. The first reason relates to the client of the study. One problem with any model of a complex system is that it is extremely difficult for the client, possibly unskilled in management science, to be fully satisfied about the validity of the model. Sometimes even the analyst is only fully convinced of its validity after subjecting the simulation results to a whole battery of statistical tests. These may also not be understood by the client.

However, the clever use of coloured graphics allows the analyst to producing a moving picture of the simulated system on a television screen. This puts the client in a much better position to assess whether the behaviour of the model is an adequate reflection of the real system. For example, the client is able to see that correct action follows the breakdown of a particular piece of equipment in the simulation. This type of display can be worth a thousand words of description.

These displays also have a direct technical value to the analyst when the simulation programs are verified and debugged. In writing the programs for the harassed booking clerk earlier in this chapter, great care was taken to ensure that each activity included a run-time print statement. Hence it is possible to check whether personal enquirers correctly have priority over phone calls when both are waiting for service. By following the print-out as the simulation proceeds, the analyst can check whether it is operating as it logically should. An enhancement of this approach is to use graphic output as well. Many people find it easier to spot incorrect logic as displayed by changes on a television screen than solely by following a trail of print-outs.

It is important to realize that as a discrete event simulation proceeds, time is moved to the next event and held there whilst all possible activity occurs at that time. The activities which occur simultaneously in the real system are simulated sequentially and this suggests that two types of display are required. Firstly, a simultaneous change display which approximates to the behaviour of the real system. Secondly, a sequential change display which shows the changes as they occur in the simulation and which is thus useful to the analyst in debugging the system.

Sadly, it is not possible to give useful examples of the implementation of such displays — except in general terms. This is because the implementation of graphics facilities varies substantially from computer to computer and their various graphics commands are even less standardized than their versions of BASIC. However, the general principles as discussed should be easily implementable on most computers offering such facilities.

5.7.2 Graphics in three phase simulation

The sequential change display is the easiest one to implement as it requires only straightforward alterations to each activity. In principle, the analyst needs only to ensure that the initialization establishes the basic layout of the screen and the symbols to be used to represent the entities. This display is then updated at the end of each activity. Thus, for the harassed booking clerk problem, an extra symbol is added to the queue as a personal enquirer arrives. As a phone caller gives up in frustration, a symbol is removed from the waiting line. In this way, the screen is gradually updated and each event generates changes to the display. On most computers, the graphics system executes such changes very rapidly.

A simultaneous change display is rather more difficult to implement as it involves the insertion of an extra phase in the executive's operation cycle. The phases are thus:

(1) redraw the screen;
(2) time scan;
(3) B phase;

phase 1 may involve redrawing virtually the entire screen. This means that the display will be redrawn sequentially as the executive will have to check each entity in turn to see whether it needs to be redrawn and then will redraw it if necessary. Thus the effect of the instantaneous change of display is lost.

This difficulty may be circumvented on those machines which allow the user to keep two or more screen images in memory at the same time. In this case, two screens are needed.

SCREEN A: sequential change display;
SCREEN B: simultaneous change display.

As the simulation proceeds, screen A is updated as described earlier and meanwhile screen B is displayed on the television. Screen B shows the simulation as it was at the end of the last C phase. At the end of the current C phase, the then current contents of screen A are copied across to the display as the new screen B. In this way the simultaneous change display is redrawn without the need to check each entity in turn. Thus the changes appear truly instantaneous as required.

5.7.3 Interactive graphical simulation

Another refinement sometimes employed in computer simulation is the addition of facilities which allow the user to run the simulation as an operational game. As the simulation proceeds, the user is allowed to interact with the model whenever the display indicates that such interaction is necessary. A useful guide to implementing these ideas on microcomputers is given by Ellison and Tunnicliffe–Wilson (1983).

To interact in this way requires access to truly interactive computer facilities. That is, to a computer which provides some means of altering the make up of a program as it is run. Various ways are possible: light pens, game paddles and the console keyboard are examples. The idea is that the user watches the progress of the simulation as displayed graphically on the television screen. If it becomes obvious that corrective action is necessary in the simulation, the user intervenes and changes the values of whichever variables are appropriate.

The principles of this sort of interaction are described by Hurrion (1976). It has two obvious applications. Firstly, it enables discrete simulations to be used as training simulators of a form similar to those employed for training pilots. Hence, a novice may learn how to operate a complex system without the potential cost of catastrophic failure. Secondly, it offers a way of reducing the number of wasted simulations carried out with the system operating in a clearly sub-optimal fashion — the user is able to home in on modes of operation close to the best.

As with the more straightforward graphical simulation it is impossible to give examples which will be generally valid as the details are dependent both on the graphics system and the mode of interaction. In the simplest case, the executive must firstly include some means of recognizing that the user is attempting to intervene as the simulation is in progress. The more sophisticated microcomputers provide facilities for this. Secondly, a further phase needs to be added to the operation cycle of the executive. This interaction phase can be placed after the C phase and should be written to allow the user to reset the values of the variables of the model. When this interaction is complete, the simulation is restarted.

EXERCISES

1. Modify the original BASIM version of the harassed booking clerk problem (Section 5.4) to simulate two clerks, both of whom can answer the phone or serve personal enquirers.

2. Change your modifications made for Exercise 1 so that one clerk attends to personal enquirers and the other answers the phone.

3. If your computer provides graphics facilities, replace the run-time print statements in Figure 5.8 with appropriate graphics commands.

4. Modify BASIM so as to use it for event based simulation. (*Hint*: you only need B activities.)

5. Modify BASIM so as to use it for activity based simulation. (*Hint*: you only need C activities).

6. Consider what B and C activities you would need to simulate the following system.
'Heavy trucks arrive randomly at a weigh bridge in a port. The trucks have just arrived from another country by ferry and are laden with many different types of goods. The weigh bridge is used to check whether the trucks are overloaded. The trucks queue for the weigh bridge and are weighed. If their load is acceptable, then they leave the port. If they are overloaded, then they move to an area in which surplus loads are removed and stored. The port authority wishes to know the following.

(1) how much space to provide for trucks queueing to be weighed;
(2) how large a warehouse to build to store surplus goods from over-loaded trucks.'

REFERENCES

Ellison, D., and Tunnicliffe–Wilson, J. (1983) *How to Write Simulations on Microcomputers*. McGraw–Hill, London.

Hurrion, R. (1976) *The Design, Use and Requirements of an Interactive Visual Computer Simulation Language to Explore Production Planning Problems*. Ph.D. thesis, University of London.

Tocher, K. D. (1963) *The Art of Simulation*. English Universities Press, London.

Chapter 6

Software tools for discrete simulation

What is the best way to program a computer simulation? Should a special purpose simulation language be used and if so, which one? Some of the broader issues were outlined in Chapter 1 and this chapter seeks to spell out some of the detail.

A huge and possibly bewildering array of computer programming languages is available. Some of these are specific to individual computers and others can be used on a wide range of machines. Some languages are designed with particular applications in mind, whereas others try to be all things to all men. Each language has had its devotees and enthusiasts who have eagerly promoted its use at some time or another. In some cases the languages were devised by committees who carefully agreed the facilities required; others were the product of an individual's vision. New languages are constantly appearing, some supposedly providing all the facilities required by any user — but even these seem to be superseded in time.

These comments are as true of the software tools devised for simulation as they are of the languages designed for more general applications. Faced with this variety, what principles emerge for selecting useful tools? Before answering this question, a quick review of the structure of programming languages is necessary.

6.1 PROGRAMMING LANGUAGES IN GENERAL

Computers are used to perform specific operations repetitively and quickly; for example, adding two numbers or comparing two strings of characters. If the machine is to carry out these operations correctly then it must be given completely unambiguous instructions. Thus, 'a computer programming language consists of sets of symbols denoting operations that a programmer wishes a computer to perform.' (Fishman, 1973). A programming language allows the programmer to give unambiguous instructions to the machine.

One simplified way of looking at programming languages is shown in Figure 6.1. Language types are shown as covering a spectrum from high level to low level. The highest level languages are those which are closest to natural language

```
HIGH LEVEL : interactive program generators
             compilers, interpreters,
             assemblers

 LOW LEVEL : basic machine language
```

Figure 6.1 Approaches to computer programming

(usually English) and thus require less specialized knowledge on the part of the programmer. At the other extreme, the lowest level languages are utterly different from natural language and have an extremely simple structure. To use a low level language, a programmer may need very detailed knowledge of the computer being used.

Languages which operate via compilers and interpreters are not necessarily very simple to use; however, they are likely to have more complex rules of vocabulary and syntax than assembly languages.

6.1.1 Basic machine language

At the lowest level, every computer has a basic machine language in which instructions can be given. Most digital computers operate with binary arithmetic which means that their basic machine language requires only two symbols, 0 and 1. Thus the structure of a basic machine language is extremely simple. A basic machine language program is a sequence of instructions to the computer, each instruction being made up of a unique string of zeroes and ones expressed in a hexadecimal or octal format. The individual instructions are not normally very powerful and are rather limited in scope. Thus an apparently simple operation may require a whole sequence of basic machine language strings.

To use a basic machine language properly requires knowledge of the make up of the computer being used. This is because the instructions each correspond to an operation carried out directly by the machine. This means that the apparently simple act of retrieving two numbers, adding them and storing the result requires a sequence of basic machine language instructions, so that writing sizeable or complex programs in a basic machine language can be a very time-consuming and fiddly task. It also requires great attention to detail, for there are many ways of confusing strings of zeroes and ones.

6.1.2 Assembly languages

For this reason and because it is simply difficult to remember the binary instruction codes, most computers also have an assembly language. Instructions written in an assembly language usually consist of strings of letters and numbers, the strings being mnemonics chosen by the language designer to make them more memorable than basic machine language code. Another difference is that assembly languages are normally more powerful than basic machine language. A single assembly language string usually instructs the machine to carry out a whole sequence of basic machine language operations. Whereas the machine itself is able to recognize basic machine language instructions — which eventually reach it as a stream of electrical pulses, it cannot inherently recognize assembly language strings. Therefore a basic machine language program, the *assembler*, is provided. This translates assembly language into the correct sequence of basic machine language instructions. These the machine can obey.

6.1.3 Compilers and interpreters

The next stage to consider is the development of problem oriented languages. Assembly languages are easier to remember and are more powerful than basic machine language instructions. However, they are still rather tedious to use for complex programs and require the programmer to have a reasonable knowledge of the internal workings of the particular computer being programmed. Problem oriented languages have vocabularies which are related to particular work. Hence one example, COBOL, is oriented towards business data processing. Thus their vocabulary is much more memorable than the assembly language mnemomics and their statements are far more powerful than assembly language strings. Typically each statement in a problem oriented language implies several assembly language commands. FORTRAN, ALGOL, Pascal, COBOL and BASIC are well known examples of problem oriented languages.

A *compiler* is a program which takes the statements of a problem oriented language and translates them into basic machine language When a program is compiled the entire program is translated into basic machine language. If this compilation is successful, then the basic machine language program is obeyed by the machine. Compilation may be unsuccessful for a host of reasons, usually because of some accidental error in the coding of the program in the problem oriented language. The version of the program produced by the programmer is often known as the *source code* and the resulting basic machine language program is called the *object code*. If a program is to be run many times, using a compiler makes sense because the object code may be stored on a computer file. This may be run whenever the program is required.

Another approach is to use an *interpreter* rather than a compiler. One widely used language which is always interpreted is APL. Most languages which are interpreted look very similar to those which are compiled. However an interpreter treats its source code in a rather different way from a compiler. Every time the interpreter encounters the instructions written in the problem oriented language it translates them and causes the machine to obey them immediately. There are thus two differences between languages implemented via compilers and those which use interpreters. Firstly, if a program which is to be interpreted contains a loop which is to be executed N times as the program is run, then this section will be translated N times on each occasion that the program is run. For example, in BASIC (which is usually interpreted)

```
100 S = 0
110 FOR I = 1 TO 100
120 S = S + 1
130 PRINT "SUM = "; S
140 NEXT I
```

A version of the same loop in a language which is compiled, for example in Pascal

```
sum: = 0;
for loop: = 1 to 100 do
  begin
    sum: = sum + loop;
    writeln("SUM = ",sum)
  end;
```

would only be translated once. Hence even for a program which is only to be run once, a compiler can produce a program which runs much faster than one written in a language which is interpreted.

A second running efficiency works in favour of compiled languages. When their source code is successfully compiled, the resulting object code may be stored permanently for later use. Thus, if the program needs to be run again there is no need to go through the compilation process because the object code may be run directly. Interpreted source code does not result in complete object code.

Why then should anyone use an interpreter in preference to a compiler? For a well-defined program which is to be run many times then a compiler makes obvious sense. However, an interpreter can have considerable advantages in program development. The first reason is that a program must be syntactically correct: for example,

in Pascal $x = x + 2$ will not do
whereas $x: = x + 2$; is correct.

If a compiler is being used, compilation is successful only if the entire source program is syntactically correct. On the other hand, an interpreted program may be executed up until the point at which an error occurs. This can of course encourage very bad programming habits, but it also allows the programmer to develop the source code in an evolutionary manner.

The second thing in favour of interpreters is that on an interactive computer system it can allow the programmer to halt execution of the program at any point. Then the values of variables may be examined and the execution continued. Thus it is easy for the programmer to interact with the machine whilst the program is being developed. If the problem being programmed is initially ill-structured, then an interpreter can be attractive.

An obvious development is to provide compiled and interpreted versions of the same language. Hence there are machines on which it is possible to use an interpreter to develop source code. Once development is complete, a compiler may be used to generate permanent object code. BASIC is an example of a language which is available in both implementations.

6.1.4 Interactive Program Generators

Interactive Program Generators (IPGs), sometimes known as pre-processors, are feasible only thanks to the widespread availability of interactive computer facilities. In these a user operates a console device which includes a display screen and a keyboard by means of which the user communicates with the machine. The generator is a program which interrogates the user about the problem which is to be programmed. The questions are displayed on the screen in natural language (whether English, French or whatever). The generator takes the responses of the user, checks their consistency and from them constructs a program in the correct syntax for a particular problem oriented language. A program generator is not a programming language but is an aid to programming. The user describes what the program is to do and then the generator writes the program in the appropriate source code. This source code is then interpreted or compiled as is necessary. The user gains two advantages from this:

(1) The IPG may be used to produce the skeleton of the program in a relatively short period of time. The time taken should be less than it would take to produce correct source code by hand.

(2) It is clear that no reasonable scale IPG could cope with the full complexity of all possible programs. However, the IPG produces conventional problem oriented code and this may be edited by the user to introduce any necessary enhancements. Hence the program can be made as complex as the application requires.

6.1.5 Problem oriented languages

The essence of a basic machine language is that the instructions should correspond precisely to the operations of the hardware of the computer. Few people who write computer programs would wish to be pre-occupied with these considerations. Consequently, most high level languages are problem oriented in that their vocabulary is suited to the applications for which the language is intended. For example, FORTRAN was intended to be a language particularly suited to the manipulation of arrays and variables. Thus, the statement

$$Y = M*X + C$$

is recognizable to most people who know some algebra. Because problem oriented languages are not related to the hardware requirements of particular computers they can be implemented on a wide range of machines by the production of compilers and interpreters for specific computers. The compilers and interpreters will obviously have to vary from machine to machine to accommodate the varying assemblers and basic machine languages, but the problem oriented languages themselves can be standardized.

Some problem oriented languages are more specific than others. For example, FORTRAN is a scientific (i.e. mathematical) language, whereas COBOL was produced for business applications. On the other hand, the promoters of Pascal claim that it is a truly general purpose language with convenient facilities for complex numerical calculation and for text processing. Simulation languages are problem oriented languages which provide the special purpose facilities needed for simulation.

6.2 SIMULATION LANGUAGES FROM THE ANALYST'S VIEWPOINT

The analyst is primarily concerned to produce a working simulation which is clearly a valid representation of the system of interest. A simulation language is useful if it enables him to do so quickly and with the minimum of effort. With some ingenuity it is possible to produce such valid simulations in most of the well known more general purpose problem oriented languages. However, a good simulation language is one which smooths the transition from model to working program.

A simulation language should have two qualities evident in its features. Firstly, its terminology should reflect the ideas and concepts used to develop the model being programmed. Hence, terms such as 'EVENT' and 'ACTIVity' commonly occur in simulation languages. Secondly it should be possible to provide adequate labels for the entities and other components of the system being simulated. Thus, a truck should be referred to as 'TRUCK' and not as 'X(21)' or something equally obscure.

As well as these syntactical features, a simulation language necessarily embodies some view of simulation modelling. Chapters 4 and 5 have described the major approaches to simulation modelling and each approach is clearly seen to embody its own world-view. For example, the process approach keeps a careful check on the individual life history of each entity as it appears within the simulation. On the other hand, the activity approach focusses on the conditions which must be satisfied before co-operative activity can begin. Because a simulation language must embody some world-view or other, it forces the user to model the system in those terms. Now this may seem a disadvantage, but in practice it appears to be a good idea. For one thing, the user has no choice but to cast the problem in terms which are known to be useful for simulation. Consider, for example, the simulation language ECSL (Clementson, 1982). This requires the user to explicitly define the classes of entity which make up the system and also the conditions under which the various activities can begin. Thus, the analyst cannot avoid these considerations when modelling. In this way, the analyst is forced to avoid the temptation of muddling through the modelling. Muddling through often produces a program which grows increasingly difficult to understand as it steadily grows in size.

As well as providing this strong conceptual framework, any system for aiding the development of simulation programs will also provide a number of specific facilities which are commonly needed. All of these features could be provided from scratch in a general purpose language such as FORTRAN, BASIC or Pascal, but it hardly seems sensible to go on re-inventing the wheel. These features are discussed below.

6.2.1 Time handling

In a discrete simulation, entities change state as the simulation progresses. Most of these state changes stem from co-operation between the various entities. It is obviously important to ensure that the state changes occur at the correct time and in the right sequence. For example, in a queueing system a service should not begin unless the server is free, having finished the service of a previous customer. If a next event technique is used, the simulation consists of a repeated cycle of

- identifying when the next state change will occur and then moving the simulation clock to that point;
- executing all activity that can occur at that time.

The first phase of event selection and time advance is usually carried out in the control program (or executive) of the simulation language. As such, it is usually hidden away from the analyst who is merely provided with instructions about the correct way of interfacing with these timing routines. Obviously the various modelling approaches described in Chapters 4 and 5 require different executives.

6.2.2 Model logic

It is crucial that the various entities of the simulation should change state in ways which accurately reflect the working of the system being simulated. To be useful, a simulation language should ease this specification of the logic. Doing so has two aspects.

(1) Allowing the analyst to easily discover the whereabouts of specific entities. For example, 'is there a 6 tonne truck available, and if so, where is it?'

(2) Having a syntax and vocabulary which correspond to the state changes occurring in the system. For example, in ECSL one can write

    SHIP A FROM PORT INTO ATSEA AFTER LOADING

The meaning of even this isolated statement is reasonably clear. Hence programs written in such languages are easier to debug.

6.2.3 Distribution sampling

The durations of the various activities and processes of discrete simulations are rarely deterministic. More often they are stochastic; that is they vary in some manner as the simulation proceeds. Thus the time to load a box trailer with 20 pallets of biscuits varies from occasion to occasion even if the conditions of operation are more or less the same. Only if a cycle of operations is entirely automatic are repeated cycles likely to take exactly the same time to complete.

These variable durations are usually simulated by probability distributions. For example, investigation may reveal that the time to load the box trailer is normally distributed with a mean of 35 minutes and a standard deviation of 5 minutes. In a simulation, a sample would be taken from this normal distribution each time the activity is due to begin. Hence it is possible to determine when the activity will finish.

Well-known methods exist for taking samples from a wide range of standard probability distributions and from histograms. These methods are discussed in Chapter 7. A good simulation provides built-in procedures using sound methods to generate the samples.

6.2.4 Random number generation

It will be seen in Chapter 7 that the sampling methods assume the existence of a stream of independent, uniformly distributed random numbers on the interval (0,1). Again the methods to produce a random number streams are well developed and are discussed in Chapter 7. Ideally, the analyst will have access to several independent streams as this will ease the problem of interpreting the simulation results (Chapter 8).

6.2.5 Initialization facilities

When interpreting the results of a simulation it is sensible to bear in mind the conditions set in the model when the run begins. For example, should the simulation of a warehouse begin with the building quiet, the vehicles empty and all the staff idle? Or should it begin with the warehouse's typical operating conditions? Conway (1963) points out the importance of giving careful consideration to these initial conditions. There is clearly a risk that they will bias the results.

Chapter 8 discusses the options open to the analyst in setting the initial conditions. Whatever the option chosen, the analyst requires some convenient way of setting up the initial conditions in the simulation. In addition, if the simulation is to be run several times to reduce sampling errors (Chapter 8) then provision must be made for re-initialization. A good simulation language should make initialization a simple matter.

6.2.6 Report generation

In management science, simulations are usually conducted for specific purposes. Thus the analyst and client wish to know the results of the simulation, that is they wish to know how the system will behave under given conditions. This has two aspects. Firstly, a simulation can be considered as an experiment (see Chapter 8) and it is important to collect data from that experiment and to analyse the results. Thus it is necessary to provide facilities which ease the task of collecting statistics and of producing attractive reports. Often the statistics will be required in graph or histogram form in the final report.

Secondly, the analyst may wish to interact with the simulation as it proceeds using the simulation as a type of operational game. Hence two facilities are required:

(1) attractive and easy to read output from the simulation as it proceeds;
(2) some way of interacting with the model as it runs.

Chapter 5 has already indicated how the three phase approach (Tocher, 1963) may be modified to allow such interaction. The method assumes that interactive computer facilities are available with graphic (preferably coloured) displays and a keyboard, light pen or game paddles to interact with the program. Whereas the provision of these hardware facilities was once expensive they are now cheap and commonplace on microcomputers.

6.2.7 Control facilities and error messages

All problem oriented languages provide control facilities and error messages, but these may not be ideal for simulation. For example, it would be useful, whilst debugging a program, to be able to follow specific entities could sometimes be useful. These tracing facilities are available only in rudimentary forms in languages such as FORTRAN. In addition, any error messages produced when the program fails should refer to the conditions within the simulation rather than to the arithmetic of the language. Messages such as 'ARRAY SUBSCRIPT ERROR' are inadequate. Unfortunately, the provision of adequate control facilities and error messages is a tedious and unrewarding task. But it is necessary.

6.3 PROVIDING SOFTWARE TOOLS FOR SIMULATION

The facilities required by the analyst are well known, but there are several ways of providing them. How best to provide them is not a question which is easily answered, the answer being related to questions other than the merely technical. Before attempting to come to any conclusion on this topic, it is necessary to describe the approaches which various designers have adopted. These may be placed in the following rough historical sequence:

collections of subroutines and procedures;
statement-description languages;
flow diagram languages;
interactive program generators.

6.4 WRITING FROM SCRATCH IN A GENERAL PURPOSE LANGUAGE

This is of course a possibility; but, as mentioned previously, it is not to be recommended except to beginners learning to produce simulations of 'toy' problems. Otherwise the analyst is constantly forced to re-invent the wheel.

6.5 COLLECTIONS OF SUBROUTINES AND PROCEDURES

Once it became clear that certain features are required in any discrete simulation program, then it seemed pointless to go on rewriting them. A useful feature of most high level problem oriented languages is that they encourage the use of subroutines or procedures for sections of program which will be used repeatedly. Consequently, an obvious step forward was to write such procedures to carry out the specific tasks necessary in most simulations. Hence specific routines were written to take samples from various distributions, for time handling, for moving entities, ..., and so on.

To use one of these collections of simulation routines, the analyst must write the skeleton of the program in the host language (e.g. FORTRAN). Hence, reasonable fluency is needed in that language. This is both an advantage and a disadvantage. The positive side is that the analyst has no other language to learn, assuming that the host language is already known. Also the organization for whom the work is being done may already have a major investment in programs written in that language. Hence it may wish to continue on familiar ground. This eases the problem of program support.

On the negative side, such collections rarely provide the full conceptual framework which is a major advantage of the 'true' simulation languages. If the analyst has to write even a few parts of the program from scratch, the temptation to cut corners may be overwhelming. It must also be said that such collections need to be of some complexity to be useful. Thus it may be a task of some difficulty to fully master an entire collection. A further snag is that the error messages generated by such systems are likely to refer to the statements of the host language. As such, they may be difficult to understand. Given that simulation programs are notoriously tricky to debug, this is a significant disadvantage.

Two well known examples of collections of subroutines for discrete simulation are SIMON and GASP. SIMON (Hills, 1965) was originally a collection of ALGOL procedures and most versions of GASP (Pritsker, 1974) are written in FORTRAN. SIMON adopts the three phase structure of Tocher described earlier in Chapter 5, whereas GASP is available in several versions, all of which are event oriented. One of the latest versions, GASP IV, also provides routines which allow the development of simulations which operate in a mixed discrete/continuous mode. Thus, GASP IV includes integration routines to simulate the continuous change of time as discussed in Chapter 2. Both SIMON and GASP allow the analyst to make use of the efficient execution offered by compiler languages.

6.5.1 GASP IV

Considering GASP IV a little further will serve to indicate the type of procedures that are found in such collections. 'A GASP IV program is made up of (FORTRAN) sub-programs linked together by an executive routine that organises and controls the performance of the sub-programs.' (Pritsker, 1974, p. 16). Specifically, GASP IV includes routines to perform the following tasks.

(1) *Time advance and status update*. Performed by subroutine GASP, the executive of the GASP IV system. Ensuring that the events of the simulation occur in the correct order at the right time.
(2) *Initialization*. Performed by several sub-programs allowing various forms of initialization. For example, during program compilation (via FORTRAN DATA statements) or from values read into the program at run-time.
(3) *Data storage and retrieval*. For maintaining the status of entity times and attributes within the simulation.
(4) *Location of state conditions and entities*. To enable the analyst to keep track of the entities and their states.
(5) *Data collection, computation and reporting*. Allowing the analyst to record data about the response variables (e.g. waiting times) during a simulation run and for generating reports based on histograms and graphs for the final output.
(6) *Monitoring and error reporting*. Simulation programs can be very difficult to verify and debug. Monitoring facilities enable the analyst to follow the progress of the entities in detail during a simulation run. The error reports are useful for debugging. Pritsker (1974) indicates that the analyst may wish to enhance these routines.
(7) *Random deviate generation*. For sampling from common distributions such as uniform, normal, erlang, etc.
(8) *Various miscellaneous routines*. To aid the general task of programming.

The analyst needs to be fully conversant with the routines provided in order to make proper use of these collections. Given that the routines are fairly complex, this is no small task and is possibly not much easier than learning a new simulation language. However, it is rather easier than writing from scratch in FORTRAN and similar problem oriented languages.

6.6 STATEMENT DESCRIPTION LANGUAGES

These are the 'true' simulation languages, whose problem orientation is towards the specifics of simulation programming. A huge number of such languages exists and the interested reader should consult the current simulation, management science or operational research literature. This section makes no attempt to present a complete survey. Other authors have tried (see for example, Emshoff and Sisson, 1970) but their efforts are quickly out of date. The main contenders for popular use seem to be SIMSCRIPT, SIMULA and ECSL. Each of these will be briefly considered in turn, with a greater emphasis placed on ECSL, to illustrate the features found in these languages. GPSS, another popularly used system, will be considered in Section 6.7.2. This section is not intended to teach the detail of any of these languages; for this, readers are referred to the texts and manuals mentioned.

6.6.1 ECSL

Extended Control and Simulation Language (Clementson, 1982), a popular British simulation language, was developed by Clementson as an extension to CSL (Buxton and Laski, 1962), which was produced by Esso in 1960. Both versions apply the simple activity scan approach described in Chapter 4. ECSL code is interpreted, the ECSL system and the interpreter being written in FORTRAN. Thus ECSL may be run on any machine which supports a FORTRAN compiler and offering sufficient storage, the amount required depending on the operating system of the computer. Though originally designed for punched card operation on mainframe computers, ECSL may also be run interactively either on a multi-user system or some microcomputers. A program generator CAPS (Clementson, 1982, see Section 6.8.1) is also available. ECSL programs normally have five sections as shown in Figure 6.2. These are as follows.

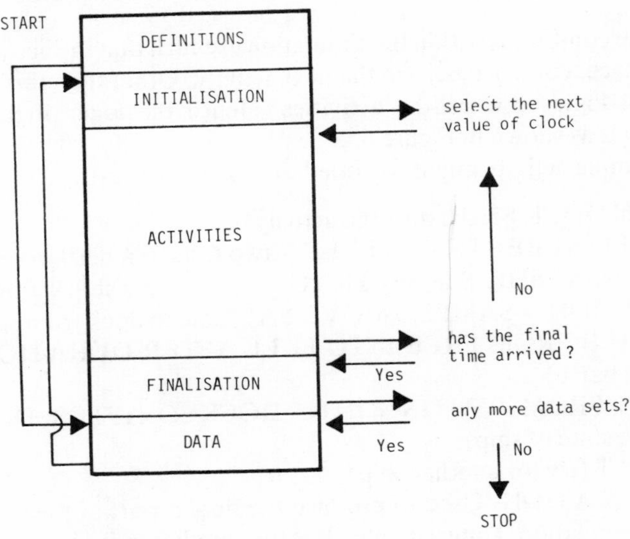

Figure 6.2 The five sections of an ECSL program

(1) DEFINITIONS: Establishing the entities and the sets of which each class may be members. For example;

THERE ARE 10 SHIPS WITH CARGO SET ATSEA HARBOUR WAITING

i.e. SHIPS is a class of entity with 10 members and each ship has an attribute CARGO and may be in any of the sets ATSEA, HARBOUR or WAITING.

The definitions section may also be used to establish any histograms or special variables required.

(2) INITIALIZATION: Setting up the initial state of the system by establishing the states of the specific entities. These are statements written in the normal syntax of ECSL.

(3) ACTIVITIES: This is the main body of the program. Each activity is regarded as a completely independent block of ECSL code. The structure of an ECSL activity is shown in Figure 6.3.

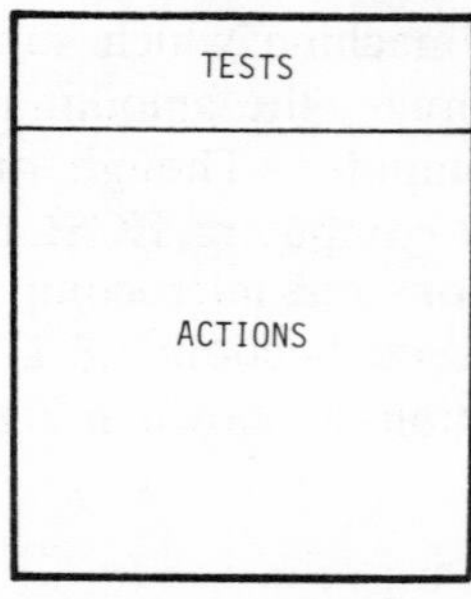

Figure 6.3 The structure of an ECSL activity

If the conditions within the simulation are such that the activity may not take place, control passes to the next activity. Other than this, there is no control logic between the activities. Hence the logic of the activities section is as shown in Figure 6.4.

A simple activity might be coded as follows in ECSL.

BEGIN DOCK SHIP (start the activity)
FIND FIRST BERTH B IN FREE (two tests: is a berth free?)
FIND FIRST SHIP S IN WAITING (: is a ship waiting?)
DURATION = SAMPLE(MOVE,SA) (time to dock from sample)
BERTH B FROM FREE INTO FULL AFTER DURATION (change state of berth)
SHIP S FROM WAITING INTO DOCKED AFTER DURATION (change state of ship)
REPEAT (try for another ship)

(4) FINALIZATION: Used to produce the final report of the performance of the simulation. Entered only after the simulation is complete.

(5) DATA: Establishes initial values of some of the variables in conjunction with the initialization section.

An example of a complete ECSL program is shown in Section 6.8.1. This was produced by the CAPS program generator and illustrates the structure of an

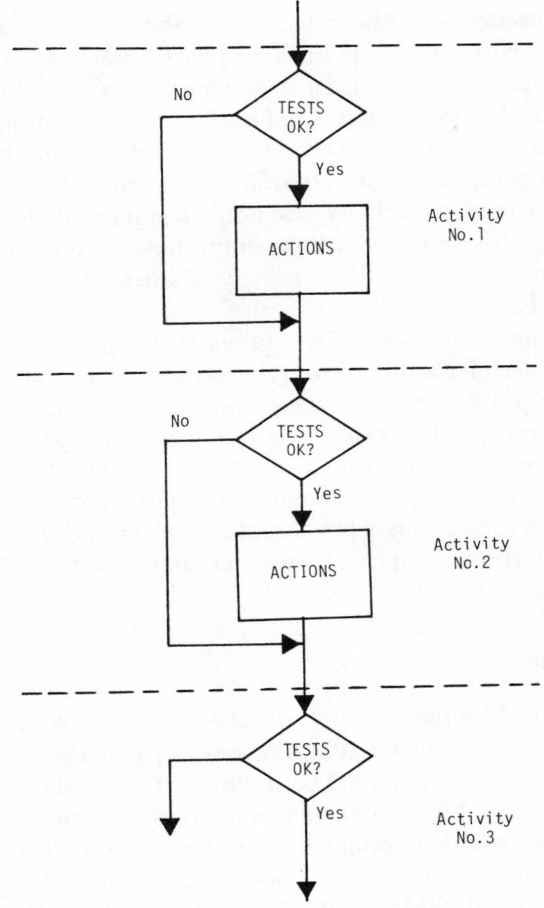

Figure 6.4 The logic of the ECSL activities section

ECSL program. When an ECSL program is executed, the following process occurs (see also Figure 6.2).

(1) The definitions section establishes the storage required for the program and details of the entities, sets, attributes, etc.
(2) The first data set is read from the data section.
(3) The initialization section establishes those initial conditions that are constant for all the data sets in the data section.
(4) The simulation proper begins and continues until the simulation duration has elapsed. During this phase there is a continued cycle of activity scans and time scans.
(5) The finalization section produces the printouts.
(6) If there are any more data sets, read the next set and return to step (3); otherwise stop.

Variations on this process are possible, but the above is the norm.

The ECSL executive has a quasi three phase approach. Firstly, the time attributes (time cells) of all entities are scanned and the minimum positive value is selected. All time cells are reduced by this amount and the clock is increased by the same amount. Secondly, any events set up by the AFTER keyword, which schedules events equivalent to 'B' activities, are carried out. Thirdly, there is a repeated activity scan until no more activities are possible at this time. If any entity begins an activity at this time, its time cell may be reset by the program to the duration of the activity. There are no true 'arrival type' B activities in ECSL.

As a simulation language, ECSL provides sampling routines, random number streams and all the other features described in Section 6.2. It is entirely oriented towards programming simulation problems and is intended to ease the modelling and programming tasks. The statements are easy to read and are powerful, each one being equivalent to several FORTRAN statements. The aim is to economize on expensive analyst and programmer time. However, because of the interpreter this is possibly at the expense of efficient execution. Despite being interpreted, an ECSL program cannot be stopped and restarted in the same way as most BASIC programs.

6.6.2 SIMSCRIPT

Probably the most popular 'true' simulation language in the USA is SIMSCRIPT. Strictly, SIMSCRIPT is a series of languages, the earliest of which was developed at the RAND corporation. This version, SIMSCRIPT I (Markowitz *et al.*, 1963) was implemented by translating the source code into FORTRAN, which was then compiled. The latest version, SIMSCRIPT II and its variants, is translated direct into assembly language and thus into object code. Hence a special SIMSCRIPT II compiler is needed. According to Markowitz (1979), SIMSCRIPT II is a general purpose programming language with simulation facilities. It may be used at any of five levels, level 1 being simple to use for beginners, though without explicit simulation facilities. At the opposite extreme, level 5 includes the simulation facilities such as sampling routines. As with ECSL, SIMSCRIPT II statements are readable, powerful and make explicit use of simulation terminology.

The basic concepts are similar to ECSL, though the approach taken is event oriented rather than activity based. A system is considered to be a set of interacting entities (e.g. SHIPS) which have attributes (e.g. CARGO) and can be members of sets (e.g. ATSEA). Sets are owned by entities and also have member entities. Hence a queue of jobs at a machine is a set, the owner of which is the machine and the jobs its members. The state of the simulation changes as the set membership changes.

Unlike ECSL, in which all entities are permanent, they can be CREATEd and DESTROYed in SIMSCRIPT II as well as moving between sets. That is, SIMSCRIPT II allows permanent and temporary entities. Both ECSL and

SIMSCRIPT II provide the full range of simulation facilities described in Section 6.2.

6.6.3 SIMULA

SIMULA was developed at the Norwegian Computing Centre and is an extension of the general purpose language ALGOL 60. Hills (1973) gives an introduction and Franta (1977) provides a rather more theoretical treatment. Whereas ECSL is activity based, SIMULA makes use of the process (or scenario) approach described in Section 4.3. Birtwhistle (1979) has developed the DEMOS package to help beginners to develop SIMULA programs by forcing them to use a simplified structure.

SIMULA uses the term 'object' to describe entities. Thus one object might be a member of the class SHIP, with attributes such as CARGO and a life history. This life history, or process, is the sequence of activities or actions in which objects of this class engage. As with ECSL, the objects must be identified in a type declaration before use.

Like SIMSCRIPT II, SIMULA claims to be rather more than a discrete simulation language. Whereas the format of SIMSCRIPT II statements is FORTRAN like, SIMULA follows ALGOL and therefore Pascal. Hence, analysts knowing one of these general purpose languages may feel more drawn to one than another.

6.7 BLOCK DIAGRAM SYSTEMS

To use a statement description language or a collection of subroutines, the analyst needs to be a reasonably proficient programmer. Block diagram systems are an attempt to ease the programming task by allowing the analyst to code the 'program' solely in terms of the blocks found on a flow diagram. Thus the task of programming is reduced to the specification of the blocks through which an entity passes in its life. This same idea is employed in the program generators discussed in the next section. Program generators produce source code in a specified language (for example, ECSL or FORTRAN) which the analyst may edit. The actual block specification is the only source code with block diagram systems.

The two best-known block diagram systems are HOCUS and GPSS, both of which are available in several versions.

6.7.1 HOCUS

Hand Or Computer Universal Simulator (Poole and Szymankiewicz, 1977) is a proprietory produce of the P–E Consulting Group, U.K. To use HOCUS the analyst must formulate the model in terms of an activity cycle diagram (see Chapter 3). A HOCUS source program consists of a block by block description of the diagram. HOCUS then calls and combines standard FORTRAN subroutines. These are then compiled and executed but they are not available for modification by the analyst. As originally devised, HOCUS was intended for use with or without a computer and in the former case it was intended for use in a punch card environment.

HOCUS programs include the following sections.

(1) ENTITIES: a list of the classes of entity in the simulation, showing the number in each class and the number of attributes. Thus;

ESHIP 20 4

ECRANE 2 2

indicates that there are 20 ships with up to 4 attributes each and 2 cranes with up to 2 attributes each.

(2) QUEUES: a list of the queue (dead state) names in order, indicating any maximum sizes.

(3) DATA FIELDS: for input of distributions and timetables for sampling, etc.

(4) ACTIVITIES: showing the conditions necessary for each activity (active state) to begin and the state changes resulting. Both should be expressed in terms of the input and output queues (dead states) to each active state. Also other information such as the duration of the active state.

(5) HISTOGRAMS: specifying those which are to be set up for the collection of data for output.

(6) INITIAL CONDITIONS: showing what should be in progress at the start of the simulation.

As well as requiring the model in this format, HOCUS allows the user to control and monitor the operation of the program by the use of standard commands.

The advantage of HOCUS is that it is extremely simple to understand and requires almost no knowledge of computing. However, there are disadvantages. Firstly, whereas program generators (Section 6.8) produce code in a specified language, the only program available to the analyst using HOCUS is the model description itself. Hence systems which are inconvenient to model via activity cycle diagrams may need to be squeezed into a HOCUS mould and the resulting program may be a rather distorted representation of the system. Secondly, even if the skeleton of the system can be modelled successfully in an activity cycle diagram, HOCUS provides no approved way of allowing the user to edit the FORTRAN code. Thus, some complexities are likely to be difficult to model. Thirdly, HOCUS provides only rudimentary facilities for distribution sampling, the user being encouraged (Poole and Szymankiewicz, 1977, p. 32) to use histogram input for many distributions. As Chapter 7 indicates, this can be a dangerous practice.

6.7.2 GPSS

The best-known block diagram system is undoubtedly GPSS (General Purpose System Simulator) which has existed in various versions since 1961. The original version stemmed from development work at the Bell Telephone Laboratory assisted by IBM. Since the IBM has continued to support GPSS and this may account for the popularity of the system. Numerous manuals and books describe its features: beginners are referred to Greenberg (1972). Those interested in GPSS in a more general simulation context should consult Gordon (1969), one of the originators of GPSS. The original version of GPSS was written to aid the development of telecommunications networks and was meant for users who were not computer specialists. These origins are clearly visible in all subsequent versions.

Like HOCUS, GPSS is based around the idea of a block diagram which models the flow of entities through a network. According to Greenberg (1972) however, there is rarely any need to actually draw the GPSS diagrams. An outline of GPSS terminology follows.

TEMPORARY ENTITY: called a TRANSACTION and seen as moving through a series of BLOCKs during its life. Each transaction begins its life in a GENERATE block and ends it in a TERMINATE block.
PERMANENT ENTITY: called a FACILITY if its operations require only a single transaction or a STORAGE if two or more transactions are required.

A GPSS source program consists of a list of the blocks through which each class of transaction should pass during its life. Each block is a distinct line of a GPSS program consisting of a block descriptor (e.g. GENERATE) followed by one or more parameters. As the GPSS translator reads the source program, it calls distinct assembly language routines for each block. This assembly program is not available to the user, who is thus strictly unable to model systems which are not easily represented as transactions flows. As a way round this, some versions of GPSS include a HELP block via which the user may write specific routines in FORTRAN or PL/1.

Consider a single server queue, GPSS being ideal for such simulations. A skeleton GPSS program might look as follows:

```
GENERATE   6,2
QUEUE      1
SEIZE      1
DEPART     1
ADVANCE    6,3
RELEASE    1
TERMINATE
```

This employs 7 blocks as follows:

GENERATE 6,2: Create transactions at a mean rate of every 6 time units, the time between transactions varying between 4 and 8.
QUEUE 1: As the transactions are created, they join queue 1.
SEIZE 1: The transactions seize facility 1 when they reach the head of the queue.
DEPART 1: When seized, the transaction leaves queue 1.
ADVANCE 6,3: The transaction remains with facility 1 for between 3 and 9 time units.
RELEASE 1: The facility is freed and available for another transaction.
TERMINATE: The transaction is destroyed.

In this example, the transactions represent customers and the facility is the server. During the simulation, the transactions move from block to block until delayed. These delays may be conditional (e.g. waiting for a server) or due to the time taken to complete an operation (e.g. service). Once the operation is complete or the conditions are satisfied, the transaction moves to the next block.

This simple skeleton program allows several comments to be made. Firstly, GPSS follows a process approach to simulation (see Section 4.3), the process of a customer being represented by the blocks in the program. This GPSS implementation of the process approach makes it difficult to model systems in which various classes of entity are competing for the same resources. In addition, Gordon (1979, p. 23) admits an error in the GPSS control program which becomes evident when complex interacting systems are simulated. To quote, 'In practice, there is a minor flaw in the algorithm ... The mechanism for automatically restarting a blocked transaction assumes that the unblocking occurs when a single specific system change occurs. There might, in fact, be several changes that can unblock a transaction ... (this) means that ... a transaction will sometimes move later than it might have been entitled to move.' GPSS users beware!

Secondly, Section 6.2 has discussed the facilities needed in a complete simulation language. Whereas the strong points of GPSS are its simple structure and its easy to use report generator, its sampling routines are all but non-existent. Virtually all distributions have to be defined in a discrete cumulative form (see Chapter 7) and set up as user-defined functions. For highly stochastic simulations, this is most unfortunate. Fishman also reports (1973, p. 183) that the random number generator of GPSS/360 (see Chapter 7) is also relatively poor and could thus lead to sampling errors. Therefore GPSS falls short of the standard set in Section 6.2.

On the other hand, GPSS does have an appealing simplicity. Hence it has an obvious application for simulating systems in which the entities follow relatively predictable paths in which their interaction is slight. Analysts modelling other types of system may wish to look elsewhere.

6.8 INTERACTIVE PROGRAM GENERATORS

A program generator is a software tool which accepts a simple description of a model and produces executable source code. A review of simulation program generators is to be found in Mathewson (1975). For convenience, most generators operate on interactive computer systems and are known as Interactive Program Generators (IPGs). The concepts are similar to those employed in the Programming by Questionnaire System of RAND (Oldfather *et al.*, 1966) which need not be interactive. The available simulation IPGs are based on the activity cycle diagram concept described in Chapter 3.

To use a simulation IPG, the user firstly draws an activity cycle diagram of the system, the diagram being as complete as possible. Obviously, no diagram could include the full complexity of all systems and still remain readable, therefore the aim is to concentrate on the essential skeleton of the model. Sitting at a console device the user is interrogated by the IPG using English (or whatever language is appropriate). From the user's responses, the IPG combines the activity cycles of the various entity classes and produces a simulation source program in an appropriate language. If the program needs to be enhanced to accommodate the full complexity of the system being simulated, this is simply done via the editing facilities of the computer.

Probably the best-known simulation IPGs are CAPS (Clementson, 1982) which produces ECSL code and DRAFT (Mathewson, 1977) which is available in versions producing ALGOL, FORTAN and SIMULA code amongst others. In principle, the same diagram may be used to generate programs using any of the modelling approaches described in Chapters 4 and 5 (Mathewson, 1975).

6.8.1 CAPS

To illustrate the use of a program generator, the following example is of CAPS and shows the activity cycle diagram (Figure 6.5), the dialogue with the IPG (Figures 6.6 to 6.9) and the resulting ECSL program (Figure 6.10). The system to be simulated is a warehouse with three loading bays, each of which can accommodate one truck or two vans. Goods enter the warehouse on fully laden trucks which are unloaded and leave empty. Empty vans arrive at the site and are fully loaded when they leave. There is no shortage of labour. If there are no free bays when either type of vehicle arrives, then they must wait in a park near the entrance until a bay is free. Should both trucks and vans be waiting, then trucks have priority when a bay is freed. The exit and entrance roads are wide and uncluttered.

Relevant data are as follows:

Warehouse capacity = 100 van loads
1 truck load = 4 van loads
Truck inter-arrival time = negative exponential with mean of 2 hours
Van inter-arrival time = negative exponential with mean of 30 minutes
Time to move from the entrance to a bay = uniform for all vehicles
Truck unloading time = normal with mean of 60 minutes, standard deviation of 5 minutes
Van loading time = negative exponential with mean of 20 minutes.
Initial conditions:
80 van loads in the warehouse, no vehicles on site.

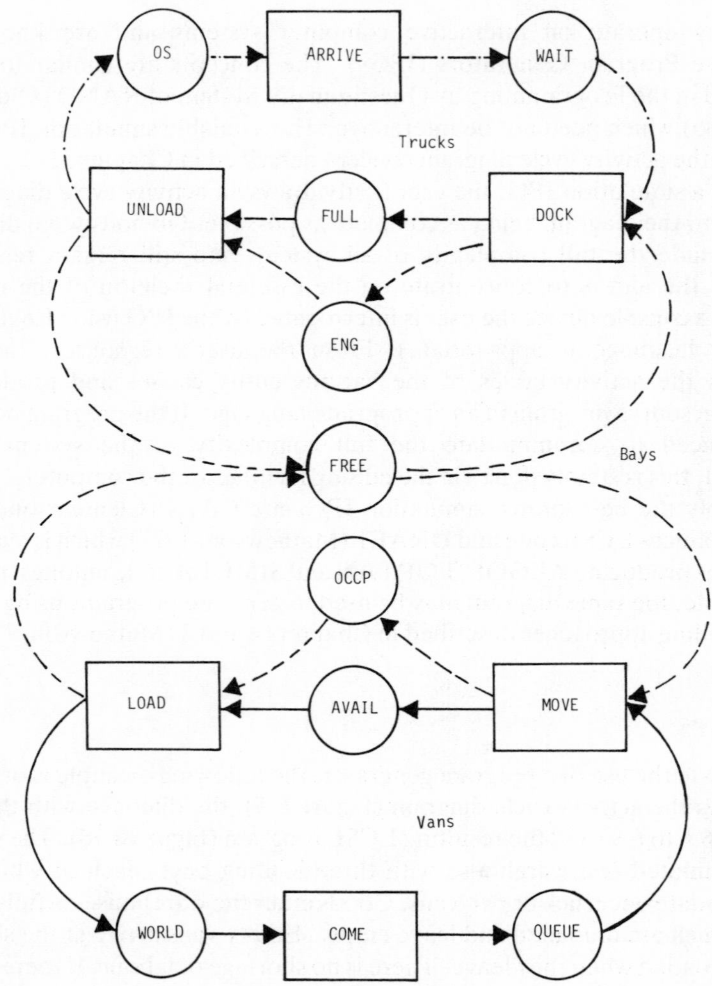

Figure 6.5 The warehouse activity cycle diagram

The CAPS dialogue

The dialogue is divided into six sections.

(1) LOGIC: in which the classes of entities are established and the logic of the system is described to CAPS.
(2) PRIORITIES: establishing whether any queues have non-FIFO discipline and sorting out the priorities of the activities.
(3) ARITHMETIC: setting up the probability distributions from which samples will be taken, and defining any attributes.
(4) RECORDING: deciding what run-time data needs to be collected for the various queues in order to record the behaviour of the model.

```
EXTENDED CONTROL AND SIMULATION LANGUAGE
--------------------------------------------
COMPUTER AIDED PROGRAMMING SYSTEM

DO YOU WISH TO HAVE INSTRUCTIONAL COMMENTS-
N
PROBLEM NAME -
WAREHOUSE
DO YOU WISH TO START A NEW PROBLEM
Y

LOGIC

TYPE NAME OF ONE KIND OF ENTITY
TRUCK
HOW MANY
8
TYPE A LIST OF THE STATES THROUGH WHICH THESE ENTITIES PASS
PRECEDE QUEUES BY Q AND ACTIVITES BY A
QOS,AARRIVE,QWAIT,ADOCK,QFULL,AUNLOAD,QOS

IS THIS CYCLE CORRECT
Y

TYPE NAME OF ONE KIND OF ENTITY
VAN
HOW MANY
15
TYPE LIST OF STATES AS ABOVE
QWORLD,ACOME,QQUEUE,AMOVE,QAVAIL,ALOAD,QWORLD

IS THIS CYCLE CORRECT
Y

TYPE NAME OF ONE KIND OF ENTITY
BAY
HOW MANY
6
TYPE LIST OF STATES AS ABOVE
QFREE,ADOCK,QENG,AUNLOAD,QFREE
AMOVE,QOCCP,ALOAD,QFREE

IS THIS CYCLE CORRECT
Y

TYPE NAME OF ONE KIND OF ENTITY
```

Figure 6.6a CAPS example: logic section

```
ARE THERE ANY (OTHER) ACTIVITIES WHICH USE MORE THAN ONE
ENTITY OF A PARTICULAR TYPE
Y
WHICH ACTIVITY
DOCK
WHICH ENTITY TYPE
BAY
HOW MANY ENTITIES PER ACTIVITY
2
WHICH ACTIVITY
UNLOAD
WHICH ENTITY TYPE
BAY
HOW MANY ENTITIES PER ACTIVITY
2
WHICH ACTIVITY


FROM WHAT YOU HAVE SAID SO FAR, THE FOLLOWING ARE THE
MAXIMUM NUMBER OF SIMULTANEOUS REALISATION OF THE ACTIVITIES.
ACTIVITY NUMBER
ARRIVE  8     LIMITED BY THE NUMBER OF TRUCK
DOCK    3     LIMITED BY THE NUMBER OF BAY
UNLOAD  3     LIMITED BY THE NUMBER OF BAY
COME   15     LIMITED BY THE NUMBER OF VAN
MOVE    6     LIMITED BY THE NUMBER OF BAY
LOAD   16     LIMITED BY THE NUMBER OF BAY
DO YOU WISH TO APPLY LIMITS WHICH ARE BELOW THESE
Y
WHICH ACTIVITY
ARRIVE
WHAT IS THE LIMIT
1
WHICH ACTIVITY
COME
WHAT IS THE LIMIT
1
WHICH ACTVITY

NOT MORE THAN   7 OF THE  8 TRUCK CAN BE ACTIVE AT ONE TIME
NOT MORE THAN  13 OF THE 15 VAN   CAN BE ACTIVE AT ONE TIME
ACTIVITY UNLOAD APPEARS TO BE BOUND TO DOCK
I.E. THE FOLLOWING QUEUES ARE DUMMIES
FULL
ENG
DO YOU AGREE
Y
ACTIVITY LOAD APPEARS TO BE BOUND TO MOVE
I.E. THE FOLLOWING QUEUES ARE DUMMIES
AVAIL
OCCP
DO YOU AGREE
Y
```

Figure 6.6b CAPS example: logic section

```
DO YOU WISH TO SEE A SUMMARY OF THE CYCLES
Y
TRUCK  8 ,QOS,AARRIVE,QWAIT,ADOCK,Q,AUNLOAD,QOS
VAN    15,QWORLD ,ACOME,QQUEUE ,AMOVE,Q,ALOAD,QWORLD
BAY    6 ,QFREE,ADOCK,Q,AUNLOAD,QFREE,AMOVE,Q,ALOAD,QFREE,
ZZARRI 1 ,AARRIVE
ZZCOME 1 ,ACOME

ARRIVE USES 1 TRUCK  1 ZZARRI
DOCK   USES 1 TRUCK  2 BAY
UNLOAD USES 1 TRUCK  2 BAY
COME   USES 1 VAN    1 ZZCOME
MOVE   USES 1 VAN    1 BAY
LOAD   USES 1 VAN    1 BAY
DO YOU WISH TO MAKE ANY CHANGES IN THE LOGIC SECTION
N
```

Figure 6.6c CAPS example: logic section

```
PRIORITIES
ARE THERE ANY QUEUES WHOSE DISCIPLINE IS NOT F-I-F-O
N
THE FOLLOWING ARE BOUND ACTIVITIES
UNLOAD
LOAD

THE ORDER OF THE FOLLOWING ACTIVITIES IS UNIMPORTANT
COME
ARRIVE

I PROPOSE PUTTING THE REMAINING ACTVITIES IN THE FOLLOWING ORDER
MOVE
DOCK
DO YOU WISH TO RAISE THE PRIORITY OF ANY ACTIVITY-
Y
WHICH ACTIVITY-
DOCK
WHICH ACTIVITY-

DO YOU WISH TO MAKE ANY CHANGES IN THE PRIORITY SECTION
N
```

Figure 6.7 CAPS example: priorities section

```
ARITHMETIC
AFTER EACH ACTIVITY NAME, TYPE FORMULA FOR ITS DURATION
IF THE DURATION MIGHT BE ZERO, TYPE 0+....
DOCK  =
RANDOM(3,SA)+1
MOVE  =
RANDOM(3,SB)+1
COME  =
NEGEXP(30,SC)
ARRIVE=
NEGEXP(120,SD)
UNLOAD=
NORMAL(60,5,SE)
LOAD  =
NEGEXP(20,SF)

IN WHICH ACTIVITY IS SA     EVALUATED

WHAT IS ITS INITIAL VALUE
5397
IN WHICH ACTIVITY IS SB     EVALUATED

WHAT IS ITS INITIAL VALUE
3579
IN WHICH ACTIVITY IS SC     EVALUATED

WHAT IS ITS INITIAL VALUE
7359
IN WHICH ACTIVITY IS SD     EVALUATED

WHAT IS ITS INITIAL VALUE
7935
IN WHICH ACTIVITY IS SE     EVALUATED

WHAT IS ITS INITIAL VALUE
3975
IN WHICH ACTIVITY IS SF     EVALUATED

WHAT IS ITS INITIAL VALUE
5973
DO YOU WISH TO DEFINE ANY MORE ATTRIBUTES FOR ENTITIES
N
DO YOU WISH TO MAKE ANY CHANGES TO THE ARITHMETIC SECTION
N
```

Figure 6.8 CAPS example: arithmetic section

```
RECORDING
WAIT  =
3
OS    =
0
QUEUE =
3
WORLD =
0
FREE  =
3
WHAT LENGTH OF RUN-IN PERIOD IS REQUIRED
120
DO YOU WISH TO MAKE ANY CHANGES TO THE RECORDING SECTION
N

INITIAL CONDITIONS
ARE THERE ANY ACTIVITIES IN PROGRESS
N

TYPE HOW MANY ENTITIES SHOULD BE IN EACH QUEUE LISTED
AFTER THE QUEUE NAME
TRUCK  -  8 ENTITIES
WAIT   -
0
OS     -
8
VAN    - 15 ENTITIES
QUEUE  -
0
WORLD  -
15
BAY    -  6 ENTITIES
 6 ENTITIES PLACED IN QUEUE FREE
PLEASE GIVE THE DURATION OF THE SIMULATION
1008
DO YOU WISH TO MAKE ANY CHANGES IN THE INITIAL CONDITION SECTION
N
LOAD  ,WHICH YOU HAVE USED AS A NAME IS AN ECSL KEYWORD
PLEASE GIVE A REPLACEMENT
FILL

SOME ENTITIES ARE APPARENTLY SUITABLE FOR AGGREGATION
I.E. THEY HAVE NO ATTRIBUTES, NO DELAY RECORDING AND USE ONLY
FIFO Q-DISCIPLINE
DO YOU WISH ME TO AGGREGATE TRUCK
N
DO YOU WISH ME TO AGGREGATE VAN
N
DO YOU WISH ME TO AGGREGATE BAY
N
YOUR PROGRAM HAS BEEN WRITTEN HAVE YOU FINISHED
Y
```

Figure 6.9 CAPS example: initial conditions section

```
THERE ARE 8 TRUCK SET WAIT OS
THERE ARE 15 VAN SET QUEUE WORLD
THERE ARE 6 BAY SET FREE
THERE ARE 1 ZZARRI
THERE ARE 1 ZZCOME
FUNCTION PICTURE NORMAL NEGEXP RANDOM
RECYCLE
RUNINZ= 120 AND PREVCLOCK = RUNINZ
SWITCH ADD ON AFTER RUNINZ
ACTIVITIES 1008
DURATION= CLOCK - PREVCLOCK
ARRAY ZAWAIT ( 445 )
FOR Z=PREVCLOCK +1 CLOCK
  ADD WAIT TO ZAWAIT ((Z-RUNINZ)/2 +1)
FOR ZZARRI WITH TIME OF ZZARRI LT 0
  ADD DURATION TO AZZZARRI
FOR ZZCOME WITH TIME OF ZZCOME LT 0
  ADD DURATION TO BZZZCOME
PREVCLOCK = CLOCK
BEGIN DOCK
FIND FIRST TRUCK A IN WAIT
EXISTS( 2 ) BAY FROM FREE
DURATION= RANDOM( 3 , SA ) + 1
ADD 1 TO DOCK
AADURATION= DURATION+ NORMAL( 60, 5 , SE )
TRUCK A FROM WAIT INTO OS AFTER AADURATION
FOR 1 TO 2
  FIND FIRST BAY B IN FREE
  BAY B FROM FREE INTO FREE AFTER AADURATION
REPEAT
BEGIN MOVE
FIND FIRST VAN A IN QUEUE
FIND FIRST BAY B IN FREE
DURATION= RANDOM( 3 , SB ) + 1
ADD 1 TO MOVE
AADURATION= DURATION+ NEGEXP( 20, SF )
VAN A FROM QUEUE INTO WORLD AFTER AADURATION
BAY B FROM FREE INTO FREE AFTER AADURATION
REPEAT
BEGIN COME
TIME OF ZZCOME LE 0
FIND FIRST VAN A IN WORLD
DURATION= NEGEXP( 30, SC )
ADD 1 TO COME
VAN A FROM WORLD INTO QUEUE AFTER DURATION
TIME OF ZZCOME = DURATION
BEGIN ARRIVE
TIME OF ZZARRI LE 0
FIND FIRST TRUCK A IN OS
DURATION= NEGEXP( 120 , SD )
TRUCK A FROM OS INTO WAIT AFTER DURATION
TIME OF ZZARRI = DURATION
ADD 1 TO ARRIVE
FINALISATION
PRINT 'DOCK   was started' DOCK ' times'
PRINT 'MOVE   was started' MOVE ' times'
PRINT 'COME   was started' COME ' times'
PRINT 'ARRIVE was started' ARRIVE ' times'
PRINT 'Utilization of ARRIVE'+4,(1-AZZZARRI/( 1. *(CLOCK -RUNINZ)))
PRINT 'Utilization of COME   '+4,(1-BZZZCOME/( 1. *(CLOCK -RUNINZ)))



DATA
OS 1 TO *
WORLD 1 TO *
FREE 1 TO *
SF 5973
SE 3975
SD 7935
SC 7359
SB 3579
SA 5397
END
```

Figure 6.10 The ECSL program generated by CAPS

(5) INITIAL CONDITIONS: setting the run-in time (see Chapter 8) and other initial conditions.

(6) HOUSEKEEPING: checking whether any ECSL keywords have been unwittingly used and suggesting improvements to the program.

In the logic section, CAPS asks for details of each entity class in turn. The cycles are described as closed loops of alternate activities (active states) and queues (dead states), each loop beginning and ending with the same queue. If the various cycles are successfully combined, CAPS tells the user the maximum number of simultaneous realizations of each activity. Thus although it is possible for all eight trucks to arrive at the same time, the user prevents this because it is highly unlikely in real life. CAPS also spots that the active states DOCK and UNLOAD need not be separated and therefore suggests the elimination of the queues FULL and ENG. The user agrees. A summary of the logic ends this section.

In the priorities section, the user is asked whether all the queues have a FIFO discipline and whether the suggested order of priorities is acceptable. In this case, it is not; DOCK needing a higher priority than MOVE.

In the arithmetic section, the user specifies how the samples for the activity durations will be taken. Thus ARRIVE is negative exponentially distributed with a mean of 120 minutes and a random number stream beginning with the value 0.7935 will be used. There are no other attributes to define.

In the recording section, the user indicates that no data is to be recorded for queues OS and WORLD. However, for the other queues, the response is '3', indicating that he wishes to record the queue lengths and the waiting times (both as histograms) as the simulation proceeds.

As for initial conditions, there are no activities in progress and all the vehicles are off the site.

Finally, CAPS checks that no ECSL keywords have been used. In this case, LOAD has been used for an activity name; thus FILL replaces it. Then CAPS suggests that the program would be shorter if certain entities were aggregated. Here, the user disagrees because he wishes to edit the resulting ECSL program.

6.9 THE BEST WAY FORWARD?

It should now be clear that there is no single best way forward. A number of factors need to be taken into account in deciding how to program a computer simulation. Firstly, there is the nature of the system being simulated. If the system consists of a series of entities flowing through a network and the degree of interaction is slight, then something like GPSS makes a great deal of sense. GPSS is extremely well documented and has a simple structure. On the other hand, a system that is characterized by complex interactions may be hard to squeeze into the GPSS mould. In such cases, the analyst would be advised to use one of the other tools available.

The analyst must also consider whether the study being undertaken merits the inevitable time investment if a new language is to be learned. Combining this with the need to maintain continuing programming support for simulations which are regularly used, it may be sensible to write in a language already well known in the organization. Thus systems such as GASP may be attractive.

On the other hand, if a complex system is to be simulated and if the project has a large potential pay-off, then the investment of time and money in acquiring a language like ECSL, SIMSCRIPT or SIMULA would seem to be well worthwhile. These statement description languages greatly ease the tasks of debugging and verification by forcing the user to adopt a suitable world view. They also allow the use of sensible variable names. For large and complex programs, these are not trivial issues. The appeal of these languages is further increased by the availability of program generators.

The question of documentation and the availability of compilers and manuals also cannot be ignored. As discussed earlier, GPSS is probably popular for two reasons. Firstly it is supported by IBM, the world's largest computer manufacturer. Secondly, GPSS is extremely well documented. It is clearly sensible to check the adequacy of the documentation and the availability of skilled support should any problems arise. Obviously, these factors are paramount for some organizations when deciding how to program a simulation.

EXERCISES

1. Find out what simulation facilities are provided by the simulation software available on your computer.

2. Study the BASIM version of the harassed booking clerk problem shown in Chapter 5. Try to see which features of the program are due to the inadequacies of BASIC as a language for simulation.

3. If you have a machine which provides a BASIC compiler as well as an interpreter, try compiling your version of the harassed booking clerk problem. See what difference it makes if you remove the run-time PRINT statements.

REFERENCES

Birtwhistle, G. M. (1979) *Discrete Event Modelling on SIMULA*. MacMillan, London.

Buxton, J. N., & Laski, J. G. (1962) Control and simulation language. *The Computer Journal*, **5**, 1962.

Clementson, A. T. (1982) *Extended Control and Simulation Language*. Cle Com Ltd, Birmingham, U.K.

Conway, R. W. (1963) Some tactical problems in digital simulation. *Management Science*, **10**(1), 47–61.

Emshoff, J. R., & Sisson, R. L. (1970) *The Design and Use of Computer Simulation Models*. MacMillan, New York.

Fishman, G. S. (1973) *Concepts and Methods of Discrete Event Digital Simulation*. Wiley, New York.

Franta, W. R. (1977) *The Process View of Simulation*. North–Holland, New York.

Gordon, G. (1969) *System Simulation*. Prentice–Hall, New Jersey.

Gordon, G. (1979) The design of the GPSS language. In Adam, N. R., & Dogramaci, A. (1979) *Current Issues in Computer Simulation*, Academic Press, New York.

Greenberg, S. (1972) *GPSS Primer*. Wiley, New York.

Hills, P. R. (1965) SIMON — A simulation language in ALGOL. In Hollingdale, S. M. (ed.) *Simulation in Operational Research*, English Universities Press, London.

Hills, P. R. (1973) *An Introduction to Simulation using SIMULA*. NCC Publication 5-Ss. Norwegian computing centre, Oslo.

Markowitz, H. M. (1979) SIMSCRIPT: Past, present and some thoughts for the future. In Adam, N. R., & Dogramaci, A. (1979) *Current Issues in Computer Simulation*, Academic Press, New York.

Markowitz, H. M., Hausner, B., & Karr, H. W. (1963) *SIMSCRIPT: A Simulation Programming Language*. RAND Corporation RM-3310-pr 1962. Prentice–Hall, New Jersey.

Mathewson, S. C. (1975) *Simulation Program Generators*. Simulation **23**(6), 81–189.

Mathewson, S. C. (1977) *A Programming Manual for SIMON Simulation in FORTRAN*. Imperial College, London.

Oldfather, P., Ginsberg, A. S., Love, P. L., & Markowitz, H. M. (1966) *Programming by Questionnaire: How to Construct a Program Generator*. RAND report RM-5129-PR.

Poole, T. G., & Szymankiewicz (1977) *Using Simulation to Solve Problems*. McGraw–Hill, London.

Pritsker, A. A. B. (1974) *The GASP IV Simulation Language*. Wiley, New York.

Tocher, K. D. (1963) *The Art of Simulation*. English Universities Press, London.

Chapter 7

Sampling methods

7.1 RANDOM SAMPLES

Random sampling is closely identified with discrete event simulation because such simulations usually include elements which are stochastic in nature. For example, in a three phase simulation, a B activity is usually scheduled after a random sample is taken from some probability distribution. In the harassed booking clerk problem (Chapters 3–5) the time taken to serve a personal enquirer was determined by taking a random sample from a negative exponential distribution with a mean of 6 minutes. Once the sample has been taken, the end of the personal service (activity B2) may be scheduled.

Using a probability distribution to represent the length of a service implies that the time taken for a particular service has two properties. Firstly that the time will lie within the range of values covered by the distribution. Secondly that the probability of particular values occurring is governed by the shape of the distribution. Hence, for a normal distribution, values near the centre of the range are most likely to occur. On the other hand, if sampled from a negative exponential distribution, values near the lower end of the range are most likely. Thus, it is known in advance how likely the service time is to take particular values. But it is uncertain precisely which value it will take.

Random sampling is used in an attempt to achieve two results. Firstly to ensure that the values taken from a distribution are randomly sequenced. Secondly in an effort to produce values in the correct proportions.

7.2 GENERAL PRINCIPLES OF RANDOM SAMPLING

The simplest method of random sampling employed in discrete event simulation is the so-called top hat method. This is used to take values from histograms: as an example consider the histogram of Figure 7.1. The top hat method will be used to illustrate the general principles of random sampling.

If this histogram were to be sampled manually, a simple procedure would be to take 100 counters and number them as follows.

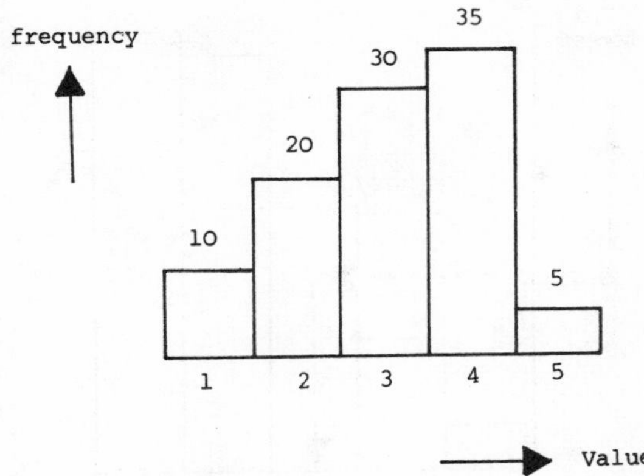

Figure 7.1 Histogram for top-hat sampling

10 numbered 1;
20 numbered 2;
30 numbered 3;
35 numbered 4;
5 numbered 5.

These could then be placed in a container (preferably a top hat) and shuffled. Counters are removed one at a time, the value on each counter is noted and it is then returned to the container. This produces a random sample from the histogram. The values produced will be randomly sequenced and, if the process continues for long enough, in more or less the correct proportions.

Rather than adopt such a slow process for simulation, an equivalent procedure is followed. For this, the histogram is converted into its cumulative form as shown in Figure 7.2. The vertical axis is relabelled as U and scaled to the values 0 to 1, where U is a value from a sequence of random digits uniformly distributed on the range 0 to 1. As each of these random digits are produced it is transformed into a random sample on the range of x. Thus, as shown in Figure 7.2,

$$\text{if } U = 0.45, \qquad \text{then} \quad x = 3.$$

In general terms, there are two requirements for random sampling in discrete event simulation.

(1) A sequence of random numbers uniformly distributed on the range 0 to 1.
(2) Some method of converting these random numbers into samples from the appropriate distribution.

From here on, the term random numbers will be used to refer to a stream of numbers uniformly distributed on the interval 0 to 1.

7.3 GENERATING RANDOM NUMBERS

So far the question, 'What is meant by random?', has been carefully ignored. However, it is important to understand what is meant by that term. An obvious

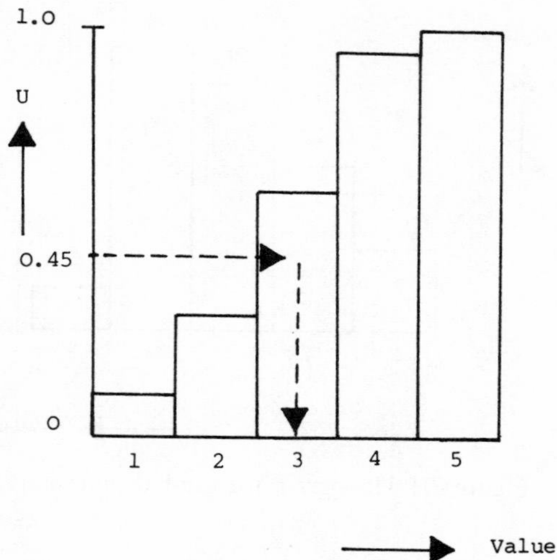

Figure 7.2 Histogram in its cumulative form

point is that it is not sensible to talk of a single value as 'random'. There is no such thing as a random number. Generally what is meant by randomness is that the process which produces the number is not deterministic. In this sense, 'randomness' is a confession of ignorance. Hence to describe a number generator as random means that no one is certain which value will be produced next. Consequently, early generators were based on physical processes thought to be random.

7.3.1 Truly random generators

Streams of numbers produced by such 'random' processes are usually described as truly random. One example would be the spinning of an unbiased roulette wheel. This is rather a slow method of producing a large stream of numbers; nevertheless some people find these devices to be of compelling interest. However, long streams of random numbers are needed for discrete event simulation and this requirement excludes all manual devices for practical purposes. It is possible to devise electronic and radio-active gadgets which produce fast streams of truly random numbers. For example, the number of particles emitted from a radio-active source in a defined period may be used for this purpose. Tocher (1963) describes several such generators which have some historical interest. However, these truly random generators are not used for a reason quite apart from the difficulty of fixing safe radio-active sources to a computer.

A discrete event simulation can be regarded as a complex sampling experiment. As the simulation proceeds, samples are taken from various distributions and combined to produce the behaviour of the model. That is, many of the conditions within the simulation are determined by the results of the random samples and their combination. If a simulation is being used to compare various ways of operating a system it is clearly important to ensure that each policy is examined under the same conditions. These conditions are at least partially determined by the samples taken and the samples are determined by the random numbers used. That is, it is important to control the results of a simulation and to ensure that a fair comparison is made. This is done by using the same random numbers each time that a different policy is simulated. For this reason it is important that the stream of random numbers should be reproducible — otherwise the comparison will not be a fair one.

One way round this problem might be to produce numbers from a truly random generator and then to store them for later use and re-use. Random number tables are sequences of values which have been produced by some truly random generator and written down. One such sequence was produced by RAND (1955) and consists of a million digits. In principle, such a sequence could be stored on a disk or other backing store and read into the computer as required in the program. Unfortunately, this is a slow process and therefore it is not usually recommended. It might also be noted that such a stored table no longer produces a 'truly' random sequence as the process of reading the next value is deterministic. This suggests that generators producing sequences which merely appear to be random might suffice.

7.3.2 Pseudo-random numbers

An alternative is to use a generator whose properties are fully understood but which produces values that look as if they were generated by a truly random process. For obvious reasons, these streams of values are described as pseudo-random numbers. They are produced by algorithms which are entirely deterministic, but the stream of values is good enough to appear random to an observer ignorant of the generation process.

In the past various generators have been employed, but the consensus nowadays is that congruential generators are the best of the available methods. These were first described by Lehmer (1951) and have the following general form.

$$X_{i+1} = aX_i + c \pmod{m} \qquad \text{for} \quad i = 0, \ldots, n \tag{7.1}$$

where $\{X_i\}$ is the stream of pseudo-random numbers,

a, c and m are constants,
X_0 is the initially specified value for the stream, usually referred to as the seed.
(mod m) means divide $(aX_i + c)$ by m and use the remainder as the result.

For example, suppose that

$$a = 3, \quad c = 0, \quad m = 5, \quad X_0 = 4.$$

The generator has the form

$$
\begin{aligned}
X_{i+1} &= 3X_i \pmod 5) \\
X_1 &= 12 \pmod 5) = 2 \\
X_2 &= 6 \pmod 5) = 1 \\
X_3 &= 3 \pmod 5) = 3 \\
X_4 &= 9 \pmod 5) = 4 \\
X_5 &= 12 \pmod 5) = 2.
\end{aligned}
$$

Notice two points from this example which apply to all congruential generators.

(1) No value of X_i can exceed m.
(2) The sequence is cyclic. In the above example

$$X_5 = X_1$$

and $X_{i+4} = X_i$ for $i = 0, \ldots, n, \ldots$

The generators produce values in the range $0, \ldots, m - 1$. To produce values on the interval (0,1), the values produced are simply divided by m.

Thus

$$U_i = \frac{X_i}{m}, \qquad i = 0, \ldots, n, \ldots.$$

It is the sequence of values U_i on the interval (0,1) which is usually called the random number stream.

The art of designing a congruential generator is to ensure that the following results occur.

(1) The cycle length (or period) should contain as many values as possible and this has two aspects. Firstly that the period should be as long as possible and this is achieved by making m as large as possible — subject to certain conditions. Secondly that a full period generator is desirable. This is one in which the number of values produced before the cycle repeats is equal to m, i.e. there are no gaps in the sequence.

(2) The sequence of values should appear to be independent. That is, all values in the range should be equally likely to occur anywhere in the sequence. Similarly, all pairs, triples and n-tuples of values should be equally likely to occur anywhere in the sequence.

(3) The stream should be produced as efficiently as possible. One way of doing this on most computers is to ensure that m is 2 raised to the power n (n integer), which allows the division operation to be carried out very swiftly.

(4) Uniform distribution. All values within the specified range of the generator should be equally likely.

Number theory provides the key to the design of good congruential generators and a useful survey is given in Knuth (1971). Rather briefer coverage is to be found in Fishman (1973) and Naylor *et al.* (1966). It should be noted, however, that some of the rules laid down are only relevant if the algorithm is to be programmed in the basic machine code of the computer being used.

7.3.3 Multiplicative congruential generators

These are simpler than the general form, having $c = 0$, thus:

$$X_{i+1} = aX_i \,(\text{mod}\, m) \qquad i = 0, \ldots, n. \tag{7.2}$$

To obtain a long period, appropriate values of a (the multiplier), m (the modulus) and X_0 (the seed) need to be selected. A full period of m values is impossible since the value zero cannot appear in the sequence. Thus the maximum period is of length $(m - 1)$.

The first rule is that X_0 and m must be relatively prime. That is, their only common divisor is 1. One simple way to ensure this is to make m a large prime number. As will be seen later, this can be a good idea on computers with 32 bits available for arithmetic.

However, if programming a binary computer in machine code, it is computationally more efficient to make m some power of 2. More specifically, the operations required to calculate the remainder are extremely quick if $m = 2^w$, where w is the word length of the computer. This allows the division operations to be replaced by a shift as follows.

Operating in decimal, the division of a large value such as 38487649 by 1 000 000 is extremely simple. As the divisor can be rewritten as 10^6 the division simply involves shifting the decimal point 6 places to the left. Thus the answer is 38.487649. Similarly, in binary arithmetic as employed in most computers, making $m = 2^B$ allows the division to be replaced by moving the binary point B positions to the left. Note too that

$$X_{i+1} = aX_i - m\lfloor aX_i/m \rfloor$$

where $\lfloor aX_i/m \rfloor$ is the integer part of aX_i/m

consists of the digits to the right of the binary point. Hence the next value in the sequence may be produced by a simple shift operation.

Knuth (1971) gives proofs for stating that

$$\begin{aligned} &\text{if} && m = 2^w \quad \text{where} \quad w \geqslant 4 \\ &\text{then } a && \equiv 3 \text{ or } 5 \,(\text{modulo } 8) \\ &\text{i.e.} \quad a && = \pm 3 + 8k, \quad \text{where } k \text{ is some positive integer.} \end{aligned} \tag{7.3}$$

Note however that a modulus of this form implies that the seed and all subsequent values must be odd. Thus the maximum period is, at most $m/2$. Fishman (1978) reports that such generators will have a period of length $m/4$.

So as to improve the computational efficiency still further, some writers have suggested using $a = 2^\alpha + 3$. Providing that $\alpha > 2$, this meets the requirements of equation (7.3). It allows the multiplication operations to be replaced by the addition of X_{i-1} and 2 shifts of X_{i-1}. Unfortunately there is strong evidence (Fishman, 1978, p. 370) that the sequences produced are distinctly non-random. Hence such generators are not recommended.

It is possible to devise multiplicative generators with rather longer periods. This is done by making m a prime number and then ensuring that a is a primitive root of m. In number theory, a is a primitive root of m if

$$a^P = 1 + mk \tag{7.4}$$

where $P = (m - 1)$, the full period of the generator

k = an integer

and P is the smallest integer for which (7.4) holds true.

Such generators have a period of length $(m - 1)$. The difficulty is in finding the primitive roots of m, the prime modulus. It is a tedious task and non-trivial, eased only by the knowledge that if a is a primitive root of m, so is a^k — provided k is relatively prime to P.

The best known multiplicative generators are used on 32-bit computers (e.g. the IBM 360/370 series). Conveniently, $2^{31} - 1$ is both prime and the largest integer available. The latter fact allows efficient arithmetic. Fishman (1978) reports 2 values for the multiplier:

$$a = 16\ 807 \qquad \text{and} \qquad a = 630\ 360\ 016,$$

both of which are in common use.

7.3.4 Mixed congruential generators

In this case, a, c, and m are all greater than zero. Thus a full period is possible as the sequence can include the value zero. Knuth (1971, pp. 15–18) gives proofs for the following assertion. A mixed congruential generator will have a full period if the conditions below hold:

(1) c is relatively prime to m;
(2) $a = 1 \pmod p$ if p is a prime factor of m,
i.e. $a = b + 1$ where b is some multiple of p.
(3) $a = 1 \pmod 4$ if 4 is a factor of m,
i.e. b is some multiple of 4.

If these conditions hold, then the choice of the seed is irrelevant.

For programming binary computers in machine code m is usually set to some power of 2. Normally,

$$m = 2^w;$$

where w is the word length, that is the number of bits available for integer arithmetic. Thus, condition (2) is subsumed by condition (3) and b should be some multiple of 4. Clearly, c must be odd for binary machines.

7.4 TESTING RANDOM NUMBER GENERATORS

It is important to realize that the values suggested for a, c, and m in the previous section give no guarantee of the 'randomness' of the generator. All they guarantee is that the period of the generators will be as long as possible and that the arithmetic will be performed efficiently. As mentioned earlier, randomness is rather a difficult property to define for pseudo-random sequences. Knuth (1971) quotes Lehmer (1951) as saying that a random sequence 'is a vague notion embodying the idea of a sequence in which each term is unpredictable to the uninitiated and whose digits pass a certain number of tests, traditional with statisticians and depending somewhat on the uses to which the sequence is put.' Knuth (1971) attempts to make this rather vague statement more precise by specifying the mathematical properties necessary if a sequence is to be considered as random. The testing of sequences produced by pseudo-random generators is mainly concerned with checking for the statistical properties that would be expected in a truly random sequence. Thus most of the tests are concerned with the uniformity of the distribution of the values of the sequence and with the lack of serial correlation in the sequence. Note that uniformity is guaranteed with a full period generator. Many tests are cited in the literature and they include variations on most standard non-parametric statistical tests. If a generator is required for a very specific purpose, then the analyst may need to design tests which are appropriate for the desired properties.

It might be imagined that most discrete simulation software systems come complete with a good generator. Sadly, this cannot be guaranteed, even if the generator is a library function provided with the computer. Fishman (1973) describes the generators used in the GPSS/360, SIMSCRIPT II and SIMULA systems. Reitman (1971) gives some results for the GPSS V generator. It is clear that some of the generators are less than perfect and care is required. The library routines provided with microcomputers are sometimes also rather poor. Brief details of a few common tests are given below and for more information, see Knuth (1971) or Fishman (1978). The tests described briefly below are not remotely novel and stem, like many others, from the work of Kendall and Babbington–Smith (1938).

It should be noted that some of the tests described in the literature are designed for sequences of integer values, whereas the stream of values $\{U_i\}$ is distributed on the interval (0,1). That is,

$$\{U_i\} = U_0, U_1, U_2, \ldots, \qquad 0 \leqslant U_i < 1 \quad \text{for } i = 0,1, \ldots$$

Hence some of the tests need to be applied to an auxiliary sequence $\{Y_i\}$ of integer values distributed on the range $(0,d)$. Thus

$$\{Y_i\} = Y_0, Y_1, Y_2, \ldots \qquad 0 \leqslant Y_i < d \quad \text{for } i = 0,1, \ldots,$$

where Y_i is the integer part of dU_i.

Knuth (1971) suggests that d is chosen bearing two things in mind. Firstly convenience: for instance, if $d = 64$ (2^6), then on a binary computer Y_i is the 6 most significant bits of U_i. Secondly, the size of d has some bearing on the statistical tests — as will be seen shortly.

7.4.1 Frequency tests

These aim to test whether the values are uniformly distributed in the sequence. A chi-square test may easily be applied to $\{Y_i\}$ or $\{U_i\}$ as follows:

(1) To $\{Y_i\}$: For each integer in the range $(0,d)$, count the number of times it occurs in a sequence of n values. For the chi-square test, this gives an expected relative frequency of $1/d$ for each value to be compared with the observed frequencies on $(d - 1)$ degrees of freedom.

(2) To $\{U_i\}$: Divide up the range (0,1) into s equal sub-intervals and count the number of values found from each sub-interval. Thus, if there are n variates in the sequence, their expected frequency will be n/s in each sub-interval if uniformly distributed. This may be compared with the observed frequencies via a chi-square test on $(s - 1)$ degrees of freedom.

Alternatively, a Kolmogorov–Smirnov test may be directly applied to the series $\{U_i\}$

7.4.2 Serial test

Using the sequence of integers $\{Y_i\}$, this test aims to check whether pairs of values are uniformly distributed in an independent sequence. A simple version is to record the frequency of occurrence of each pair of integers. A goodness of fit test (e.g. chi-square) may be used to compare the observed and expected frequencies.

This requires a sequence of length $2n$ and works as follows:
For $0 \leqslant k \leqslant n$ count the numbers of occurrences of the pair of values

$$(Y_{2k}, Y_{2k+1}) = (l,m)$$

where l,m are integers and $0 \leqslant l,m < d$. Note that only the pairs (Y_0,Y_1), (Y_2,Y_3), (Y_4,Y_5), ... are used.

There are d^2 distinct pairs of values in the integer interval $(0,d)$. Hence a chi-square test with $(d^2 - 1)$ degrees of freedom may be used to compute the observed frequencies with the expected relative frequencies. The latter obviously equal $1/d^2$.

Obviously the test could be extended to consider triples and higher k-tuples. In all cases, the value of d needs to be chosen so as to avoid small observed frequencies.

7.4.3 Gap test

This is used to examine the gaps between occurrences of the values in a specified range and is thus applied direct to $\{U_i\}$. Consider two real numbers a and b, where

$$0 \leqslant a < b \leqslant 1.$$

For a gap of size r, there is a subsequence of r successive values for all of which $a \leqslant U_k < b$.

A sequence of length n may be examined for gaps of length 0,1,2, ..., $(t-1)$ and also for $r \geqslant t$. The number of occurrences of each gap of length r gives the observed frequencies for a chi-square test.

If $P = \Pr(a \leqslant U_k < b)$, then $P_g = P(1-P)^g$ is the probability of a gap of length g, if the sequence is uniform and independent. Hence a chi-square test on t degrees of freedom may be applied.

7.4.4 Poker test

This applied to $\{Y_i\}$ and involves examining the sequence for combinations of five values, that is groups of five successive integers

$$(Y_{5k}, Y_{5k+1}, \ldots, Y_{5k+4}).$$

In such combinations there are seven possible outcomes, namely:

all different; one pair; 3 of a kind; 2 pairs;
one pair and 3 of a kind, 4 of a kind; all the same.

A chi-square test may be used to compare the observed and expected frequencies of these combinations. Knuth (1971) suggests a simplified version which is easier to program.

7.4.5 Other tests

Many other tests are mentioned in the literature. Most commonly these are:

RUNS TESTS: examining the sequence for segments in which successive values are all increasing or decreasing,

and PERMUTATION TESTS: examining the permutation of values possible in a group of successive values.

Knuth (1971) gives details, together with information on other tests.

7.5 GENERAL METHODS FOR SAMPLING FROM CONTINUOUS DISTRIBUTIONS

Section 7.2 pointed out that random sampling in discrete event simulation requires a sequence of random numbers uniformly distributed on the range

(0,1) and some means of transforming these random numbers into samples from the appropriate distributions. The transformations that are available can be divided into two groups. There are general methods which can be applied to a variety of distributions and other methods which are used for specific distributions. This section is concerned with general methods suitable for continuous distributions.

7.5.1 Inversion

This method is applicable to certain continuous distributions and is almost equivalent to the top hat method. Consider a random variable X which takes values x in the range $-\infty$ to $+\infty$. Thus;

$$\Pr(x < X < x + \delta x) \simeq f(x)\,\delta x,$$

where $f(x)$ is known as the probability density function (p.d.f.). Now

$$F(x) = \Pr(X \leqslant x) = \int_{-\infty}^{x} f(t)\,\mathrm{d}t$$

where $F(x)$ is known as the cumulative distribution function (c.d.f.). For a particular random variable, the p.d.f. as defined above might be as shown in Figure 7.3 and the c.d.f. might be as shown in Figure 7.4. Consider Figure 7.4

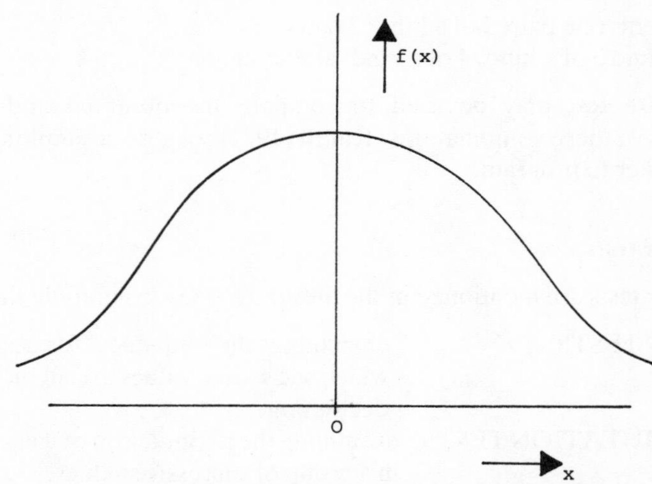

Figure 7.3 A probability density function

and suppose that, on the vertical axis, $F(x)$ is replaced by u, where u is a random variable uniformly distributed on the interval (0,1). Hence, any value of u may be transformed into a value of x, the horizontal axis. Algebraically

$$\text{if}\quad u = F(x) = \int_{-\infty}^{X} f(t)\,\mathrm{d}t,\qquad \text{then}\quad x = G(u),$$

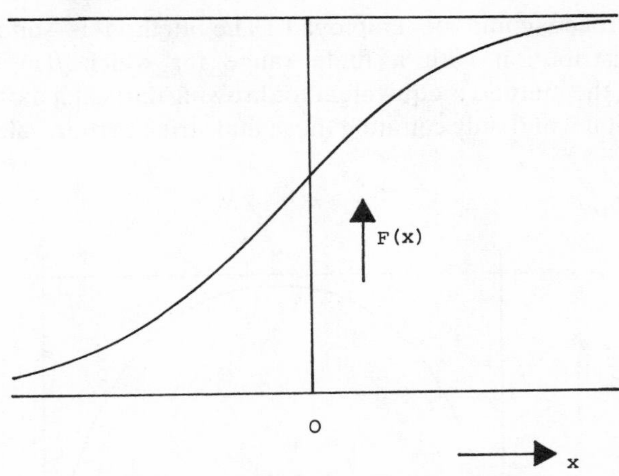

Figure 7.4 A cumulative density function

where $G(u)$ is known as the inverse cumulative function. Thus, $G(u)$ is employed to transform u into x. That is, $G(u) = F^{-1}(x)$

The most common example of sampling by inversion is the negative exponential distribution, for which

$$f(x) = \frac{1}{\lambda} e^{-x/\lambda} \qquad \text{for } 0 \leqslant x < \infty,$$
$$= 0 \qquad \text{elsewhere,}$$

$$F(x) = \int_0^x \frac{1}{\lambda} e^{-t/\lambda} \, dt$$
$$= 1 - e^{-x/\lambda};$$

thus
$$u = 1 - e^{-x/\lambda},$$
$$(1 - u) = e^{-x/\lambda},$$

and $\log_e (1 - u) = -x/\lambda$

$\therefore \; x = \lambda \log_e (1 - u)$.

Now, if u is a uniform variate, so is $(1 - u)$

$\therefore \; x = -\lambda \log_e (u)$ is equivalent.

An inverse transformation may be employed if two conditions hold. Firstly that $f(x)$, the probability density function, is known. Secondly that $f(x)$ can be successfully integrated. Fishman (1973) gives inversion methods for various Gamma and Beta distributions.

7.5.2 Rejection

For some continuous distributions it is impossible to integrate $f(x)$; in this case a rejection approach could be employed. The method is suitable for any continuous distribution with a finite range for which $f(x)$ is tractable. Conceptually, the method is equivalent to throwing darts at a dart board (such that they all hit it!) and only counting those that strike certain values.

(1) Basic method

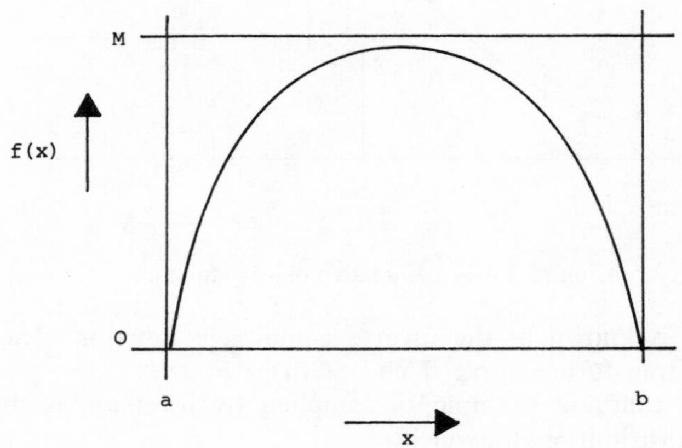

Figure 7.5 Rejection sampling

Consider the bounded p.d.f. shown in Figure 7.5. Thus

$$0 \leqslant f(x) \leqslant M \qquad \text{for} \quad a \leqslant x \leqslant b$$

and $\qquad f(x) = 0 \qquad$ elsewhere.

Take two uniformly distributed random variables.

r on the range (a,b)

s on the range $(0,M)$

Use these as co-ordinates of a point within the bounding region of Figure 7.5 and reject any pair lying above the $f(x)$ curve. If the pair is acceptable, use r as the sample x.

(2) Practical procedure

(i) Choose a constant c such that

$$cf(x) \leqslant 1 \quad \text{for} \quad a \leqslant x \leqslant b.$$

(ii) Redefine x as follows:

$$x = a + (b - a)u.$$

(iii) Generate pairs of uniform (0,1) deviates u_1 and u_2.

(iv) If $u_2 \leqslant cf(a + (b - a)u_1)$, accept u_2, and use $x = a + (b - a)u_1$ as the sample.

Otherwise reject u_2 and repeat the procedure until u_2 is acceptable.

Since the area under $f(x)$ is 1, a proportion

$$\frac{(b - a) - c}{(b - a)}$$

of the pairs is rejected.

7.5.3 Composition

The idea here is to decompose a complicated function into others which are more easily sampled by one of the previous methods. The most common examples are the methods of Marsaglia, MacLaren and Bray (1964) for sampling from Normal distributions.

7.6 THE NORMAL DISTRIBUTION

This is probably the most common non-uniform and continuous distribution. Not surprisingly, therefore, considerable effort has been made to devise suitable methods for the generation of Normal deviates. The most common methods are described below. For other continuous distributions see Fishman (1973,1978) and Atkinson and Pearse (1976).

7.6.1 Box–Muller Method

This is a fast method due to Box and Muller (1958) which produces random normal deviates in pairs. The samples are exact and not an approximation.

The joint distribution of two independent normal variables x and y, both with mean = 0 and variance = 1, is

$$f(x,y)\mathrm{d}x\,\mathrm{d}y = \frac{1}{2\pi}\,\mathrm{e}^{-(x^2+y^2)/2}\mathrm{d}x\,\mathrm{d}y.$$

Transforming x and y into polar forms gives

$$x = r\cos\theta \qquad \text{and} \qquad y = r\sin\theta.$$

Thus

$$r^2 = x^2 + y^2 \qquad \text{and} \qquad \theta = \tan^{-1}(y/x).$$

Now it can be shown that the joint distribution of r and θ is

$$f(r,\theta)\,\mathrm{d}r\,\mathrm{d}\theta = \frac{1}{2\pi}\,\mathrm{e}^{-r^2/2}r\,\mathrm{d}r\,\mathrm{d}\theta$$

$$= \frac{\mathrm{d}\theta}{2\pi}\,\mathrm{e}^{-r^2/2}\mathrm{d}(r^2/2),$$

which implies that θ and $r^2/_2$ are independently distributed:

θ with a uniform distribution over $(0,2\pi)$, and
$r^2/_2$ with a negative exponential distribution, whose mean is 1.

Suppose U_1 and U_2 are uniform (0,1) random variants.

$$\text{Put} \quad U_1 = e^{-r^2/2} \therefore r = \sqrt{(-2 \log_e U_1)}$$

$$\text{and} \quad U_2 = \theta/2\pi \quad \therefore \theta = 2\pi U_2$$

This leads to a pair of independent standard normal deviates

$$x = \sqrt{(-2 \log_e U_1 \cos 2\pi U_2)}, \qquad y = \sqrt{(-2 \log_e U_1 \sin 2\pi U_2)}.$$

Thus a pair of uniform (0,1) variates leads to a pair of standard normal deviates.

7.6.2 Box–Muller Polar Method

Trignometric function are slow to calculate and a polar variation on the Box–Muller method is as follows. Consider V_1 and V_2, both independent uniform random variates on the range $(-1,+1)$. Also consider W, a uniform random variate on the range (0,1) such that $W = V_1^2 + V_2^2$ and $W \leqslant 1$. Hence the trigonometric functions of the original Box–Muller method can be replaced as follows:

$$\cos 2\pi U_2 = \frac{V_2}{\sqrt{(V_1^2 + V_2^2)}}, \qquad \sin 2\pi U_2 = \frac{V_1}{\sqrt{(V_1^2 + V_2^2)}}$$

Hence

$$x = V_1, \sqrt{\frac{(-2 \log_e W)}{W}} \qquad \text{and} \qquad y = V_2, \sqrt{\frac{(-2 \log_e W)}{W}}$$

Atkinson and Pearse (1976) reported that this method was faster than the original method and no more difficult to program. It is therefore preferable. For either version, it is important that the pair of uniform variates are independent of one another. If the random number generator is perfect, this is no problem. However, it is probably safer to use separate generators for each variate of the pair. If this is impossible, the values should at least be obtained from separate parts of the same sequence. That is, via different seeds from the same generator.

It should also be noted that the original Box–Muller method may not be satisfactory on microcomputers. Fishman (1978) reports that the samples produced are inexact on computers with short word lengths.

7.6.3 Composition

This is due to Marsaglia and Bray (1964) and is a simpler version of the method proposed by Marsaglia, MacLaren and Bray (1964). It produces fast perfect samples, though the programming is more complex than that of the Box–Muller method or its polar variant. The method is favoured by Atkinson and Pearse (1976) as offering speed without too much programming complexity. The normal distribution is decomposed into a series of other densities such that

$$f(x) = \sum_{i=1}^{4} g_i(x) r_i,$$

where $f(x)$ is the p.d.f. of a standard normal variable x. In the original 1964 paper, the values of r_i are as follows:

$r_1 = 0.8638$, $r_2 = 0.1107$, $r_3 = 0.0228002039$, $r_4 = 0.0026997961$.

The idea is to take a single uniform (0,1) random variate U_0:

(1) if $U_0 \leqslant r_1$
then sample from $x = 2(U_1 + U_2 + U_3 - 1.5)$,
which is a set of rectangles.

(2) If $r_1 < U_0 \leqslant (r_1 + r_2)$,
then sample from $x = 1.5(U_1 + U_2 - 1)$,
which is a set of triangles.

(3) If $(r_1 + r_2) < U_0 \leqslant (r_1 + r_2 + r_3)$,
then use a rejection method to sample from the residual density for $x < 3$.

(4) If $(r_1 + r_2 + r_3) < U_0 \leqslant 1$,
then use a modified form of the polar Box–Muller method to sample for $x > 3$, i.e. the tails of the distribution.

U_1, U_2, U_3 are independent (0,1) random variates.

Thus for about 97% of the samples, the value of X is proxuced very quickly. Hence the method is fast.

7.6.4 Via the central limit theorem

The central limit theorem states that the probability distribution of the sum of n independently distributed deviates from the same distribution approaches a normal distribution as n becomes large. If the n deviates are uniformly distributed on the (0,1) interval, then their sum is approximately normally distributed with

$$\text{mean} = 0.5 \qquad \text{and} \qquad \text{variance} = n/12.$$

Hence, this method requires a set of n uniform (0,1) variates to be added together. In some implementations of this method, $n = 12$ for reasons of computational efficiency. This is rather a small value and it means that the samples produced are only approximate. This can cause difficulties if the simulation requires accurate samples from the tails of a normal distribution. If samples from the tails are required, the analyst would do well to check what method is being used if employing a commercial software system.

7.7 SAMPLING FROM DISCRETE DISTRIBUTIONS

Not all random variables are continuous. Some are discrete, that is they take only certain integer values. For example, the number of vehicles arriving at a repair shop each day is a discrete random variable. On the other hand, the time inverval between successive arrivals is a continuous random variable. General methods for sampling from discrete distributions are similar to those for continuous variables. The most common are rejection and inverse transformation. In the latter case, the inversion may be implicit.

7.7.1 Implicit inverse transformation

As a simple example of the method, consider the histogram of Figure 7.1. Previously, samples were taken from this by the top hat method. Another approach is shown in Figure 7.6. In this U, which is a sample from a uniform (0,1) distribution, is compared with successive values of $\Pr(X \leqslant k)$ from $k =$ 0,1 ... When $U \leqslant \Pr(X \leqslant k)$, then the desired sample is $X = k$.

To sample from discrete analytical distributions, it is not necessary to store explicitly the values of the cumulative probabilities for all values of k. Instead, consider that for any such distribution

$$\Pr(X = x + 1) = A_{x+1} \Pr(X = x), \qquad x = 0,1 \ldots,$$

where A_{x+1} depends on the distribution of X

and $\Pr(X \leqslant x + 1) = \Pr(X \leqslant x) + \Pr(X = x + 1)$.

Using the correct A_{x+1} for the distribution being sampled, samples from a uniform (0,1) distribution can be compared with successive values of $\Pr(X \leqslant k)$ for $k = 0,1 \ldots$ This is shown in Figure 7.7. The variables are as follows:

$$P = \Pr(X = k) \qquad \text{for } k = 0,1 \ldots,$$

$$B = \Pr(X \leqslant k)$$

$$A = A_{x+1}$$

Hence an implicit inverse transformation may be made.

7.7.2 Geometric distribution

This can be considered as the discrete equivalent of a negative exponential distribution. It has

$$\Pr(X = x) = p(1 - p)^x \qquad x = 0,1, \ldots,$$

where p is the probability of some event occurring

and x is the number of independent trials before its occurrence.

Hence $\Pr(X = x + 1) = p(1 - p)^{x+1}$

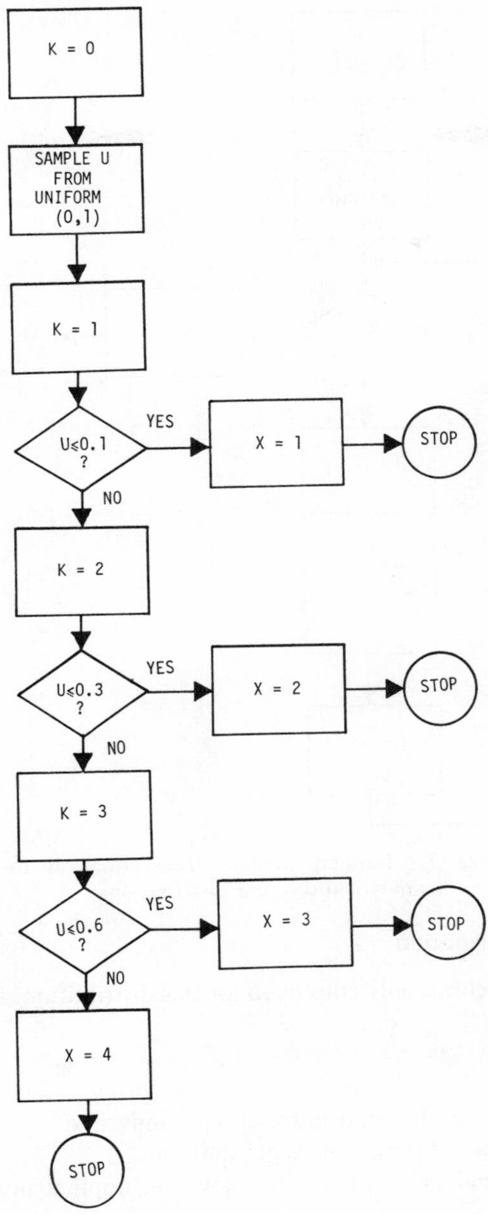

Figure 7.6 Implicit inverse transformation for histograms

Therefore $A_{x+1} = (1 - p)$

Hence an implicit inverse transformation is easily made.

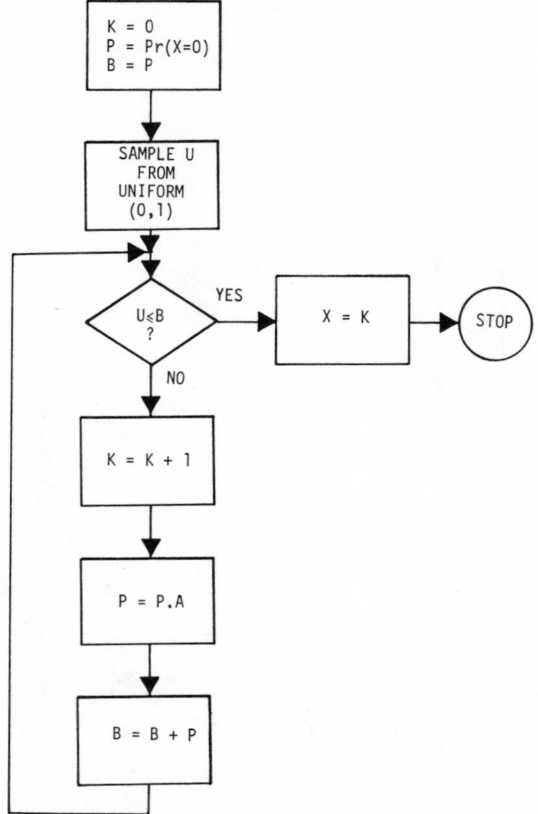

Figure 7.7 Implicit inverse transformation for analytical discrete distributions

7.7.3 Poisson distribution

Two methods are commonly employed for this distribution, for which

$$\Pr(X = x) = \frac{e^{-\lambda}\lambda^x}{x!}, \qquad x = 0,1 \ldots ,$$

where λ = mean number of occurrences per unit time
x = number of occurrences per unit time.

Obviously $A_{x+1} = \lambda/(x + 1)$, which allows an implicit inverse transformation.

The second method utilizes the well-known result that if the numbers of occurrences per unit time are represented by a Poisson distribution, then the times between occurrences follow a negative exponential distribution as follows:

$$f(y) = \frac{1}{\lambda} e^{-y/\lambda}, \qquad 0 \leqslant y \leqslant \infty.$$

A rejection method utilizes this negative exponential distribution as follows.

Generate successive negative exponential deviates using the inverse transformation of $f(y)$, giving variates T_0, T_1, ..., until

$$\sum_{j=0}^{x} T_j \leq 1 < \sum_{j=0}^{x+1} T_j, \qquad x = 0,1 \ldots;$$

that is, until the sum of their times exceeds the unit interval at which point X has a Poisson distribution with mean λ.

The condition above can be conveniently re-written as

$$- \sum_{j=0}^{x} \log_e U_j \leq \lambda < - \sum_{j=0}^{x=1} \log_e U_j.$$

Hence

$$\prod_{j=0}^{x+1} U_j < e^{-\lambda} \leq \prod_{j=0}^{x} U_j.$$

This allows the algorithm shown in Figure 7.8 which results in X, a sample from a Poisson distribution with mean λ.

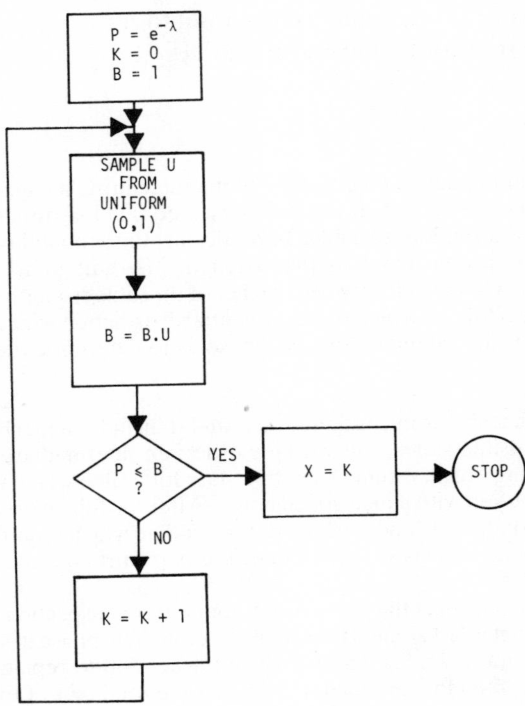

Figure 7.8 Poisson implicit inverse transformation

7.7.4 Binomial distribution

This has the following p.d.f.

$$f(x) = \binom{n}{x} p^x(1-p)^{n-x}, \qquad x = 0,1, \ldots, n,$$

where p is the probability that some event will occur.

(1) For large n
In this case, a normal approximation may be employed as described in any statistics text.

(2) Via a tabulated c.d.f.
As a binomial variate can take only a finite set of values, then a table of the cumulative probabilities could be constructed. From this, samples may be taken via a top hat procedure. If n is large, this is obviously rather tedious.

(3) Using Bernoulli trials
This is also not recommended for large n, but for other values it works as follows, given some value of p and n. A counter is employed and initially set to zero. For each random number, the counter is increased by 1 if the number is less than or equal to p. Thus a rejection method is employed. After n random numbers have been used, the value of the counter gives the sample of x. The counter is then reset to zero.

(4) An inverse transformation is also possible.

EXERCISES

1. A company is in the development stage of manufacturing a chemical and no batch can be guaranteed to be perfect. It has been observed that its strength, measured on a scale from 0 to 1, is a random variable. In particular, the probability of obtaining any specific strength is proportional to that strength. To add to their problems, the manufacturing time varies even between batches of the same strength. The manufacturing time (in minutes) follows a negative exponential distribution with a mean of 10 times the strength scale value. Simulate this system so as to determine the expected hourly production rate.

2. An expensive machine is in continuous use and it includes a mechanical part which can be in three possible states: full working order, an intermediate phase, or failed. When in full working order, it remains in that state for a time which follows a negative exponential distribution with a mean of 20 hours. After the fully working state, the part enters the intermediate state and remains thus for a time which is uniformly distributed between 0 and 5 hours inclusive. After that, the part fails and must be immediately replaced.

Current policy is to inspect the part every 8 hours. If, on inspection, the part is in full working order, then it is left alone. If it is in the intermediate phase it is replaced straight away. Each inspection costs \$20 and it costs a further \$40 to replace the part. If the part fails in service, then lost production increases the total cost of the replacement to \$200.

The company are considering whether it would be cheaper to inspect the part every 4 hours. Simulate both policies for 10 replacements and calculate which policy is cheaper over this short period.

3. Use a programming language with which you are familiar to write a program which generates variates from a normal distribution with mean of 10 and variance of 6. Use the Box–Muller polar method and employ the random numbers available on your computer.

4. Apply the serial and gap tests to the random numbers shown in Figure 2.5.

5. Apply the serial and gap tests to the random number generator available on your computer.

6. Develop an inversion formula for sampling from the following continuous uniform distribution:

$$f(x) = 1/(b - a),$$

where x takes values in the range a to b.

7. Write a BASIC program to generate normal variates using the Box–Muller polar method.

REFERENCES

Atkinson, A. C., & Pearse, M. C. (1976) The computer generation of beta, gamma and Normal random variates. *Jnl R. Stat. Soc. A.* **139**, 431ff.

Box, G. E. P., & Muller, M. E. (1958) A note on the generation of Normal deviates. *Ann. Math. Stat.* **28**, 610–611.

Fishman, G. S. (1973) *Concepts and Methods in Discrete Event Digital Simulation*. Wiley-Interscience, New York.

Fishman, G. S. (1978) *Principles of Discrete Event Simulation*. Wiley-Interscience, New York.

Kendall, M. G., & Babbington–Smith, B. (1938) Randomness and random sampling numbers. *Jn.. R. Stat. Soc.*, **101**, 147–166.

Knuth, D. E. (1971) *The Art of Computer Programming*, Vol 2: *seminumerical algorithms*. Addison–Wesley, Reading, Mass.

Lehmer, D. E. (1951) Mathematical methods in large-scale computing units. *Ann. Comp. Laboratory*, Harvard University, **26**, 141–146.

Marsaglia, G., & Bray, T. D. (1964) A convenient method for generating Normal variables. *SIAM Review*, **6**(3), 260–264.

Marsaglia, G., MacLaren, M. D., & Bray, T. D. (1964) A fast procedure for generating Normal deviates on a digital computer. *Jnl. Assoc. Comp Mach*, **7**, 4–10.

Naylor, T. H., Balintfy, J. L., Burdick, D. S., & Chu, K. (1966) *Computer Simulation Techniques*. Wiley, New York.

RAND Corporation (1955) *A Million Random Digits with 100,000 Normal Deviates*. The Free Press, Glencoe, Ill.

Reitman, J. (1971) *Computer Simulation Applications. Discrete Event Simulation for Synthesis and Analysis of Complex Systems*. Wiley-Interscience, New York.

Tocher, K.D. (1963) *The Art of Simulation*. English Universities Press, London.

Chapter 8

Planning and interpreting discrete simulations

8.1 BASIC IDEAS

The usual purpose of a computer simulation is to bring about an improvement in the system being simulated. Hence the output of the simulation should be interpreted with some care, the risk being that wrong decisions will be taken. Assuming that the simulation model is considered valid and that the computer programs have been verified, further difficulties remain in most discrete event simulations because they commonly include stochastic elements. Figure 8.1 shows that a simulation experiment involves subjecting the model to inputs (or factors) at various levels and interpreting their effect on the outputs (or responses).

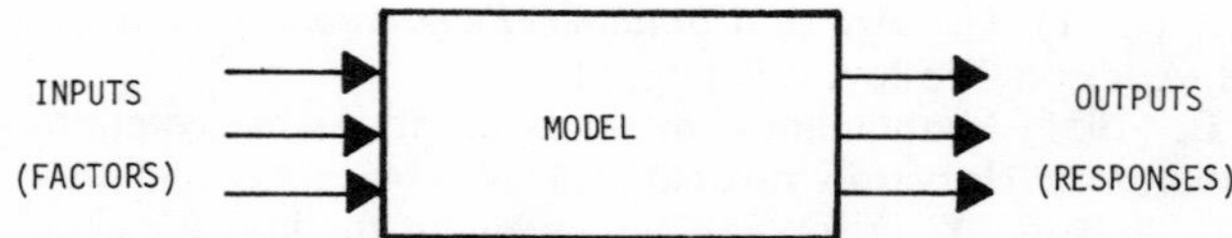

Figure 8.1 Simulation experimentation

As a simple example, consider again the problem of the harassed booking clerk introduced in Chapter 3 and subsequently developed. Possible measures of performance might be the average waiting times of personal enquirers or the number of them waiting for service. Thus the queue lengths and the average waiting times are the response variables for which estimates need to be found. The inputs whose effects are being investigated are in two groups. Firstly, those parameters which define the configuration of the system — for example, the number of clerks or the priority rules for different types of customer. Secondly, the random samples from the various probability distributions such as those for the inter-arrival and service times. Some of these samples are exogeneous, that is they stem from outside the controlled system (e.g. arrivals). Others are part of the controlled system and are thus endogeneous.

Suppose that the management wishes to investigate the effect of a variety of system configurations such as one or two clerks, or no priority to personal enquirers. The inputs include stochastic elements, that is the random samples. Therefore, simulating the same configuration with different sets of random numbers will produce results that differ at least slightly. This effect, due to the sampling variation, is clearly seen in Figure 8.2. This shows the length of the

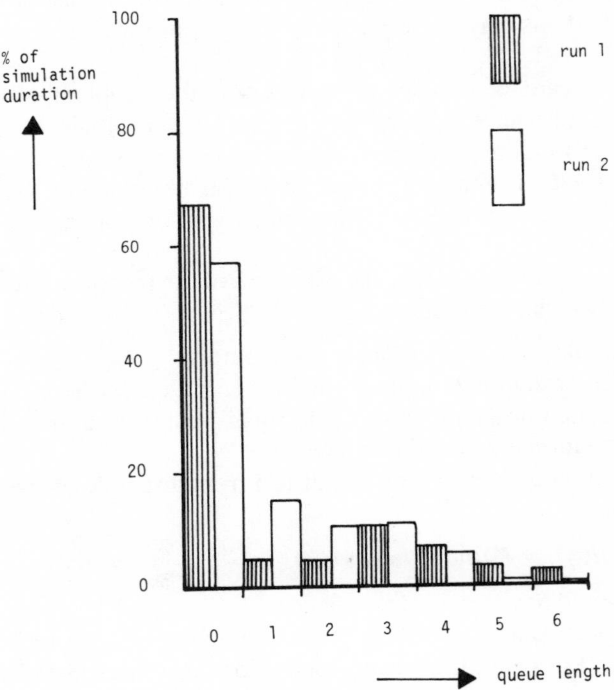

Figure 8.2 Histogram of waiting times

queue of personal enquirers during two simulations employing different sets of random numbers. Thus the analyst simulating even such a simple system needs to be sure that different estimates of the average queue length are due to the system configuration and do not result from sampling variation.

Generalizing from this simple example, it is important to distinguish clearly between the effects of the sampling variation and the effects of the system configuration. This is the major task of planning a discrete simulation and then interpreting its results.

It should be clear from this preamble that the response variables are random variables whose estimation requires careful statistical analysis. Detailed descriptions of possible analyses are given in Kleijnen (1974) and Fishman (1973; 1978). In a book of this nature, it is only possible to give some indication of the styles of analysis which are required and of some of the pitfalls that await the unwary.

8.1.1 Estimation and comparison

Given that the response variables are random variables, simulations are occasionally used solely to determine the parameters of their distributions. One example might be a simulation of an airport in order to determine its operational capacity. Another possible use for a simulation is, as indicated earlier, to compare different policies or system configurations. This too involves the estimation of response variables. But it also requires their comparison and this may be rather easier than acquiring a precise estimate of a single variable.

Comparison can, of course, be reduced to the problem of estimating a statistic which is defined to be the difference of two variables. However, in the case of comparison, the problem of bias is not so great as long as both variables are equally biased. The task of comparison is further eased by the existence of methodologies for hypothesis testing and experimental design in classical statistics.

It seems generally agreed that the estimates of the response variables should have at least two characteristics.

(1) They should stem from unbiassed estimators.
Consider a random variable X with p.d.f. $= f(x;P)$, where P is a vector of parameters. For example, if X is normally distributed, then P consists of the population mean and variance.

Then if an estimator p of P is drawn from a sample of size n, then p is unbiassed

$$\text{if} \quad E(p) = P \text{ for all values of } n.$$

(2) They should have minimum variance.
This is particularly important when comparisons have to be made, for the risk of drawing the wrong conclusions increases as the variances of the response variables increase. One simple way of reducing the variance is to use an enormous sample, that is to run the simulation for over-extended time periods. This luxury is rarely available in practice due to pressing deadlines and competition for computer time. Consequently, so called variance reduction techniques have been developed. These aim to produce estimates with a rather lower variance without taking too long over the job. Kleijnen (1974) gives a useful detailed survey of these methods. See also Ehrenfield and Ben–Tuvia (1962) for a rather more abbreviated description. A mathematical analysis of the causes of variance in discrete simulations is to be found in Saliby (1980).

The problem of comparison is further increased in most realistic simulations because there are several input variables. These may each operate at different levels and they will most probably interact. For example, there is bound to be some interaction between the effect of the number of booking clerks in the theatre and the effect of the priority accorded to personal enquirers. The only way to sort out these interactions is by careful experimental design. The literature of classical statistics is replete with texts and papers which describe experimental design methodology. However, it should be noted that simulation experiments differ from those on which most experimental design methodology is based.

A simulation experiment is controlled. Usually the creator of the model and the subsequent programs is also responsible for the simulation experiments. The analyst thus occupies a privileged position. Most classical experimental designs treat the experiment as a game against malevolent nature and the process itself is regarded as a black box. The aim of the design is to minimize the effect of this, albeit random, malevolence. That is, the aim is to achieve complete control. In a simulation experiment the analyst already has this complete control and should already understand the nature of the black box — the model in this case. The unpredictability stems from the sampling variation and, in this sense, a simulation experiment involves fewer difficulties then a 'real' experiment, although that is not to say that the tasks of design and analysis of simulation experiments are easy. Simulation experiments can involve a large number of interacting variables which all operate at various levels. A detailed description of the important ideas relevant to simulation is given in Kleijnen (1975).

8.1.2 Steady state and transience

It is important to distinguish between transient and steady state behaviour in a discrete simulation. Even those systems which do achieve a steady state necessarily pass through a transient phase en route. Some of the transient effects are due to the starting conditions for the simulation — for example, whether any enquirers were waiting when the booking office opened. Methods of dealing with the problem of starting conditions are given in Section 8.3.

A simulated system is considered to be in a steady state if its current behaviour is independent of the starting conditions and 'if the probability of being in one of its states is governed by a fixed probability function' (Kleijnen 1974, p. 69). This does not mean that the system does not change state but that the probability of being in any of its possible states can be determined. Thus, at steady state, the number of enquirers waiting to be served by the harassed booking clerk vary somewhat. Some systems never achieve a steady state — a target-seeking missile in flight is one example, particularly if its target weaves in an attempt to escape. Needless to say, steady state and transient responses may need to be analysed differently.

Whether or not steady state conditions within the simulation are desirable depends on the purpose of the simulation. If a job shop is being simulated, then an estimate of the mean waiting time of the jobs is best taken when the system is in a steady state. On the other hand, Fishman (1973) points out that the aim of a simulation of an outpatient clinic may be to find a queue discipline for the patients, given that the clinic opens with 50 people waiting. One feature of a steady state is that the effects of the initial conditions are no longer noticeable.

In the above outpatient clinic, the effect of the initial conditions on the queue discipline is one of the points of the experiment.

8.1.3 Terminating and non-terminating systems

Another important distinction should be made between those systems which could, in principle at least, be simulated for infinite time and those which are self-terminating by a particular event. A civil airport operating 24 hours each day is one of the former non-terminating systems. The flight of a missile has a definite termination.

When simulating systems which are non-terminating, the analyst can affect the variance of the response variables by controlling the sample sizes. This is done by altering the run length of the simulation either by simulating for a specified time duration or by simulating for a specified number of activities. In the latter case, an example is the number of arrivals. Terminating systems allow no such control and thus replication is the only 'sample increasing' strategy open to the analyst in these cases.

8.2 LACK OF INDEPENDENCE

Estimation is usually simplest when the observations are independent and identically distributed. In such cases, the central limit theorem can be used to estimate confidence limits for the random variables. In many simulations, the results are not mutually independent. That is, observations of a single variable are likely to be autocorrelated. For example, consider a simple queueing system. It is clear that the waiting time of customer n depends on the number of people waiting when customer n arrives. Thus, the waiting time of customer n is in some way dependent on the waiting time of the preceding customers. In such simulations, appropriate analyses must be used. Before doing so, it is important to ensure that bias due to initial conditions is removed (see Section 8.3).

8.2.1 Simple replication

An obvious way of handling the problem of autocorrelated results is to make several replications of the same run. Hence, the simulation is repeated several times with the same conditions — except that different random number streams are used for each run. This ensures that the replications will be independent of each other. Thus for a random variable X resulting from n replications of the same simulation, the mean value is the overall mean of the n replications. Similarly, the overall variance is the mean of the n variances.

8.2.2 Batching

A second approach is to use a single long run. The results are batched by dividing the run into segments such that each segment contains the same number of observations. The hope is that the batches will be independent. If this is achieved, then elementary statistics apply.

In practice, the batches are likely to display autocorrelation unless consecutive batches are separated by intervals whose results are discarded. With large batch sizes, this is less of a problem because the autocorrelation ought to decrease as the separation between data points increases. However, unless 'dead' periods are employed, then the batches ought to be examined for significant autocorrelation.

8.2.3 Regenerative methods

A third approach can be used in some simulations. These are systems in which identical conditions (i.e. system states) recur from time to time during a simulation. For some queueing systems, an obvious example is the state in which all servers are idle and all waiting lines are empty. Such a recurrence is called a REGENERATION POINT. The time interval between consecutive regeneration points are called EPOCHS.

The idea is that the sequence of activities that occur during epochs should be independent of one another. If this is the case, then observations of random variables made during different epochs should also be independent. This allows the use of the central limit theorem for establishing confidence intervals. Fishman (1973 & 1978) gives more information.

8.3 ACHIEVING STEADY STATE

This is one aspect of computer simulation which is presented in stark clarity by Conway (1963). The easiest way of bringing a simulated system to a steady state, assuming that this is possible, is by setting the starting conditions of the simulation. In any simulation, the simplest course open to the analyst is to begin the simulation with no activity occurring and with the queues empty. Thus no activity begins until the first temporary entity arrives for processing. Though this tactic is extremely simple it is inefficient and possibly misleading. This is because the system being simulated may never ever have been in such an idle state — thus bizarre transient effects are not impossible. Whatever initial conditions are chosen it is obvious that they will bias the results of the simulation, if only for a short period.

Once this difficulty is acknowledged, there are 2 approaches recommended for consideration.

(1). Using a run-in period
or (2). using typical starting conditions.

8.3.1 Using a run-in period

Accepting that any starting conditions impose initial bias on the simulation, one obvious remedy is to run the simulation for a period long enough to remove the effect of the bias. During this run-in period no attempt is made to record the output of the simulation, the results are thrown away. The simulation proper begins at the end of the run-in period, from which point of time the response variables are collected for analysis. The aim is thus to begin the experiment when the transient phase is over. Obviously, this method is only appropriate when steady state results are required.

The practical question to be asked is, 'how long should the run-in period be?' If it is too long then time is wasted (though computer time is an increasingly cheap resource). If it is too short then transient effects will be evident and the results will be biassed. There is no straightforward technique which will determine a suitable run-in period, though some general principles are clear.

Access to interactive computer facilities which allow the simulation to be monitored as it runs are a help in this regard. With such systems, data on important response variables can be plotted on a television screen as the simulation proceeds. Such a pattern display can give a useful indication as to whether the transient phase is over. For example, if queue lengths are continually increasing, then no steady state has been reached. Once something approaching a steady state has been reached, the simulation can be switched over to a data collection mode if the programs are implemented via an intepreter (Section 6.1.3). Alternatively, the run may be stopped at this point and restarted from scratch with the same random number seeds, though this time with a switch in the program to turn on data collection at the simulation clock time noted in the run-in period experiment.

In the absence of interactive facilities, the answer is to record all the data throughout an entire run. Its subsequent analysis as a time series should indicate when gross transience is no longer present. Data collected before this steady state is then rejected and only that data collected after the now defined run-in period is used in the analysis of the simulation experiment.

Another possibility, though less recommended, is to determine the run-in period in advance and use the same run-in period for all the experiments. A switch in the program turns on the data collection at the appropriate time. The run-in period may be determined by hunch, from an initial simulation or by analysis of a simplified (e.g. queueing theory) model.

8.3.2 Using 'typical' starting conditions

An obvious thought is to begin each run of the simulation with non-zero conditions which are typical in some sense or other. Thus the model might be in a steady state right at the start of the simulation. These 'typical' conditions could, in theory, be determined from knowledge of the system being simulated. The difficulty is that if the steady state conditions were known, then the simulation might not be necessary. Alternatively, use may be made of observations of the conditions within the simulation at the end of previous run-in periods.

The attraction of the idea is that computer time need not be wasted by having a run-in period for each run of the simulation. The snag is that bias is inevitable, though this time due to the non-zero initial conditions. Thus it is important to ensure that all runs of the simulation begin with the same initial conditions. Conway (1963) puts this extremely clearly.

'I would be extremely reluctant to report on an investigation in the following manner:

(1) I wished to compare two systems, A and B.
(2) I anticipated that system A would yield a greater mean value of attribute M than would system B.
(3) I performed an experiment in which the initial value of attribute M for system A was greater than for system B.
(4) The experimental results demonstrate that the mean value of attribute M for system A is significantly greater than for system B.'

However, a problem with using the same initial conditions for all the simulation runs is that they may not be 'typical' for all configurations of the system. For example, if a simulation were being used to investigate the effect of an extra runway at an airport it seems unlikely that the typical operating conditions would be the same before and after the new runway. However, giving in to the temptation to vary the starting conditions lands the analyst right in the above trap described by Conway (1963).

8.4 VARIANCE REDUCTION

8.4.1 An overview

When considering the variance reduction techniques advocated by Kleijnen (1974) and others, it is well to bear in mind the purpose of the simulation. Some of the techniques are aimed at increasing the precision of response variable estimates. Others aim to ease the problem of comparison. Kleijnen (1974) lists the following variance reduction techniques:

stratified sampling;
selective sampling;
control variates;
importance sampling;
antithetic variates;
common random numbers.

Of these, only common random numbers (Section 8.4.3), control variates (Section 8.4.4) and antithetic variates (Section 8.4.5) are widely used in discrete simulation. Selective sampling (Section 8.4.6), which has been rather neglected, will be shown to have some potential.

For the purposes of the ensuing discussion it will be assumed that an estimate of the mean values of a response variable is being sought. Thus a decrease is sought in the variance of the estimator of the mean. The reliability of the estimator (its confidence interval) can be expressed as in equation (8.1):

$$\bar{X} \pm a\,(\sigma/\sqrt{n}), \tag{8.1}$$

where $\bar{X}$ is the average of n independent runs of the simulation,
a is some constant,
σ is the standard deviation, and
$\sigma/\sqrt{n}$ is the standard error.

Thus, the reliability of the estimate depends on the standard error, which should decrease as the square root of n increases. Variance reduction techniques are used to increase the reliability of the estimate without resort to the blunderbuss of massive samples.

8.4.2 Sampling variation

The sampling process described in Chapter 7 has two stages.

(1) generate one (or several) uniform random variates;
(2) transform the uniform random variate(s) into a variate from the appropriate distribution.

In this way samples are taken from the appropriate distributions as the simulation proceeds. Thus the random numbers are used for two purposes. Firstly to select values from the distribution in more or less the correct proportions. Secondly to ensure that the set of values produced are in a random sequence. Following Saliby (1980) there are thus two sources of sampling error in a discrete simulation.

(a) The set effect

These are errors due to the set of values produced by the sampling process. They are characterized by the differences between the sample distribution (or histogram) and the theoretical distribution (or frequency function). With random sampling as described in Chapter 7, some sampling error due to the set effect is inevitable. That is, the sample moments will differ from the population moments. There will never be perfect correspondence between the sample distribution and the theoretical sampled distribution. For example, it is highly unlikely that the sample mean and variance will equal those of the distribution.

(b) The sequence effect

These are errors due to the sequence in which the set of values is produced. These errors are rather more subtle than those due to the set effect. As will be seen in Section 8.4.6, it is possible to virtually eliminate errors due to the set of values. That is, samples can be taken so that the sample and population moments are equal. However, even if this is the case, the sequence effect still remains — though the larger the sample size, the less marked are the errors.

To illustrate the point, consider a simple example. Suppose there are two uniform distributions of integer values as follows:

X, producing values 0,1,2,3,4,5,6,7,8,9;
Y, producing values 0,−1,−2,−3,−4,−5,−6,−7,−8,−9.

Suppose a sampling experiment were carried out to determine the mean value of XY.

Consider samples in groups of 10. Suppose that the set effect is eliminated by ensuring that each set of 10 values consists of

0,1,2,3,4,5,6,7,8,9 for X and
0,−1,−2,−3,−4,−5,−6,−7,−8,−9 for Y.

In both cases the values are randomly shuffled for each new group of 10, the sequence of X being independent of the sequence of Y. Thus

$$E(XY) = -20.25.$$

If the shuffling produces the following first groups of 10:

2,1,3,0,5,6,7,4,9,8 for X

and

−9,−6,−5,−3,−4,−2,−8,0,−7,−1 for Y.

Taking the values of X and Y in pairs gives a value of −19.8 for the mean of XY and a standard error of 6.97.

Taking a second pair of 10 shuffled values might produce

6,3,0,9,7,4,2,8,5,1 for X

and

−5,0,−4,−8,−7,−6,−1,−3,−2,−9 for Y.

From these 20 pairs of values, the mean of XY is −20.9 and the standard error is 4.96. Obviously, as the sample size increases, the standard error falls. Thus the reliability of the estimator increases. This is of course very elementary statistics, but the point is that it is solely due to the sequence effect in this case.

The sequence effect is caused by the fact that a simulation can only produce finite samples, whereas definitions of probability distributions assume an infinite population of values.

It is important to recognize that sampling errors are undesirable in a simulation. What are desirable are good estimates and error-free comparisons. Neither is possible if there is much sampling error. It so happens that sampling error due to the set effect is easily controllable given that the analyst has full control over the sampling process. The sequence effect is, however rather more difficult to control. The variance reduction techniques discussed in the following sections are effective mainly because they allow control of the set effect (Saliby, 1980).

8.4.3 Common random numbers

This, the simplest of all variance reduction techniques, is used when two or more policies or system configurations are being compared. In such cases it is obvious that the sampling variation should as far as possible be held constant across all the policies being compared. If this can be achieved, then the observed differences in the response variables will be due to the policies or system configurations. The method involves ensuring that each source of variation with the model has its own unique stream of random numbers, each within a defined seed.

Consider the example of the harassed booking clerk and imagine that the management wish to know the difference in performance between one and two clerks. The longer the service times, the longer the queue will appear to be. The longer the inter-arrival times, the shorter the queue will appear to be. Now suppose that only a single stream of random numbers were to be employed and suppose further that a very low value appears in the stream. It is possible that on one run (with 1 clerk say) this small value is used to produce an inter-arrival time and this will lead to a smaller queue because of the resulting long inter-arrival time. It is also possible that on another run (this time wth two clerks) the same small value is used to produce a service time. Again this will be a large value (being sampled from a negative exponential distribution), thus increasing the delays of subsequent customers and increasing the queue length! Thus the resulting estimate of the difference between the queue lengths for the two policies will be rather difficult from what might be expected.

On the other hand, if each activity has its own random number stream, then the following streams are needed.

1 — for arrival of personal enquirers
1 — for arrival of phone calls
m — for m clerks' service times for personal enquirers
m — for m clerk's phone conversation times,

giving $2(1 + m)$ streams for a simulation involving m clerks. For each run of the simulation, each of the streams is restored to its seed value. In this way, each of the clerks remains the same peculiar individual from run to run and the environmental effects (arrivals) are also kept the same. Also, the effect of the sampling variation is contained. Thus the estimate of the differences between the policies should be rather more precise. Common random numbers allow almost complete control over the set effect and partial control of the sequence effect.

What the method does is to introduce positive correlation between the two runs of the simulation. Suppose that the experiments are to compare two policies which result in random variables X and Y, where

X gives results in the variates x

and

Y gives results in the variates y.

Hence an estimate

$z = x - y$ is sought.

For completely random sampling (i.e. no common streams)

$$\text{var}(Z) = \text{var}(X) + \text{var}(Y).$$

For correlated sampling (i.e. common random numbers)

$$\text{var}(Z) = \text{var}(X) + \text{var}(Y) - 2\text{cov}(X,Y).$$

If cov (X,Y) is high, then var (Z) is much lower for correlated sampling than for completely random sampling.

In practice, the correlation is likely to be less than perfect because the behaviour of the model is likely to vary somewhat for each of the policies under comparison. Even with perfect streaming, a sample on one run will not necessarily be used for the same purpose on another run. Thus the sequence effect is only partially controlled, though the set of values remains the same from run to run if the sample size is not changed. Kleijnen (1974, p. 204) reports a variance reduction of 34% on a simulated maintenance system. Other authors have claimed larger reductions.

How easy it is to implement common random numbers depends to a large extent on the software system in use. Sadly, not all give a wide choice of streams. The random number generators commonly provided with micro- and minicomputers are often quite unsuitable as they do not allow any forms of streaming. In any case, it should be noted that several unique streams often means in practice that the same stream is accessed at different points via different seeds. Provided that the generator has a long period (see Chapter 7) then this is effectively the same as having several unique streams. The advice has to be to aim for as much control as possible.

8.4.4 Control variates

As well as comparing policies, it is important to ensure that reliable estimates of the response variables are produced. Control variates make use of the fact that a simulation model is not a black box but is something which should be completely understood by the experimenter.

As an example consider a simple queueing system. If the service time increases, then the queue length would also be expected to rise, provided that the inter-arrival times do not change. The following variables are defined:

Q is the random variable, queue length, which takes values q_i, $i = 0,1, \ldots, n$.

μ_Q = the 'true' mean queue length from the distribution
$\bar{q}$ = the observed mean queue length from the simulation
μ_s = the 'true' mean service time from the distribution
$\bar{s}$ = the observed mean service time from the simulation,

where

$$\bar{q} = \sum_{n=1}^{n} qi/n \quad \text{and} \quad \bar{s} = \sum_{i=1}^{n} si/n.$$

The temptation is to use $\bar{q}$ as an estimator of μ_Q because $E(\bar{q}) = \mu_Q$, i.e. it is unbiassed.
However, this simple estimator can be improved upon.
If $\bar{s} > \mu_s$, then this ought to lead to longer queues and this knowledge can be put to good use in constructing a better estimator for μ_Q. The new estimator is

$$\hat{q} = \bar{q} - \lambda(\bar{s} - \mu_s), \tag{8.2}$$

where λ is a number with some value, yet to be chosen.

$$\text{Note that } E(\hat{q}) = E(\bar{q}) - \lambda E(\bar{s} - \mu_s)$$
$$= \mu_Q - \lambda(\mu_s - \mu_s);$$

therefore $E(\hat{q}) = \mu_Q$, i.e. it is unbiassed.
Consider the variances:

$$\text{var}(\hat{q}) = \text{var}(\bar{q} - \lambda\bar{s})$$
$$= \text{var}(\bar{q}) + \lambda^2 \text{var}(\bar{s}) - 2\lambda \text{cov}(\bar{q},\bar{s});$$

$$\text{therefore } \text{var}(\hat{q}) - \text{var}(\bar{q}) = \lambda^2 \text{var}(\bar{s}) - 2\lambda \text{cov}(\bar{q},\bar{s}) \tag{8.3}$$

The variance is reduced if $\lambda^2 \text{var}(\bar{s}) - 2\lambda \text{cov}(\bar{q},\bar{s}) < 0$; that is, if

$$2 \text{cov}(\bar{q},\bar{s}) > \lambda \text{var}(\bar{s}). \tag{8.4}$$

Therefore the variance may be reduced by selecting a suitable value for λ so as to satisfy inequality (8.4). λ may be chosen after a few runs when something is known about the dependence of $\bar{q}$ and $\bar{s}$. Whether λ is positive or negative depends on whether $\bar{q}$ and $\bar{s}$ are negatively or positively correlated.

A further improvement may be gained in this example by controlling the effect of the inter-arrival times too, as they clearly affect queue lengths. Thus a new estimator q' may be used, where

$$q' = \bar{q} - \lambda(\bar{s} - \mu_s) + \beta(\bar{A} - \mu_A), \tag{8.5}$$

where β is a constant
μ_A is the 'true' mean inter-arrival time from the distribution
$\bar{A}$ is the 'observed' mean inter-arrival time from the simulation.

As with (8.3), this is an unbiassed estimator and will result in a variance reduction provided suitable values of β and λ are chosen.

This method can clearly be extended to include more than two control variables.

In the control variate technique, the observed values of the input variables realized by the simulation are compared with the expected or theoretical values. Any deviation, which must be due to the set effect, is thus controlled. This provides a method of reducing the variance of an estimator within a single run of the simulation. There is no control of the sequence effect.

8.4.5 Antithetic variates

This is another attempt to control the variance of an estimator, this time by introducing negative correlation between successive simulations of the same system configuration. There is some disagreement about the value of this technique. One thing is certain: if used, then caution is necessary.

Tocher proposed a simple implementation of this technique for simulations by generating one simulation run from the random numbers $u_1, u_2, u_3, u_4, \ldots$ and the second, antithetic run from the random numbers $(1 - u_1)$, $(1 - u_2)$, $(1 - u_3)$, $(1 - u_4)$, ..., the idea being that this complementary sampling should ensure negative correlation between the responses of the two simulations.

Thus, in the simplest case the simulation response variable X is dependent only on a single sequence of random numbers. Consider the antithetic technique in such an example.

Suppose the random variable X_1 results from the first run and the random variable X_2 results from the antithetic run. Thus

$$\bar{X} = \tfrac{1}{2}(X_1 + X_2)$$

is an unbiassed estimator of $E(x)$ and

$$\text{var}(\bar{X}) = \tfrac{1}{4}[\text{var}(X_1) + \text{var}(X_2) + 2\text{cov}(X_1,X_2)]$$

which is to be compared with the variance from two non-correlated runs.

Hence a reduced variance is to be expected provided strong negative correlation is introduced between the two runs.

Page (1965) proposed a different antithetic procedure for a simple queueing problem in which he interchanged the random streams for service and arrivals. Saliby (1980) gives experimental and theoretical results for a simple queueing system using both the Tocher (1963) and Page (1965) approaches, and these show a greater variance reduction for the interchange of streams.

Antithetic sampling has always been regarded with some suspicion in discrete simulation. This is mainly due to the obvious difficulty of ensuring that any of the negative correlation between the input variables finds its way to the response variables. For it must be borne in mind that realistic simulations effect complex transformations on the input variables. Thus it seems unlikely that there will be much direct correspondence between events in successive runs. As it happens, this is a good thing! Saliby (1980) demonstrates experimentally that any correspondence between events on antithetic runs actually produces positive correlation due to the sequence effect. Hence he observes that, for a simple queueing system, the observed overall negative correlation is rather lower than that which might be predicted theoretically.

Hence, if antithetic sampling is to be used, which seems doubtful, it should be employed in conjunction with common random numbers and control variates. In this way the set effect and some of the sequence effect may be controlled.

8.4.6 Selective sampling

This is a technique first mentioned by Brenner (1963) and enhanced by Saliby (1980). Brenner's work was criticized by Kleijnen (1974) who argues that it produces biassed samples. Saliby (1980) calls his version of the procedure descriptive sampling.

The method requires access to the inverse of the distribution function. According to Saliby (1980) it is applicable to discrete, continuous or even mixed distributions. In some cases, e.g. the normal distribution, a numerical approximation will be necessary. Tocher (1963) gives an approximation for the normal distribution.

The sampling procedure is as follows.

Consider a random variable X which takes values x in the range $-\infty$ to $+\infty$:

$$\Pr(K \leqslant X < K+1) \simeq f(x),$$

$\Pr(X \leqslant k) = F(x) = \int_{-\infty}^{x} f(t)\, dt$ (the cumulative distribution function).

$$\text{Putting} \quad U = F(x), \quad \text{where } U \sim \text{uniform } (0,1)$$

$$\text{gives} \quad x = G(U) \quad \text{the inverse function}$$

Thus to obtain a descriptive (or selective) sample of size n:

(1) divide the range (0,1) into n equiprobable sub-intervals. Thus, for $i = 1, \ldots, n$,

$$U_i = \frac{1}{2n} + (i - n)\frac{1}{n}$$

where U_i is the mid point of each of the n sub-intervals;

(2) transform these U_i into samples from the distribution:

$$U_i = G(U_i), \qquad i = 1, \ldots, n;$$

(3) randomly shuffle these x_i to give a randomly sequenced sample of size n.

As an example, consider a negative exponential distribution with a mean of 5. Suppose a sample of size 10 is required. The midpoints and thus the sample values are easily calculated and are shown in Table 8.1. In this case $x_i = -5 \log_e (U_i)$

Table 8.1

midpoints (U_i)	Sample Values (x_i)
0.05	14.98
0.15	9.49
0.25	6.93
0.35	5.25
0.45	3.25
0.55	2.99
0.65	2.15
0.75	1.44
0.85	0.81
0.95	0.26

Descriptive sample of size 10 from a negative exponential distribution mean 5.

This gives a sample mean of 4.77 and a standard deviation of 4.60. The corresponding values for the distribution are both 5 exactly. For a negatively exponential distribution, the procedure will always result in an underestimate of the moments. This is because the use of the centre of the sub-intervals on the interval (0,1) excludes values close to 0 unless n is large. Thus very large values of X are excluded from the sample.

Any random variable with a monotonically decreasing distribution function will produce underestimates of the moments for small samples. The opposite applies to monotonically increasing function.

Descriptive (or selective) sampling has yet to be applied in a 'real' simulation for two reasons. Firstly, the sample sizes need to be determined beforehand— though this should be no problem. Secondly, there is no obvious way of implementing the procedure, which is a form of sampling without replacement, without storing all the values. For a simulation involving 12 random variables each requiring 5000 values, this suggests that 60 000 values need to be stored somewhere. Given that mass storage devices are increasingly cheap, this may not turn out to be a problem in the near future. However, currently no language incorporates such sampling procedures.

8.5 EXPERIMENTATION

8.5.1 Basic ideas

Many simulations are carried out to compare system configurations or policies for operating the system. The inputs which are controllable and which are thought to affect the system response are called FACTORS. These factors can be quantitative variables — for example, having one, two, or three booking clerks in the example used earlier. As well as this, the factors may be qualititative, that is they reflect different policies. An example of such qualitative factors might be the priority rules which define whether or not personal enquirers have priority over phone callers. A simulation experiment could thus be used to investigate the effect of the number of clerks (quantitative) and the priority rules (qualitative).

In the simplest comparison experiments there are just two things to compare. These could be two LEVELS at which a single factor can operate, for example having one or two booking clerks. Alternatively it might be a comparison of two factors, each of which operates at only a single level and are known not to interact. For example, the length of the clerk's lunch break and the priority rule. In either case the experiment is designed to assess which of the two factors or two levels produces the most favourable response. The results of the experiments may be analysed by straightforward parametric tests. For example, if two values of the mean number of tickets sold are to be compared, then a Student's *t*-test may be employed if the two estimates are independent. Note that most variance reduction methods ensure that this assumption of independence is invalid.

However, things are often more complicated. There may be more than two factors or levels and the factors may be thought to interact and jointly affect the behaviour of the system. In such cases, the normal recourse is to a factorial experiment whose results are assessed via the analysis of variance. Factorial experiments aim to compare the effects of each level of each factor with each level of each of the other factors. Only via a factorial experiment may the effects of interacting factors be assessed.

The problem with factorial experiments is that, in simulation terms, they require many runs of the model. If there are three factors each of which has three levels, then this means that there are 27 factor–level combinations. Because of the stochastic variation inherent in discrete simulations each factor level combination should be repeated several times, i.e. there must be replication. If each policy is replicated 3 times, this requires 81 separate runs! So this is potentially a time-coming process.

Suppose that there are n such factors, each of which operate at L_f levels ($f = 1, \ldots, n$). Then the number of possible combinations in a fully factorial experiment is

$$\prod_{f=1}^{n} L_f.$$

Now if each factor has the same number of levels L, then the number of combinations is L^n. If each factor has two levels, then the experiment is described as a 2^n factorial experiment.

In a factorial experiment there are two types of effect due to the various factors. Consider a 2^3 factorial experiment which aims to analyse the influence of three factors X, Y, Z.

(1) The main effects: these are due solely to the factors X, Y and Z as they are individually changed without changing the other factors.
(2) The interaction effects: due to simultaneous changes in two or more of

the factors. If two factors change, this is called a second order effect (in the 2^3 experiment these are due to XY, XZ, or YZ). The third order effect (XYZ) is due to simultaneous change in all three factors.

These effects are usually unscrambled via the analysis of variance in which the observed variation of the response variable is split into independent components. The variation is usually expressed in terms of sums of squared deviations from the means. The total sum of squared deviations is separated into independent components, each of which represents one of the main effects or one of the interaction effects. Statistical tests are then employed to determine whether any of these component sums of squares is statistically significant. If any are significant, then it is believed that the corresponding factors have a real effect on the response variables.

In a book of this type it would clearly be inappropriate to provide a detailed exposition of experimental design or the analysis of variance. For a lucid account of the principles of experimental design, readers are referred to the seminal work by Fisher (1951). For detailed accounts of the mathematics and statistics see Kleijnen (1975) who discusses some ideas that may be of value in simulation. More general discussions are to be found in any text on experimental design: for example, see Cochran and Cox (1957).

The next section provides a description of a simple factorial experiment and its analysis. Though this particular design is obviously unlikely to be of value in specific simulations, it does display the general principles. It should also be clear how to use similar approaches for particular applications.

8.5.2 A factorial experiment

As an example consider a simulation experiment in which two factors are to be evaluated. Suppose that each of the factors A and B is operated at n levels (i.e. separately with n distinct values) and that each of these 2^n combinations is replicated m times. Thus a total of $m.2^n$ runs of the simulation are required. The experiment is to determine whether either of the factors or their combination affects the response variable. If significant effects are found, then the aim is to find which of the levels (or values) produce the most satisfactory results. The analysis proceeds in two phases.

(1) An analysis of variance of the experimental results — assuming that sensible tabulation of results does not immediately identify the important effects.
(2) A multiple comparison of the factor levels if significant effects are obvious or are found in the analysis of variance.

The analysis of variance

Most factorial experiments of this type assume the following model for the response variable and the effects:

$$Y_{ijk} = \mu + \alpha_i + \beta_j + \theta_{ij} + \varepsilon_{ijk}, \tag{8.6}$$

where Y_{ijk} is the result of the factor combination A_i and B_j at its kth replication;
- μ is the overall average effect (the grand mean);
- α_i is the main effect of factor A at level i;
- β_j is the main effect of factor B at level j;
- θ_{ij} is the interaction effect of the factor combination A_i and B_j;
- ε_{ijk} is the unexplained variation (the residual, or error term).

Most analyses also assume the following

(a) The ε_{ijk} are all independent Normal $(0,\sigma^2)$ variables

(b) $\sum_{i=1}^{n} \sigma_i = \sum_{i=1}^{n} \beta_j = 0$

$\sum_{i=1}^{n} \theta_{ij} = 0$ for all j, $\sum_{j=1}^{n} \theta_{ij} = 0$ for all i;

i.e., the effects represent the difference between the factors at each level i or j and some average μ.

As with all statistical testing, it is important to carefully define the hypotheses under consideration. In this experiment, interaction effects are expected and so it is necessary to firstly check whether these are significant. If they are, there is no point in examining the main effects.

Thus the null hypotheses are:

$H_0(1)$: the interaction of A and B has no effect. i.e. $\theta_{ij} = 0$ for all i and j;
$H_0(2)$: factor A has no effect. i.e. $\alpha_i = 0$ for all i;
$H_0(3)$: factor B has no effect. i.e. $\beta_j = 0$ for all j.

The alternate hypotheses are

$H_1(1)$: $\theta_{ij} \neq 0$ for some i,j;
$H_1(2)$: $\alpha_i \neq 0$ for some i;
$H_1(3)$: $\beta_j \neq 0$ for some j.

The usual procedure is to find least squares estimates of the parameters α_i, β_j, θ_{ij} and μ by minimizing

$$S_{\mathrm{E}}^2 = \sum_{i=1}^{n} \sum_{j=1}^{n} \sum_{k=1}^{m} (Y_{ijk} - \hat{\mu} - \hat{\alpha}_i - \hat{\beta}_j - \hat{\theta}_{ij})^2, \tag{8.7}$$

where the caret over the symbols indicates a least squares estimate. The result is that

$$S_{\mathrm{E}}^2 = S^2 - S_A^2 - S_B^2 - S_{AB}^2, \tag{8.8}$$

where S_{E}^2 = the error (or residual) sum of squares;
S^2 = the total sum of squares;
S_A^2, S_B^2, S_{AB}^2 = the sum of squares due to A, B and AB.

These sums of squares are then used to provide estimates of the proportion of the variance due to each factor and factor combination.

The results are depicted in Table 8.2 which shows the nature of the comparison. Factor A takes n values, each of which is replicated m times. Thus, if the mean of these m replications is used, there are $(n-1)$ degrees of freedom associated with the resulting statistic. Similar arguments apply to factors A and B.

Table 8.2

Source	Degrees of freedom	Sum of squares	Mean sum of squares
A	$(n-1)$	$S_A^2 = \sum_{i=1}^{n} y^{i}_{..}/nm - y_{...}^2/n^2m$	$S_A^2/(n-1)$
B	$(n-1)$	$S_B^2 = \sum_{j=1}^{n} y_{.j.}^2/nm - y_{...}^2/n^2m$	$S_B^2/(n-1)$
AB	$(n-1)^2$	$S_{AB}^2 = \sum_{i=1}^{n} \sum_{j=1}^{n} y_{ij.}/m - \sum_{i=1}^{n} y_{i..}^2/nm - \sum_{j=1}^{n} y_{.j.}^2/nm + y_{...}^2/n^2m$	$S_{AB}^2/(n-1)^2$
Error	$n^2(m-1)$	$S_E^2 = S^2 - S_A^2 - S_B^2 - S_{AB}^2$	$S_E^2/[n^2(m-1)]$
Total	(n^2m-1)	$S^2 = \sum_{i=1}^{n} \sum_{j=1}^{n} \sum_{k=1}^{m} Y_{ijk}^2 - y_{...}^2/n^2m$	

$$y_{...} = \sum_{i=1}^{n} \sum_{j=1}^{n} \sum_{k=1}^{m} Y_{ijk} \qquad y_{i..} = \sum_{j=1}^{n} \sum_{k=1}^{m} Y_{ijk}$$

$$y_{.j.} = \sum_{i=1}^{n} \sum_{k=1}^{m} Y_{ijk} \qquad y_{ik} = \sum_{j=1}^{m} Y_{ijk}$$

Thus the hypothesis testing proceeds as follows:

$H_0(1)$: is $\theta_{ij} = 0$ for all i and j

$$\text{Reject } H_0(1) \text{ if } \frac{S_{AB}^2}{(n-1)^2} \Big/ \frac{S_E^2}{n^2(m-1)} > F_{(n-1)^2, n^2(m-1)}.$$

If $H_0(1)$ rejected, there is no point in testing $H_0(2)$ and $H_0(3)$.
If $H_0(1)$ is accepted, then the model simplifies to

$$Y_{ijk} = \mu + \alpha_i + \beta_j + \varepsilon_{ijk}. \tag{8.9}$$

$$\text{Thus: Reject } H_0(1) \text{ if } \frac{S_A^2}{(n-1)} \Big/ \frac{(S_E^2 + S_{AB}^2)}{(n^2m - 2n - 1)} > F_{(n-1),(n^2m-2n-1)}$$

$$\text{Reject } H_0(2) \text{ if } \frac{S_B^2}{(n-1)} \Big/ \frac{(S_E^2 + S_{AB}^2)}{(n^2m - 2n - 1)} > F_{(n-1),(n^2m-2n-1)}.$$

8.5.3 Multiple comparison

If an analysis of variance has demonstrated that a set of effects $(\alpha_1, \alpha_2, \ldots, \alpha_n)$

are significantly different, then it will be important to compare the effects. In this way, the factor–level combinations which produce the best results may be identified. The procedure attempts to group the effects into subsets, each of which may be regarded as the same.

Requirements: the estimates ($\hat{\alpha}_1, \ldots, \hat{\alpha}_n$) of the effect parameters, plus those of the other factors if more than a single factor at several levels is involved and

: an unbiassed estimate of the error variance $\hat{\sigma}^2$

: d the error sum of squares degrees of freedom.

The simple model has a single factor operated at n levels, each level being replicated m times.

Thus

$$\hat{\alpha}_i = \frac{Y_{i.}}{m} - \frac{y_{..}}{nm}$$

$$\therefore \hat{\alpha}_p - \hat{\alpha}_q = \frac{Y_{p\cdot}}{m} - \frac{Y_{q\cdot}}{m}, \qquad p \neq q,$$

$$\therefore E(\hat{\alpha}_p - \hat{\alpha}_q) = \alpha_p - \alpha_q$$

$$\text{VAR}\,(\hat{\alpha}_p - \hat{\alpha}_q) = \frac{2\sigma^2}{m}$$

Now if $\alpha_p = \alpha_q$

$$\therefore \hat{\alpha}_p - \hat{\alpha}_q \sim N\left(0\,, \frac{2\sigma^2}{m}\right)$$

$$\therefore \frac{\hat{\alpha}_p - \hat{\alpha}_q}{\sqrt{2\sigma^2/m}} \sim N(0,1)$$

which suggests that

$$\frac{\hat{\alpha}_p - \hat{\alpha}_q}{\sqrt{2\sigma^2/m}} \sim t_d$$

Hence, under H_0: $\alpha_p = \alpha_q$

Reject H_0 if $|\hat{\alpha}_p - \alpha_q| > t_{s,\alpha} \cdot \sqrt{\dfrac{2\sigma^2}{m}}$

Where $t_{d\alpha}$ is the α significance point for a 2-tailed t test on m degrees of freedom

and $t_{d,\alpha} \cdot \sqrt{\dfrac{2\hat{\sigma}^2}{m}}$ is known as the Least Significant Difference at the α level.

In this case, Least Significant Difference tests should be performed on all $(n-1)n/2$ pairs of difference effects α_i.

For a 2-way design without significant interaction.

$$\hat{\alpha}_i = \frac{y_{i.}}{m} - \frac{y_{..}}{nm}$$

$$\hat{B}_j = \frac{y_{.j}}{m} - \frac{y_{..}}{nm}$$

and both sets of effects must be tested.

For a 2-way design with significant interaction

$$\mu_{ij} = \mu + \alpha_i + \beta_j + \theta_{ij}$$

where μ_{ij} is the average response to the factor combination α_i, β_j.

$$\text{Use } \hat{\mu}_{ij} = \frac{Y_{ij}}{m}$$

and test for significant differences.

EXERCISES

1. Using the final BASIC version of the harassed booking clerk problem, investigate the effect of starting conditions on the queue lengths.

2. Use the BASIC version of the harrassed booking clerk to select values for the parameters of control variates suitable for the estimation of queue lengths.

3. Use descriptive sampling to take a sample of size 10 from a triangular distribution.

4. Investigate the effect of streaming the random numbers used in your version of the harassed booking clerk program.

REFERENCES

Brenner, M. E. (1963) Selective sampling — a technique for reducing sample size in simulations of decision making problems. *J. Ind. Eng.* **14**, 291–296.

Cochran W. G. & Cox, G. M. (1957) *Experimental Designs*. Wiley, New York.

Conway R. W. (1963) Some tactical problems in digital simulation. *Mgt. Sci.* **10**, 47–61.

Ehrenfield S. & Ben-Tuvia S. (1962) The efficiency of statistical simulation procedures. *Technometrics* **4**, 257–275

Fisher R. A. (1951) *The Design of Experiments*. Oliver & Boyd, Edinburgh.

Fishman G. S. (1973) *Concepts and Methods in Discrete Event Digital Simulation*. Wiley-Interscience, New York.

Fishman G. S. (1978) *Principles of Discrete Event Simulation*. Wiley-Interscience, New York.

Kleijnen J. P. C. (1974) *Statistical Techniques in Simulation*, Part I. Marcel Dekker, New York.
Kleijnen J. P. C. (1975) *Statistical Techniques in Simulation*, Part II. Marcel Dekker, New York.
Page E. S. (1965) On Monte Carlo methods in congestion problems: II. Simulation of queueing problems. *Ops. Res.* **13**, 300–305.
Saliby E. (1980) *A Reappraisal of Some Simulation Fundamentals*. Ph.D. thesis, University of Lancaster.
Tocher K. D. (1963) *The Art of Simulation*. English Universities Press, London.

PART III

SYSTEM DYNAMICS

Chapter 9

Modelling feedback systems

9.1 FEEDBACK SYSTEMS

9.1.1 Hierarchical feedback systems: an example

Consider a company which produces spares and replacement parts for the motor trade. Suppose that it does not produce original equipment and is dependent on the large number of motor factors and retailers. Thus the company has two groups of final consumers of its produced:

(1) garages who fit the parts to their customers' vehicles;
(2) DIY motorists who fit the parts themselves.

The company has no direct contact with either of these groups of consumers.

To make its products, the company buys in raw materials and processes them. Thus it creates two distinct sets of stocks within its own boundary. These are:

raw materials;
finished goods.

All of these stocks must be financed and will thus be subject to some control.

The finished goods are sold to motor factors who themselves hold stocks as wholesalers. The motor factors buy in large lots from the manufacturer and sell in smaller batches to the retailers or the garage trade. The DIY motorists buy in units from the retailers. This produces the overall hierarchical system shown in Figure 9.1.

DIY motorists enter a retail outlet to buy parts, and as the individual sales occur the retailer's stocks are reduced. In time, possibly as a result of a call from a salesman, the retailer places an order with the motor factor. As several such orders are met, the motor factor's stocks are also run down. Thus the motor manufacturer receives an order from the factor. In this way, the finished stocks of the manufacturer are depleted. Eventually, the effect is felt in the raw material stocks and so an order is placed on the raw material supplier. Most

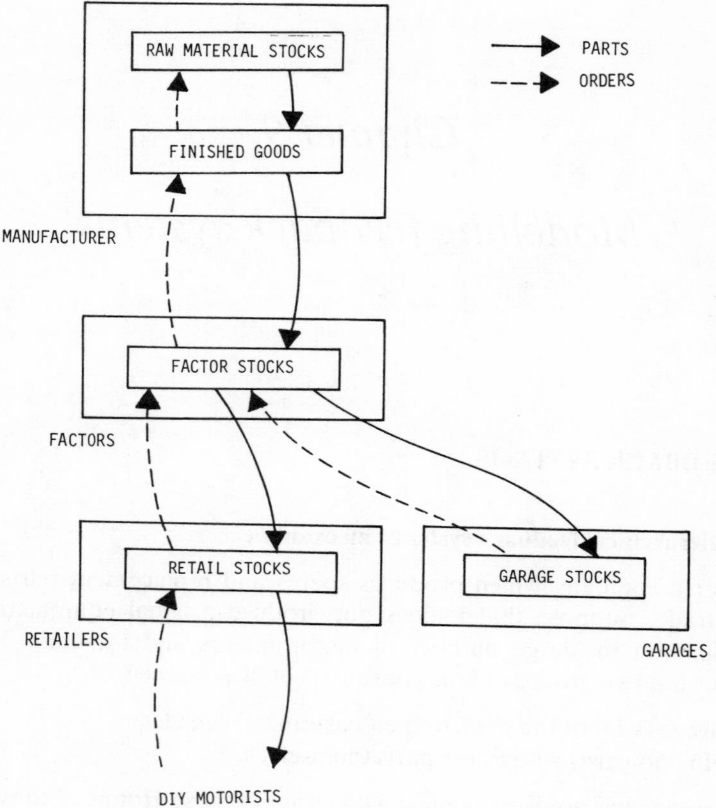

Figure 9.1 The motor parts distribution system

likely, the parts manufacturer operates a production plan which calls for production of particular parts in batches at regular time intervals.

Several things are apparent in moving up this chain of supply from the DIY motorist to the manufacturer. Firstly, the batch sizes of stock replenishments increase. Thus mistakes are more costly higher up the chain. Secondly, the purchasing decisions move further and further away from the consumers' behaviour. Hence, both the cost and the risk of wrong action increase higher up the chain. A third feature is the presence of delays in the system. For example, the manufacturer does not respond to individual orders from factors by attempting to maintain a constant finished stock level. Rather, batches are made and added to the stocks at intervals. Similarly, the retailer may place weekly or monthly orders on the factor.

Suppose, for example, that the DIY motorists suddenly reduce their demand for parts. What happens?

(1) The depletion of the retailers' stocks slows down. This occurs immediately.

(2) Rather later, the factors' stocks are also higher than normal. If parts ordered from the manufacturer a month earlier begin to arrive in stock, then this makes things even worse. Eventually, the factors reduce their orders to the manufacturer. If things get too bad, they may stop ordering for some time.

(3) Meanwhile, in the absence of market intelligence, the manufacturer may be blissfully unaware of all this. Whilst the downturn in DIY demand is happening, the regular production plan of the manufacturer continues. Then suddenly, to the unaware manufacturer at least, demand dries up. This causes severe problems. Raw material stocks are too high and more supplies are already on order. Finished stocks are also mounting and there is no prospect of moving the stock. Thus the manufacturer has either to reduce production, which will create severe labour problems, or must devise some way of shifting the stocks. One way might be to offer a special price promotion.

(4) Remember that these problems hit the manufacturer some time after the original downturn in DIY demand. If their luck is bad, and sometimes it is, the price promotion may coincide with a resumption in DIY demand. The price promotions may inflate this demand still further. This causes frantic calls for deliveries at all levels in the hierarchy. Thus there is a risk that the manufacturer may end up over-producing to meet this artificial demand. What happens next? That depends, but there is a clear risk of catastrophic overshoot in production.

Of course, this scenario is not entirely realistic. However, similar effects do occur in systems of this type. Small decisions at a low level can have much amplified effects further up the system. Such multi-level systems need to be modelled with the aim of exploring their stability and response.

9.1.2 Causal loop diagrams

These offer a simple way of mapping out the interacting elements of feedback systems. As will be seen in Chapter 10, Forrester (1961) put forward a rather more complicated system of flow diagrams to aid system dynamics modelling. For present purposes the simpler causal loop diagrams will suffice. The idea is to show which factors cause other factors to change.

As a simple example, consider a thermostatically controlled domestic central heating system. This is shown in simplified causal loop form in Figure 9.2. Gas is burned to provide heat; heat input to the room causes the room temperature to rise; as the temperature rises, this trips a thermostat which cuts off the gas supply. If the temperature drops below some pre-set temperature, the thermostat causes the gas supply to be restored.

Notice the following conventions:

(1) The direction of the arrow head indicates causality. For example, an

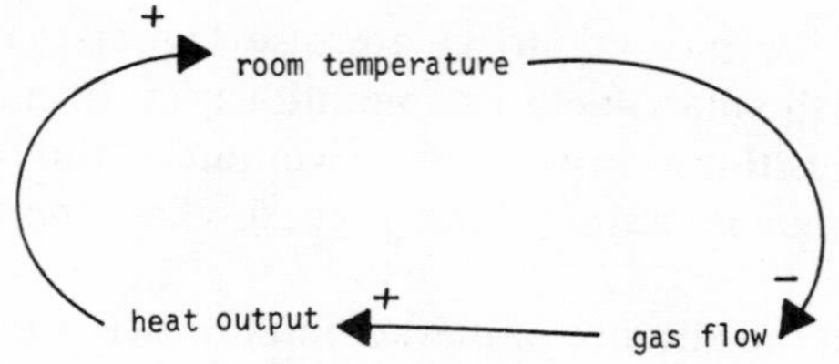

Figure 9.2 Causal loop for central heating system

increase in room temperature causes (via the thermostat) the gas supply to be cut off.

(2) The sign at the arrow head indicates the effect of the causality. If an increase in one factor causes an increase in another, other factors remaining unchanged, then a plus sign is correct. If an increase in one leads to a decrease in another, other factors being unchanged, then a minus sign is called for. Sometimes both effects are possible and a question mark should be used. In the central heating example, increased heat output should lead to an increase in room temperature — hence a plus sign is shown.

Of course, the systems investigated by management scientists are much more complex than this simplified central heating system. The control function in particular is much more complicated and, most likely, is fairly diffuse. At one extreme, control may be exercised via simple programmed rules or procedures which are rigorously followed. For example, jobs of certain types may always be allocated to specified machines in a job shop. At the other extreme is the adaptive behaviour by which any organization ensures its continued existence. This is characterized by conscious responses to changes in the organization's environment which present both threats and opportunities. For instance, companies which were manufacturing clockwork watches around 1973 needed to be ready for the micro-electronics revolution. Some were not.

Hence it would be wrong to regard organizations as machines or even as directly analogous to machines. Only low level control is exercised by simple procedures. Thus the causal links for organizational control are shown as dashed lines on the diagrams. This is to emphasize that control is usually exercised via policies which can be changed without affecting the causality of the 'material links'. Most likely, the purpose of the simulation is to explore the effect of current and alternative policies on the rest of the system. Dashed lines are also used to indicate information flows.

Section 2.3.1 included a simulation of a simplified manufacturing company. Figure 9.3 and 9.4 are causal loop diagrams of the two versions of the system considered. Figure 9.3 shows the original, and rather unstable version of the system. Figure 9.4 shows the revised version of the system which turned out to be rather more stable — at least in the limited terms of

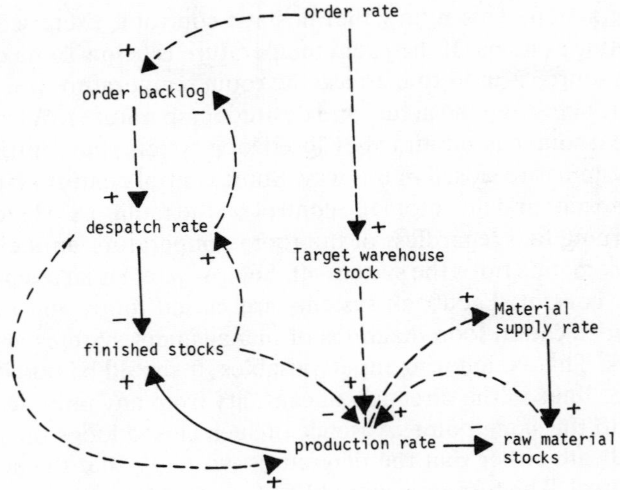

Figure 9.3 Causal loop diagram for the original system

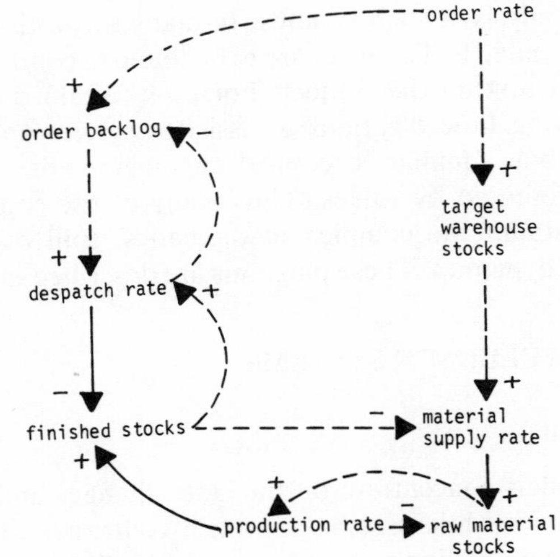

Figure 9.4 Causal loop diagram for the revised system

Section 2.3.1. Notice that the more stable system has a rather simpler set of loops.

9.1.3 Closed and open loops

A feedback system is one which incorporates a loop from the output to the input. In simple homeostats, this feedback path allows control to be exercised by comparing the difference between the output and some desired result. In negative feedback systems this difference, or error term, is reduced by taking appropriate action. This is how thermostatic control is exercised in domestic central heating systems. If the room temperature is below some desired level, then a heat source is used to increase the room temperature (i.e. to minimize the difference between the actual and desired temperature). When the error is zero, the heat source is withdrawn. Closed loop systems have intrinsic control.

Not all systems are closed in this way. Some central heating systems have no room thermostats and no automatic control on the radiators. Hence the system goes on burning fuel regardless of the room temperature until either the fuel runs out or someone turns the system off. Such a system is an open loop and has no intrinsic control. Feedback systems are closed loops and offer intrinsic control. Hence causal loop diagrams of management systems always include closed loops. That is, ignoring input variables, it should be possible to follow the influence links in the direction of causality from any point in the diagram and return to the same point. Absence of such closed loops on a causal loop diagram indicate either that the diagram is wrong or that the system has no intrinsic control. The former is more likely.

The analysis of mechanical, electrical and electronic systems is a major pre-occupation of design engineers. Control theory offers a mathematical approach to the analysis of such systems. In many ways, the roots of system dynamics as propounded by Forrester are to be found in control theory and this is clear in the first text on the subject (Forrester, 1961). Indeed, Forrester recommends drawing flow diagrams to assist in system analysis and these diagrams use symbols familiar to control engineers. For example, control functions are represented by valves. Thus many of the concepts of control theory, though without the complex mathematics, spill over from control theory into system dynamics. These diagrams are described in Section 10.1.

9.2 ANALYSING FEEDBACK SYSTEMS

9.2.1 Level of detail

Discrete event models concentrate on the state changes and interactions of individual entities. This microscopic approach contrasts with the approach usually taken to the modelling and simulation of feedback systems. Here it is normal to operate at a much more aggregate level by concentrating on the rates of change of populations of entities. For example if the distribution system of the motor parts manufacturer were being simulated, it would not be sensible to follow each individual stock item through the system. Instead, a simulation model would most likely be used to analyse the changes in rates of demand and production in the system.

To build the model it would be normal to regard these rates as varying continuously through time. In some cases, this is a reasonable assumption. For example, suppose that the parts flowing through the system are cheap and common items such as screws. To all intents and purposes, the variable 'number of screws' is continuous even though the figure '234.675 screws' has no meaning in the real system. For other systems, for example the cases described in Chapter 11, any assumption of continuity requires careful consideration.

In order to model feedback systems for simulation, it is important to concentrate on their structure rather than their content. The structure defines how the variables interact, the content is the meaning of those variables for the organization. Two systems may have similar structures but quite different content. For example, a supermarket and the control room of a fire station may both be analysed in terms of their queueing structure. Both systems have customers who are served, but the meaning (and importance) of the customers differ. In the fire station the customers are calls awaiting a response, whereas in the supermarket the customers are the shoppers. Causal loop diagrams are concerned with system stucture. Coyle (1977) points out that the management scientist has to maintain two views of a system at the same time. To model it, the system must be seen in terms of its structure, but to consider making changes it is crucial to keep in mind the meaning of the variables. Only then will it be clear which changes are feasible. Thus a rounded approach is needed.

9.2.2 Simulating feedback systems

Engineering students are familiar with the modelling of feedback systems by differential equations. Indeed, the design of servo-mechanisms is still a feature of many engineering curricula. Once such systems become realistically complex, then their direct analysis is often impossible. Various means are resorted to so as to get round this difficulty. One approach is to use analogue computers to simulate the behaviour of the system being studied. Such a computer employs a network of electrical components whose behaviour can be described by the same differential equations as the system of interest. Analogue computers allow continuous variables to be represented by continuous properties such as voltage and current. In one sense therefore, analogue simulators offer a more accurate way of simulating feedback systems than system dynamics. The simulation is carried out by subjecting the selected electrical circuits to specified inputs and observing the behaviour of the model system. The components are then rearranged or tuned to design systems which perform in the way required.

A major difficulty with analogue computers is that they require a reasonable expertise in the design of electrical circuits — otherwise, the selection and assembly of the correct components is impossible. Another problem is that few commercial organizations possess analogue computers. However, most do have digital computers. An obvious development was therefore the production of digital computer packages which simulate analogue computers. To use the current versions of such systems, the analyst formulates the problem in terms of differential equations. These digital–analogue packages, such as SLAM (1972) and the later versions of CSMP, use standard integration routines to simulate the behaviour of the system of equations given certain inputs.

9.3 SYSTEM DYNAMICS MODELLING

To analyse feedback systems in system dynamic terms it is normal (Forrester, 1961) to concentrate on three aspects of system structure. These are:

delays;
levels;
rates.

The meaning of these is discussed in the sections below.

9.3.1 Delays

It is important to realize that information and materials (or whatever make up the 'stuff' of the system) are rarely transmitted and received instantaneously. To give a simple example, orders may be sent by customers to their supplier by ordinary mail, thus introducing a delay of at least one day. Similarly, a company may have good reason to increase its production by 30% but face a lead time of four weeks to do so because of the need to train more staff. Delays occur for all sorts of legitimate reasons and often these may be reduced at a cost. For example, a company with geographically dispersed distribution depots may choose to transmit information about stock levels by facsimile transfer rather than by using the normal mail.

Delays, of whatever type, can have profound effects within feedback systems. As a trivial example, most people have had the distressing experience of trying to control the temperature of a shower which has a manual mixing valve. Typically, such a valve mixes water from separate hot and cold sources. The mixed water then passes to the shower head and thence drops onto the person in the shower. Unfortunately it takes time for the water to travel from the mixing valve to the shower head. Hence the familiar pattern of events unfolds:

(1) bather enters shower area and turns on the water, but the water is too cold because the shower was last used some time ago;
(2) bather turns the mixer valve so as to increase the water temperature;
(3) no immediate effect, therefore the bather turns the mixer valve further towards hot;
(4) scalding water now hits the bather who frantically turns the mixer valve to the cold side;
(5) water still too hot, so the bather turns the mixer valve still further towards the cold side;
(6) bather now hit by cold water! Therefore the bather turns the mixer valve towards hot, but with no immediate effect.

And so the process continues.

With stable water flows and an intelligent bather, the temperature oscillations decrease in amplitude until the right temperature is achieved. All this because of a delay in a simple system. Figure 9.5 shows the temperature oscillations and their eventual damping. To avoid such oscillation, the answer is to reduce the delay. Thus the temperature should be sensed as close to the mixing valve as possible. Hence if a thermostat is to be used, it should be placed in the circuit immediately after the valve.

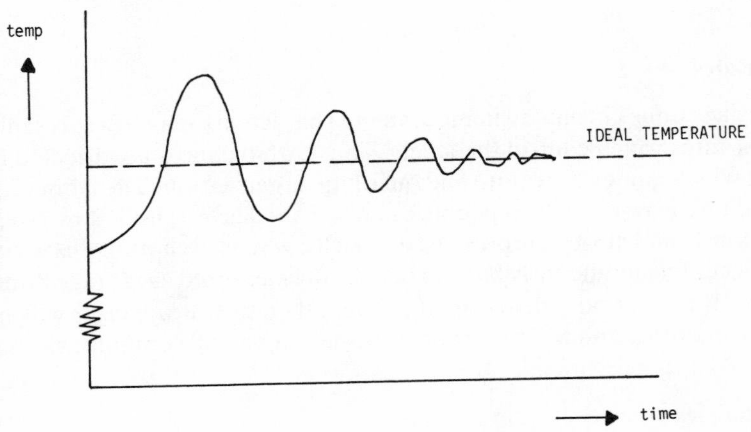

Figure 9.5 Temperature variations under a shower

Let us return to organizational systems. The motor parts manufacturer (Section 9.1.1) has real difficulties in trying to control production runs and stock levels. As it stands, the system includes far too many delays; also decisions about the production rates are too far removed from the behaviour of the consumers. One objective of the manufacturer, if more control is required, may be to reduce the effect of these delays. That is, the manufacturer must be more in touch with the state of the market. This does not mean that the management must respond to every fluctuation in the market. However, they ought to be in a position to decide whether or not to react.

Thus the consideration of delays is an important part of the analysis of feedback systems. Sections 10.3 and 10.4 discuss how different types of delay are handled in system dynamics.

9.3.2 Levels

Organizational systems contain accumulations of one kind or another. In system dynamics, these are usually called *levels*. The current conditions of the levels within a system correspond to the system state. Often, levels are clearly recognizable as such; for example, stocks of various types. Another example might be cash balances which are produced by inflows and outflows of funds. A slightly less obvious example might be a labour force with numbers of employees at different levels and experience. This too could be regarded as a level or accumulation within the system. Levels continue to exist (in principle, at least) even if all activity ceases (Forrester, 1961).

In modelling feedback systems, it is important to identify the relevant levels of the system. Generally, these levels are subject to some control by the management of the organization. By examining the levels within the system, the system state can be understood and appropriate corrective action may be taken.

9.3.3 Rates

Activity continues in any dynamic system. This activity may be represented by the flow rates which control the levels. Thus cash balances are affected by the rates at which money flows into and out of the organization. The labour force is affected by the rate at which people are hired and leave. These flow rates vary continuously and must be represented in such a way as to capture this variation. Flows occur instantaneously but can be usefully measured as average rates over a period. If the period is made small enough, then the rate changes will appear to occur smoothly and will thus capture something of the continuous variation.

9.3.4 Policies

It should now be clear that the system dynamics method views feedback systems as interconnected sequences of levels and flows. Matter and information flow from one level to another. Thus, the levels are affected by the flow rates and the flow rates may be affected by the levels. As an example, a manufacturer's finished stocks are determined by at least two flow rates:

(1) despatch rate to customers;
(2) production rate of finished goods.

In turn, the production and despatch rates are affected by the level of finished stocks. Goods cannot be despatched if they have not been made. Thus the despatch rate depends, in some sense, on the level of finished stocks. Similarly, if the finished stocks are too high, the management may decide to cut production.

Thus, in system dynamics terms, policies are explicit statements as to how levels affect rates and rates affect levels. In feedback systems, polices are expressed as decision rules stating what action is to be taken so as to achieve a given state. Hence they might state the flow rate necessary to achieve (it is hoped) a certain level.

9.4 ORIGINS OF SYSTEM DYNAMICS

It ought to be clear that simulating hierarchical feedback systems calls for methods which are rather different from the discrete event approaches covered in Chapters 3–8. With such systems, the major concern is often with stability — that is, how does it respond to changes in its inputs? For example, what will happen if demand increases briefly and then settles down again? Or, what effect would the doubling of certain stocks have on production rates in the short term? To answer these and similar questions calls for a simulation method which can cope with delays, with flows of information as well as 'material' and which lends itself to the study of transient phenomena.

System dynamics was first called 'industrial dynamics' from the book of that name by Forrester (1961). Despite its long history, in simulation terms at least, many management scientists are sceptical of its value. Possible there are two reasons for this. Firstly, *Industrial Dynamics* was an ambitious book. Possibly it was too ambitious. This is particularly seen in Forrester's claim that it presented a revolutionary approach to management. With hindsight, this does seem rather an exaggeration. Even at the time of publication, its mechanistic approach must have seemed a limiting factor to practising managers.

Another possible reason for the commonly found scepticism is that system dynamics is definitely not a highly refined and accurate tool. The aim is to explore the dynamics of feedback systems in terms of their stability and responses to external shocks. In many cases, the presenting instability may be so gross that exact analyses are not required. System dynamics presents a way of approximately simulating such systems. For the purist, the approximation may seem too great.

As mentioned in Section 9.2.2, the analysis of feedback systems via differential equations has long been the concern of engineers. System dynamics adopts a rather simpler approach in which the differential equations are replaced by first order difference equations. As will be seen in Section 10.5, this results in an integration approach which needs to be used with some care, otherwise the results of a simulation could be misleading. Nevertheless, its simplicity can be a great asset in communicating with managers.

The idea of modelling socio-economic systems in feedback terms is not original to Forrester. Forrester gives credit to Tustin (1953) for considering in detail the analogy between servo-mechanisms and economic systems. Forrester's contribution was to provide a simple and systematic way of simulating such systems.

REFERENCES

Coyle, R. G. (1977) *Management System Dynamics*. Wiley-Interscience, London, U.K.
Forrester, J. S. (1961) *Industrial Dynamics*. M.I.T. Press, Cambridge, Mass.
SLAM (1972) *A Simulation Language for Analogue Modelling*. ICL, UK.
Tustin, A. (1953) *The Mechanism of Economic Systems*. Harvard University Press, Cambridge, Mass.

Chapter 10

System dynamics simulation

10.1 INFLUENCE DIAGRAMS

In order to understand the system being simulated, it can be useful to sketch out the system components to show their interactions. Whether such diagrams are always useful for detailed modelling is a moot point. However, they can be valuable if they clearly display the major interactions. Chapter 3 described how activity cycle diagrams could be used for this purpose in discrete event simulations. For system dynamics, two types of diagram have been recommended.

Firstly there are the causal loop diagrams described in Section 9.1.2. Goodman (1974), who worked with Forrester at M.I.T., argues that they are a useful preliminary to modelling. He suggests mapping out the system roughly with causal loop diagrams and then drawing a detailed level-rate diagram as described below. Coyle (1977) regards causal loop diagrams as being all that is necessary for modelling before writing down the equations. That is, he does not use the detailed level-rate diagrams. Certainly, causal loop diagrams do provide a useful link between a verbal description of a system and its representation as difference equations.

Forrester (1961) recommended level-rate diagrams in which each different type of system element has its own symbol. Figure 10.1 shows the principal recommended symbols, many of which would be recognizable to control engineers. For example, a decision function is shown as a valve. This reflects Forrester's view that a policy (or decision function) is something that immediately affects flow rates. Correspondingly, levels are shown as rectangles — presumably reflecting the view that they are tanks or reservoirs. The levels are depleted by out-flows and increase as a result of in-flows. The flows themselves are the arrow lines of the diagrams and link together the levels and decision functions. In Forrester (1961) there were six types of flow. However, two types should suffice for most purposes.

The symbols are defined as follows:

LEVELS: accumulations within the system;

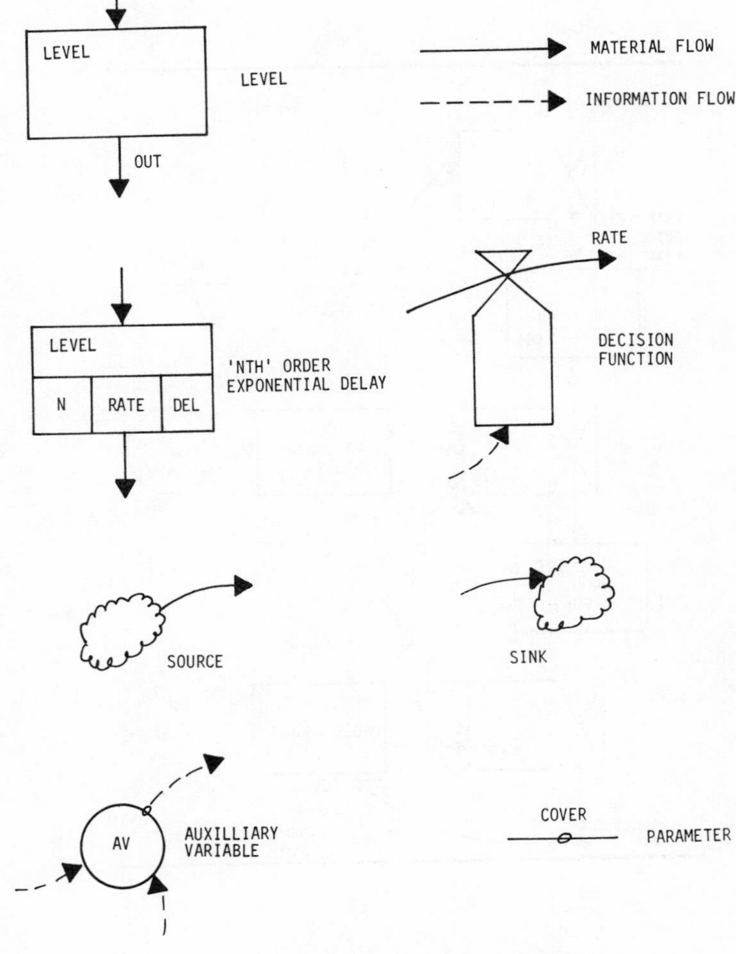

Figure 10.1 Forrester's influence diagram symbols

FLOWS: the movement of materials and information within the system;
DECISION FUNCTIONS: the ways in which the flows are controlled. These are usually defined by management policy;
DELAYS: as defined in Sections 9.3.1 and 10.3;
SOURCES: the beginning of a flow, if that flow begins outside the system being modelled;
SINKS: the final destination of a flow, if that destination is outside the model;
AUXILIARY VARIABLES: used when it is convenient to perform some algebraic operation;
PARAMETERS: constants.

Consider the system described in Section 2.3.1. This was of a simplified

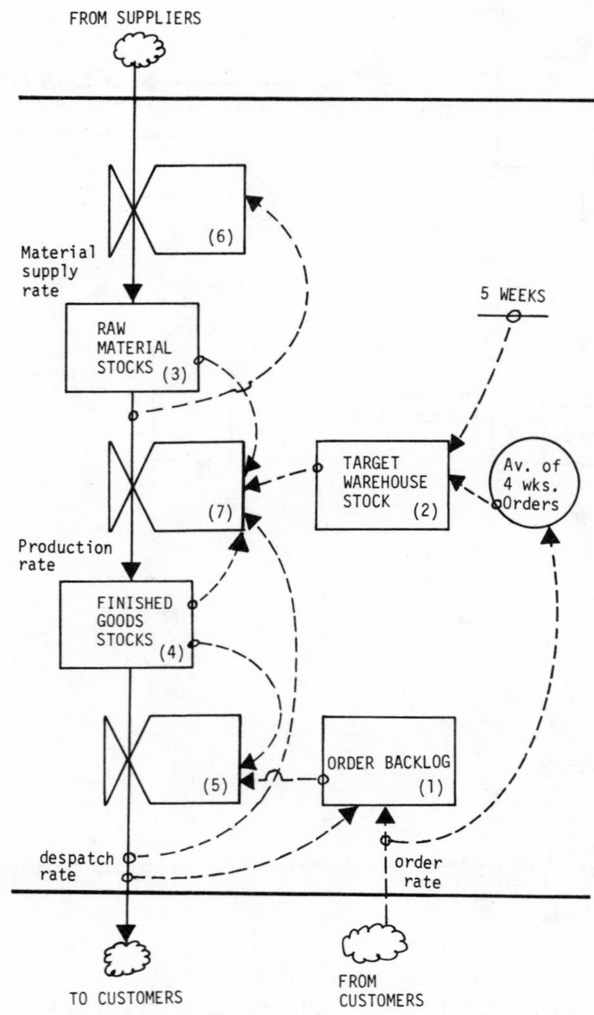

Figure 10.2 Level-rate diagram for original system

manufacturing company whose operations were to be simulated deterministically. As it happens, the simulation method used in Section 2.3.1 was very similar to the system dynamics method — as will be clear shortly. A level-rate diagram constructed using Forrester's symbols might be as shown in Figure 10.2. This shows the first version of the system, which turned out to be extremely unstable. A number of feedback loops are in evidence and some of these are probably the cause of the trouble. Strictly speaking, an auxiliary variable was not used to calculate the target warehouse stock: however, its use does make the diagram clearer.

Figure 10.3 shows a level-rate diagram for the second version of this system.

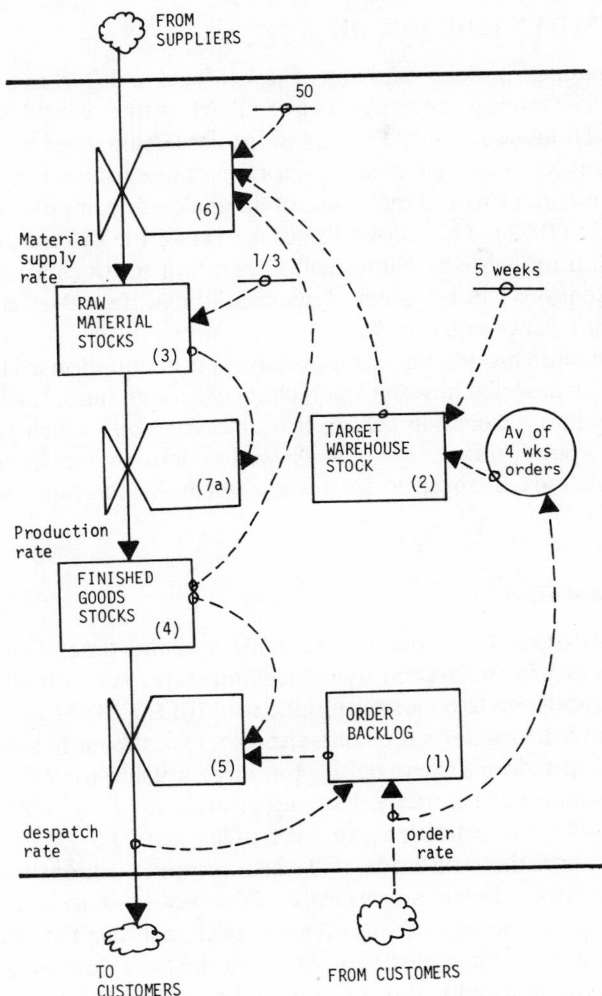

Figure 10.3 Level-rate diagram for revised system

This turned out to be more stable, at least in the limited investigation made in Section 2.3.1.

For both types of diagram, the description so far has been back to front. Diagrams have been drawn for models which already existed in an algebraic form in Section 2.3.1. The normal purpose of the diagrams is to assist in the first stages of modelling; thus they are produced before the sets of equations and this raises a difficulty for causal loop diagrams. Whereas Forrester's symbols map directly onto the equations, this is not true of causal loop diagrams, as they do not clearly distinguish between levels and rates. Coyle (1977) describes a method of labelling causal loops so as to sort this out. This is less important if they are regarded as a preliminary to drawing full level-rate diagrams.

10.2 SYSTEM DYNAMICS MODELS

A system dynamics model is made up of several sets of difference equations. A control engineer attempting to model a feedback system would most likely do so with differential equations. The equations describing most realistic systems can only be solved by numerical means, for direct integration is rarely feasible. Usually, the engineer would make use of an analogue computer or a package such as SLAM (1972). This allows the user to state the differential equations which make up the system. Numerical integration routines are then used to solve the equations. For system dynamics, the differential equations are replaced by difference equations.

System dynamics models have two primary sets of equations. There are *level equations* which describe how the levels change through time. Each level has its own level equation. Secondly, there are *rate equations* which represent the management's policy on rate changes. As well as these two sets, there are other equations which are introduced for convenience. All the types are discussed below.

10.2.1 Time handling

Time is moved forward in fixed increments and the time slice is normally referred to as DT in the system dynamics literature. As with all time slicing methods it is important to choose a suitable value of DT. If DT is too long, then the behaviour of the model is too coarse and some of the more subtle transient effects will be lost. More importantly, too large a value for DT can result in serious errors due to the method of integration used by DYNAMO type packages. Details of this problem are given in Section 10.5.

If DT is too short then the model will waste computer time (though this may not matter greatly). More importantly, this may lead to a model whose parameters require excessive data collection and analysis. The usual advice is to choose DT so that it is realistic to regard all the flow rates as constant over that time interval. Normally, it is safest to make DT small, as computer time is rarely a constraint. But see Section 10.5 for more specific advice.

The simulation proceeds as follows. Imagine three points of time J, K and L, where

$$K = J + DT$$

$$\text{and } L = K + DT.$$

Suppose that time is about to reach point K. The level equations will be computed at time K, using the flow rates evaluated at time J, the assumption being that the flow rates are constant over the interval JK. When the levels have been evaluated, the rate equations are computed. This gives the rates which will apply over the interval KL. Time is then moved to point L and the process repeats. Figure 10.4 shows the basic idea. Hence a system dynamics simulation proceeds as follows:

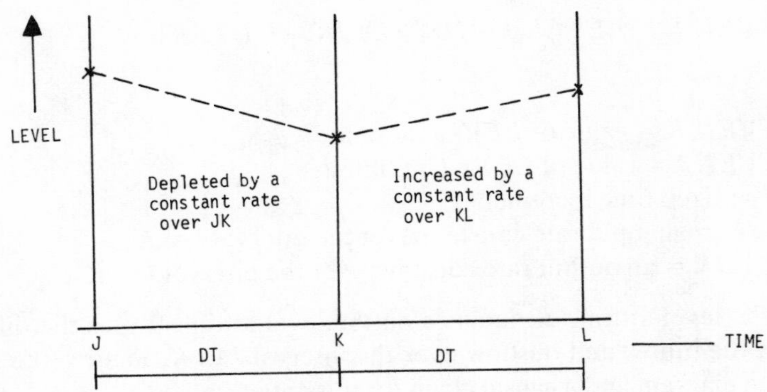

Figure 10.4 Time handling in systems dynamics

increment time to K;
evaluate level equations at time K;
evaluate rate equations, the rates to be held constant over the interval KL;
relabel the rates and levels so that K is now J and L is now K;
increment time by DT, call this new time K (previously regarded as L);
and so on until the simulation is over.

Thus what are in reality smooth changes of the levels are simulated as small linear changes as shown in Figure 10.5.

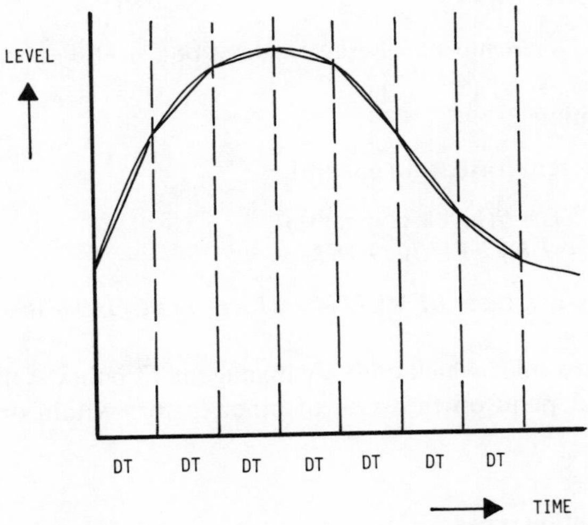

Figure 10.5 Linear approximations in systems dynamics

10.2.2 Level equations

A typical level equation might have the following format, using DYNAMO conventions:

$$LEVEL.K = LEVEL.J + (DT)(IN.JK - OUT.JK),$$

where

$LEVEL.K$ = value of $LEVEL$ at time K,
$LEVEL.J$ = value of $LEVEL$ at time J,
DT = fixed time increment,
$IN.JK$ = an input rate constant over the interval J to K,
$OUT.JK$ = an output rate constant over the interval J to K.

Hence the level at time K depends on the level at time J plus the difference between the inflow and outflow over the interval J to K. Figure 10.6 shows a level-rate diagram and a causal chain for this equation.

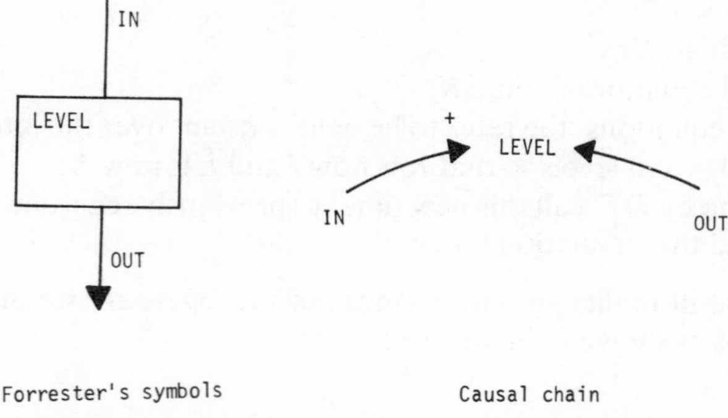

Figure 10.6 Representations of a level

10.2.3 Rate equations

These have a different format. In general,

$$RATE.KL = f(\text{levels constants})$$
e.g. $$R1.KL = LEVEL.K/CONST$$

where $R1.KL$ is a flow rate, $LEVEL.K$ is a level and $CONST$ is some constant (parameter).
Rate equations are rules which embody management policy. Obviously, this policy may also depend on the state of other factors within or outside the organization.

10.2.4 Other equation types

Following DYNAMO conventions, various other types of equation are to be found in system dynamics models.

(1) Auxiliary equations

Used to avoid very complicated equations by breaking down rate equations into subsidiary equations. Clearly they must be executed after the level equations but before the rate equations. Hence the value of the auxiliary equations can be substituted into the rate equations proper. The order of evaluation of rate equations can be important.

(2) Supplementary equations

Introduced to define variables needed for the output but which are not actually part of the dynamic model. For example, one measure of performance might be the average order backlog in each 4 week period, and this would be defined in supplementary equations.

(3) Initial value equations

As the name suggests, these set up initial values for all levels and some rates. Obviously these are only computed once in each run.

10.3 MODELLING DELAYS

As discussed in Chapter 9, delays cause many problems in dynamic systems. They occur when some process or other receives information or material and transmits it

at a slower rate;
or later, but at the same rate;
or both.

Hence delays are special cases of the level concept introduced in Section 9.2.2. Various commonly occurring types of delay are described in the following sections because it is useful to know how to incorporate them within system dynamics models. DYNAMO, DYSMAP and MICRO-DYN B all provide built-in functions for delays.

The initial discussion will assume that delays to information and material are treated identically. Later, this assumption will be relaxed.

10.3.1 First order exponential delays

Figure 10.7 shows the influence diagram for a first order exponential delay. It consists of a *LEVEL* which is increased by some input rate (*IN*) and depleted by some output rate (*OUT*). There are information flows from the level to the decision function controlling *OUT*. There is also a constant delay (*DEL*) exerting its influence. This represents the average time taken by the flow to traverse the delay. The resulting *DYNAMO* style equations are shown below:

$$LEVEL.K = LEVEL.J + (DT)(IN.JK - OUT.JK) \quad 10.1,L$$
$$OUT.KL = LEVEL.K/DEL \quad 10.2,R$$

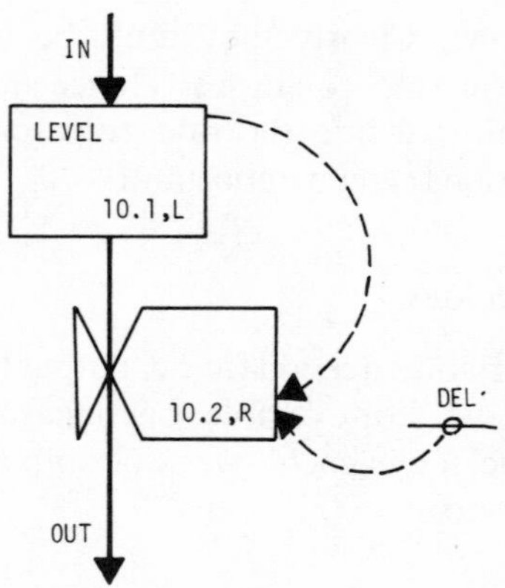

Figure 10.7 First order exponential delay

Equation 10.2,*R* states that a fixed proportion of the level becomes the new value of the output rate.

Delays have important consequences for the dynamics of feedback systems. Figure 10.8 shows the transient response of a first order exponential delay to two specific inputs. The following initial values are used;

$$\begin{aligned} LEVEL &= 0, \\ OUT &= 0, \\ DT &= 1 \\ \text{and } DEL &= 6 \end{aligned}$$

The system is in balance before being perturbed.

(a) IMPULSE: equivalent to the receipt of an unexpectedly large single consignment at a warehouse. In this case, *IN* suddenly rises to 1 and then returns immediately to zero.
(b) STEP: equivalent to a sudden increase in receipts. Unlike the impulse, the input rate remains at the new level. In this case, *IN* suddenly rises to 1 and remains at that value.

As can be seen, the impulse causes the output rate to rise quickly to a peak way above its original value. It then decays exponentially towards zero. The step causes the output rate to climb assymptotically towards the new value of the input rate. This is what would be expected given that *OUT* is a fixed proportion of *LEVEL*.

10.3.2 Third order exponential delays

Following the same principles, delays of higher order are constructed by subjecting the flows to a series of first order delays. The number of first order delays in this cascade gives the order of the delay. Figure 10.9 shows a third order exponential delay whose equations are as follows:

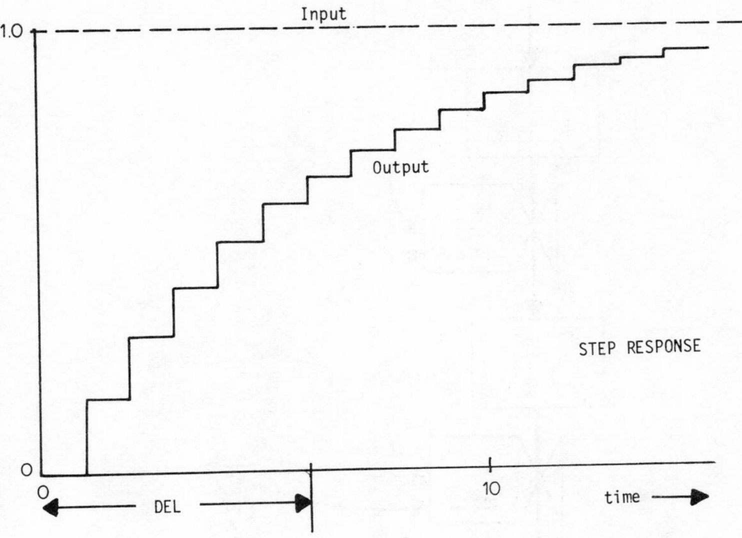

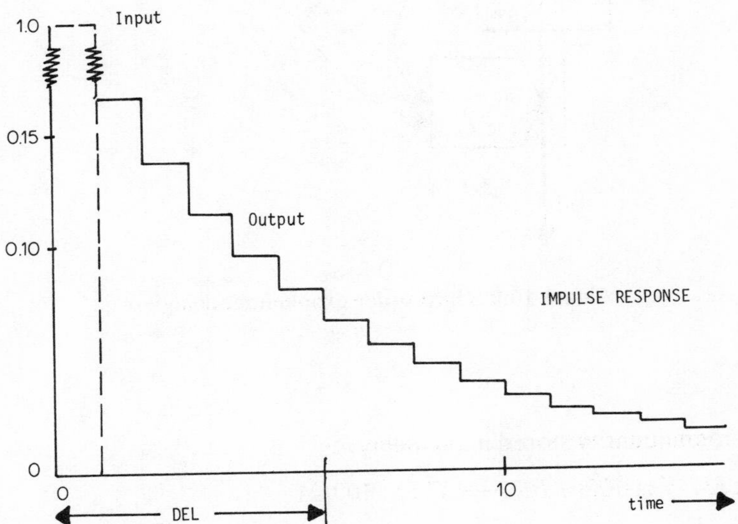

Figure 10.8 Step and impulse responses: first order exponential delay

$$LA.K = LA.J + (DT)(IN.JK - RA.JK) \quad 10.3,L$$
$$LB.K = LB.J + (DT)(RA.JK - RB.JK) \quad 10.4,L$$
$$LC.K = LC.J + (DT)(RB.JK - RC.JK) \quad 10.5,L$$
$$RA.KL = LA.K/(DEL/3) \quad 10.6,R$$
$$RB.KL = LB.K/(DEL/3) \quad 10.7,R$$
$$RC.KL = LC.K/(DEL/3) \quad 10.8,R$$

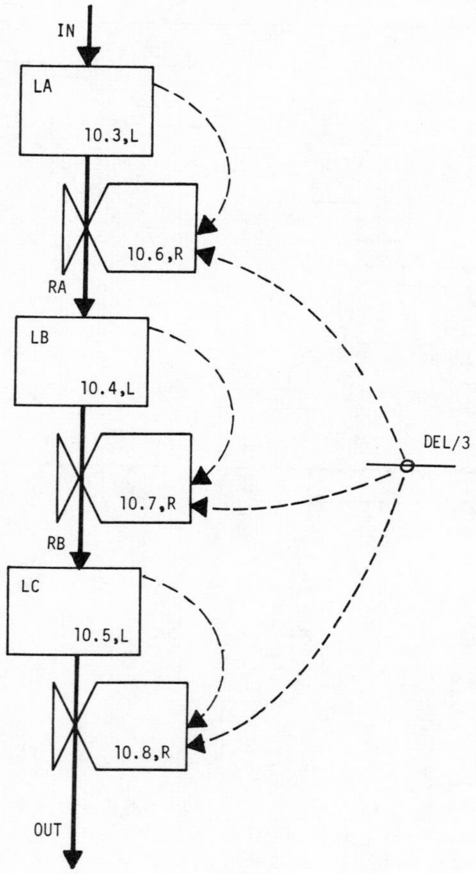

Figure 10.9 Third order exponential delay

And the total quantity stored in the delay is

$$LEVEL.K = LA.K + LB.K + LC.K \quad 10.9,A$$

Note that the total delay is divided equally between each step of the series. Figure 10.10 shows the step and impulse responses from this delay; the step produces an 'S' shaped curve. The same initial conditions apply as for the first order delay. The step produces a gradual climb including an inflexion point.

Forrester argues that third order exponential delays are good models of the delays experienced when goods are shipped in a quasi-continuous fashion. Increases in the shipping rate are followed by third order dynamic behaviour in the receipt rate.

10.3.3 Pipeline delays

These occur when an increase in an input is exactly reflected in an increase in the output rate but at a later time. If such delays exist, they can be modelled via what corresponds to an infinite order exponential delay. In effect, the 'S' shaped step response is replaced by a gap followed by a vertical climb to the new value. Impulse and step responses are shown in Figure 10.11.

10.3.4 Incorporating delays into models

Rather than writing out a tedious sequence of level and rate equations, DYNAMO and its imitators provide standard functions in their libraries. In DYNAMO format, a third order exponential delay is expressed as

$$LEVEL.K = LEVEL.J + (DT)(IN.JK - OUT.JK) \qquad 10.10,L$$

$$OUT.KL = DELAY3(IN.JK,DEL) \qquad 10.11,R$$

Obviously a function is necessary for a pipeline delay.

An important part of system dynamics modelling is the selection of appropriate delays. The aim is to produce delays of the same type as observed in the system being modelled. Coyle (1977) describes a method due to Holmes (1970) for accurately estimating the appropriate order of a delay. Its application requires estimates of the mean and variance of the distribution of the delay times. Both Coyle (1977) and Forrester (1961) suggest that it is rarely crucial to be precisely correct in modelling the order of a delay. This is particularly true of simulations in which the interest surrounds the pattern of fluctuating behaviour rather than an attempt to make accurate estimates. For most purposes, first, third or infinite order delays will suffice.

10.4 INFORMATION SMOOTHING

Recognizing when significant change has occurred is a significant problem when controlling any dynamic system. For example, a company selling biscuits will have a daily sales rate that varies considerably. The management must decide whether any of these fluctuations mark the start of a significant change in the pattern of demand. If sales have significantly increased, then production will have to be increased if they wish to satisfy their customers. The management do not wish to make gross responses to what turns out to be day to day variation, they only wish to respond to significant and continuing changes.

As a way of handling this problem, attempts are usually made to forecast the value of the variable in question. Operations are then planned on the basis of that forecast. The management are not so naïve as to assume that the forecast will be absolutely correct, but it should give some indication for future behaviour. Many of the statistical methods used for such forecasting are based on the concept of information smoothing.

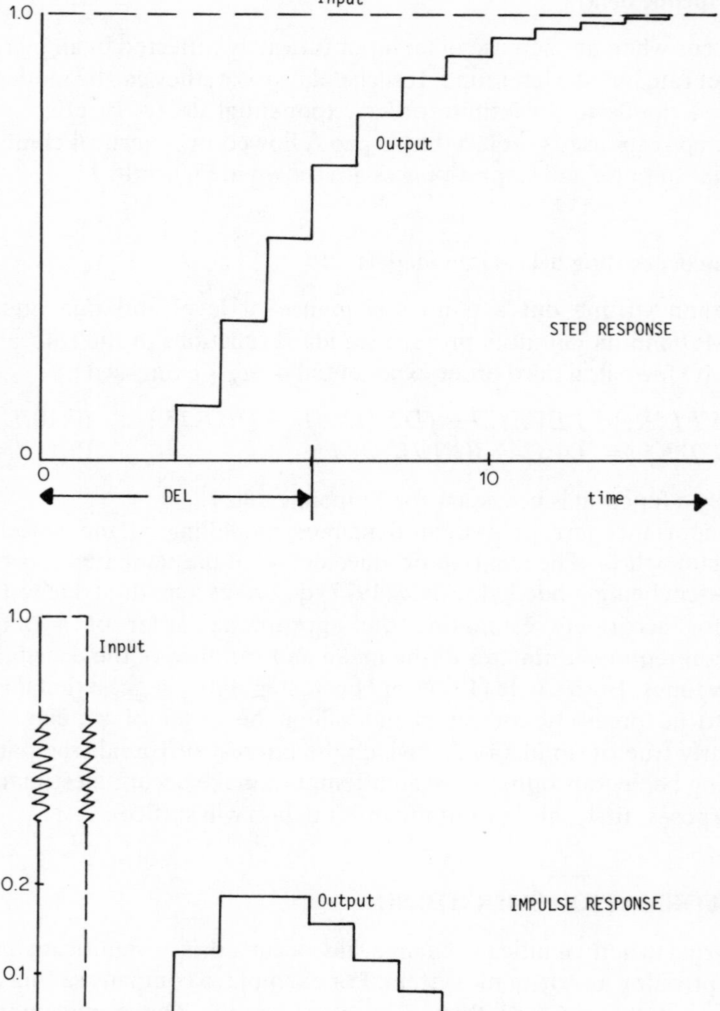

Figure 10.10 Step and impulse responses: third order exponential delay

Consider a variable Y whose value y_i is measured at regular intervals. The problem is to forecast the next value y_i. Smoothing methods do this by using the past behaviour of the time series and averaging the changes.

The simplest approach is to put

$$\hat{y}_i = y_{i-1},$$

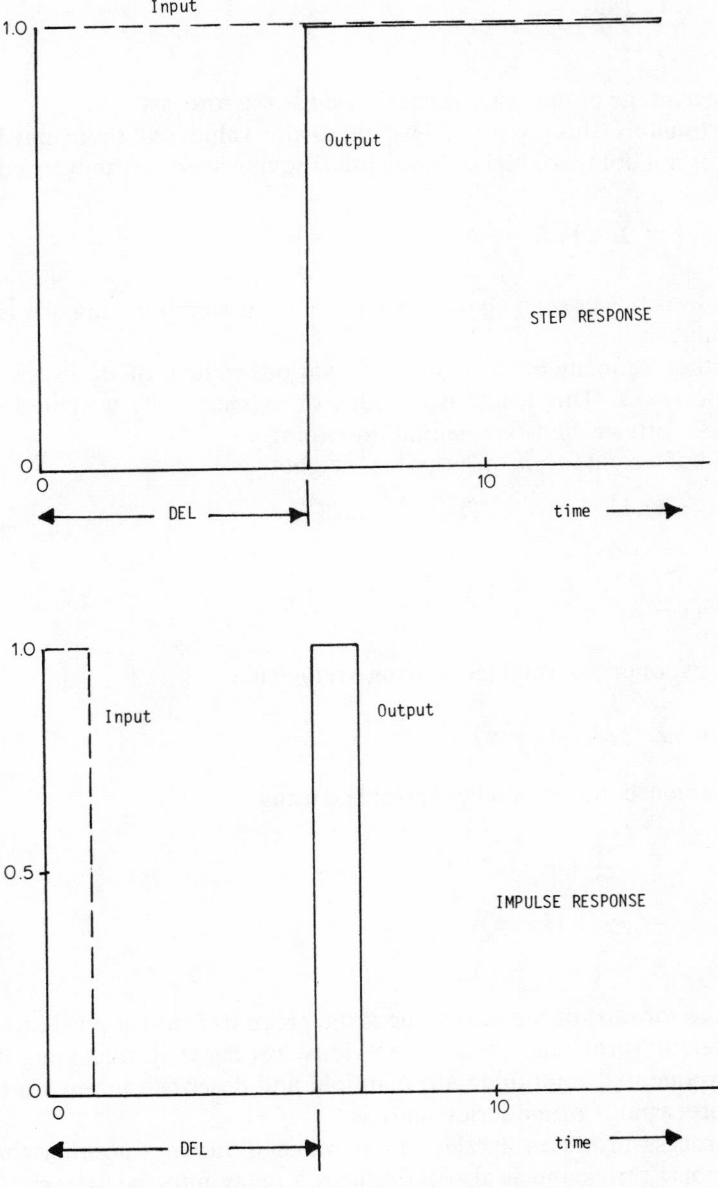

Figure 10.11 Step and impulse responses: pipeline delay

where $\hat{y}_i$ is the forecast of the value of y_i (not yet known). That is, use the last known value as the forecast of the next value. This crude method works surprisingly well sometimes. Unfortunately all the noise (i.e. short run random variation) is transmitted to the forecast. To avoid this, moving averages can be employed:

$$\hat{Y}_i = \frac{1}{n} \sum_{k=1}^{n} Y_{i-k}.$$

Thus the average of the last n values is used as the forecast.

Unfortunately, this gives equal weight to all n values and there may be good reason for not doing so. Hence a weighted moving average can be used:

$$\hat{Y}_i = \frac{1}{n} \sum_{k=1}^{n} a_k Y_{i-k} \quad \text{and} \quad \sum_{k=1}^{n} a_k = 1.$$

Hence if a_1 is bigger than all other values of a_k, then more emphasis is put on recent values.

A further refinement is to link the various values of a_k in an infinite geometric series. This leads to the idea of exponentially weighted moving averages — often called exponential smoothing.

Instead of weights $a_1, a_2, \ldots$, this has weights

$$1, (1 - \alpha), (1 - \alpha)^2, \ldots, (1 - \alpha)^n, \ldots,$$

where

$$\sum_{k=0}^{\infty} (1 - \alpha)^k = 1/\alpha$$

Thus the exponential weighted moving average is

$$\hat{y}_i = \alpha \sum_{k=0}^{\infty} y_{i-1-k}(1 - \alpha)^k.$$

For convenience, this is usually rearranged using

$$\begin{aligned} \hat{y}_{i+1} &= \sum_{k=0}^{\infty} y_{i-k}(1 - \alpha)^k \\ \therefore\ \hat{y}_{i+1} &= \alpha y_i + (1 - \alpha)\hat{y}_i \\ \therefore\ \hat{y}_{i+1} &= \hat{y}_i + \alpha(y_i - \hat{y}_i). \end{aligned}$$

That is, the forecast of the next value is the previous forecast plus α times the forecast error (previous actual $-$ previous forecast). Refinements on this simple exponential smoothing are manifold and described in any up-to-date text on forecasting or time series analysis.

This process produces a sales graph which is rather smoother than the original noisy series and it also introduces a delay into the system, for the smoothed series must always lag behind the noisy series.

In system dynamics terms, this exponential smoothing process can be expressed as in the following equations.

$$Y.K = Y.J + (DT)(A)(S.JK - Y.J)$$

where Y is some smoothed value of S
and A is the smoothing constant.

This can easily be incorporated into a system dynamics model. More complex forms of smoothing are treated similarly.

10.4.1 Material delays

Delays to information and materials were assumed to have identical forms in Section 10.2. However, if the delay constant becomes a variable, then information and material delays need to be distinguished.

For a first order material delay

$$LEVEL.K = LEVEL.J + (DT)(IN.JK - OUT.JK)$$
$$OUT.KL = LEVEL.K/DEL.K$$

where $DEL.K$ is now a variable.

Thus because no material must be lost in the delay (the principle of conservation), as DEL increases

$OUT.KL$ decreases
and $LEVEL.K$ ultimately increases.

Assuming, that is, that the delay was previously at some steady state in which

$IN.JK = OUT.JK$
and $LEVEL.K = OUT.KL*DEL.K$.

10.4.2 Information delay

Information on the other hand behaves rather differently. A value transmitted as information does not change merely because it is delayed. Consider again the exponential smoothing equation

$$Y.K = Y.J + (DT)(A)(S.JK - Y.J)$$

At the steady state, $S.JK = Y.J$
thus, $Y.K = Y.J$.

Hence the value of A, which is equivalent to $1/DEL$, can be varied with no effect on the smoothed outputs at the steady state.

Information delays ought then to be modelled in this way if there is a risk that the delay will be variable.

10.5 CHOOSING A SUITABLE VALUE FOR *DT*

The J, K and L notation of DYNAMO forces the simulation model to consist of a series of first order difference equations. Forrester (1968) refers to these as integral equations. They are integrated numerically in DYNAMO by the Euler–Cauchy method. This is a simple first order method which is well known to be error prone and is, at best, only approximate. To avoid some of the possible problems it is important to choose the value of DT with some care. As an example, consider the following pair of DYNAMO equations.

$$L.K = L.J + (DT)(I.JK - O.JK) \quad (1)$$

$$O.KL = L.K/A \quad (2)$$

In system dynamics terms, this constitutes a simple first order exponential delay, where $L.K$ is the level at time K, $I.JK$ and $O.JK$ are the input and output rates over the interval J to K. The same function could easily be expressed as the following differential equation.

$$L' = I - L/A, \quad (3)$$

for which the Euler–Cauchy integration formula is

$$L(n+1) = L(n) + DT.(I(n) - L(n)/A), \quad (4)$$

where DT is the step size
and $F(n)$ is the value of variable F at integration step n.

Equation (4) is clearly equivalent to the DYNAMO pair of equations (1) and (2).

As Forrester (1961) suggests, it is instructive to consider the effect of the size of DT on the evaluation of such a delay. This will illustrate the limitation of the Euler–Cauchy integration method. As an example, consider a first order exponential delay with

$A = 4$,
both L and I set initially to 0
and 0 rising to a value of 10 at time 0 and remaining there.

It is clear that small values DT produce more accurate results. As DT exceeds 2, then the errors increase markedly. When DT reaches 8, then the solution is unstable and, for the longer values of DT, the errors increase in amplitude. For this reason, Forrester (1961) recommends that the value of DT should not exceed $DEL/(2d)$, where d is the order of the highest order delay in the model and DEL is the total length of that delay. If there are several such delays, choose the delay with the shortest total length.

In general, the Euler–Cauchy integration method needs care in use because it is highly sensitive to the size of the integration step and it tends to propagate errors. Hence, system dynamics modellers who observe strange behaviour in a model whose equations are sensible would do well to test the effect of smaller values for DT.

10.6 COMPUTER PACKAGES

The most widely known package for system dynamics is DYNAMO developed by Pugh (1973) at M.I.T. This was the first such package, Pugh being a colleague of Forrester. Consequently, the nomenclature of DYNAMO has stuck with system dynamics ever since. DYNAMO is usually available for I.B.M. computers. It compiles into machine code.

DYSMAP was developed by Ratnatunga (1980) at the System Dynamics Research Group of the University of Bradford, England. Its features are described extensively by Coyle (1977) who argues that it is simpler to use than DYNAMO and also has extensions which make it preferable. DYSMAP requires a FORTRAN compiler.

A recent development is MICRO-DYN B, developed by Parker and Croston (1982) at the University of Lancaster, England. This is a package for Apple microcomputers. It employs DYNAMO format (as does DYSMAP) and produces very similar output. MICRO-DYN B requires a 48K Apple II with Applesoft, a printer and at least one disk drive.

As always, the possibility of writing in FORTRAN, APL, BASIC or similar languages remains. The pros and cons of these as simulation languages have been rehearsed in Chapter 5. It is not at all difficult to use them to produce system dynamics models. The difficulty comes, according to Coyle (1977) when the programs need to be enhanced. FORTRAN etc. require the equations to be in the correct sequence for computation and this causes problems if equations are added or deleted. Such changes are desirable if the analyst is following the 'Principle of Parsimony' described in Section 3.3. The translators of the special purpose system dynamics packages can sort the equations into the correct sequence — provided they are correctly labelled. To counter this point, interactive computer systems usually have sophisticated editors. These make the addition, deletion and shifting of equations a trivial matter.

A further point to bear in mind is the type of output required. In a system dynamics simulation, the aim is usually to study the transient behaviour of the system. This is best displayed graphically, and DYNAMO etc. make this an easy task; with FORTRAN etc. this is more difficult. Considering this interest in transient behaviour, it is perhaps surprising that at the time of writing (mid-1983) there are no packages available that allow convenient and direct interaction with a system dynamics model as it runs. Ellison and Tunnicliffe–Wilson (1982) describe the value of this approach to discrete simulation and show how easy it is to implement on microcomputers. This is an obvious development which could enhance system dynamics as an approach to simulation.

EXERCISES

1. Draw a causal loop diagram of the following system.
A biscuit company sells its biscuits to retailers, most of whom demand a price discount. The bigger the discount, the more biscuits the retailers will buy. At the same time, a large discount produces lower (or negative) profits for the manufacturer. Low discounts result in low sales and sometimes to no sales. Low sales result in low market share which makes the retailers reluctant to stock the company's biscuits. This leads the retailers to demand yet larger discounts if they are to stock the company's biscuits.

High sales lead to reduced unit costs in production and distribution and thus to higher profits.

2. Investigate the effect of different values of *DT* on the behaviour of a third order exponential delay.

3. Use DYNAMO format equations to rewrite the models of the simple production/distribution systems of Section 2.3.1.

4. Consider the types of delay which might be appropriate in the following:

(a) the rate at which children reach school age, assuming negligible mortality after they are one year old;
(b) the rate at which ordinary mail reaches its destination;
(c) a production rate which aims to deplete work in progress stocks by a fixed proportion each week.

5. Rewrite the models of Section 2.3.1 as a set of differential equations.

6. Use an analogue package such as CSMP to simulate the equation set of question (5) above.

REFERENCES

Coyle, R. G. (1977) *Management System Dynamics*. Wiley-Interscience, London.
Ellison, D., & Tunnicliffe–Wilson, J. (1982) Interactive simulation on a microcomputer. *Simulation*, May 1982.
Forrester, J. W. (1961) *Industrial Dynamics*. M.I.T. Press, Cambridge, Mass.
Forrester, J. W. (1968) *Principles of Systems*. Wright–Allen, Cambridge, Mass.
Goodman, M. R. (1974) *Study Notes in System Dynamics*. Wright–Allen, Cambridge, Mass.
Holmes, D. S. (1970) *A Probabilistic Interpretation of the Delays of Industrial Dynamics*. Union College, Schenectady, New York.
Parker, B. J., & Croston, K. C. (1982) *Micro-dyn B Users Manual*. Lancord Ltd, University of Lancaster.
Pugh, A. L. (1973) *Dynamo Users Manual*. M.I.T. Press, Cambridge, Mass.
Ratnatunga, A. (1980) *Dysmap Users Manual*. University of Bradford.
SLAM (1972) *A Simulation Language for Analogue Modelling*. ICL, UK.

Chapter 11

System dynamics in practice

Note: The companies involved in these studies are given pseudonyms so as to protect their competitive positions. As well as changing their names, it has been necessary to disguise their products so as to make identification even more difficult. Both belong to multi-national organizations with turnovers in excess of \$500 000 000 per annum. All the divisions involved in these studies are located in the UK.

11.1 ASSOCIATED SPARES LTD.

Associated Spares Ltd. (ASL) makes and sells parts for domestic appliances and the motor trade. They supply original equipment and spares.

11.1.1 The problem as originally posed

In 1977, the general manager of the UK distribution division of ASL put it something like this:

'The economy seems to fluctuate by about 5% over a 5 year cycle. What I don't understand is why the demand at the central warehouse fluctuates much more than this. Mind you, we have so many products at different stages of their life cycles that I can't prove that this really happens. But I'm fairly certain that it does and it creates enormous problems for my business. Is there any way in which you can help?'

As is so often the case, the initial brief was rather vague and some effort had to be put into problem structuring. After visiting a number of retail outlets and after extensive discussions it looked as though a system dynamics approach could be of some use. In particular, it could be used to identify the effect of the various decision rules used in the distribution division of ASL. It could also show the effect of changes in the market.

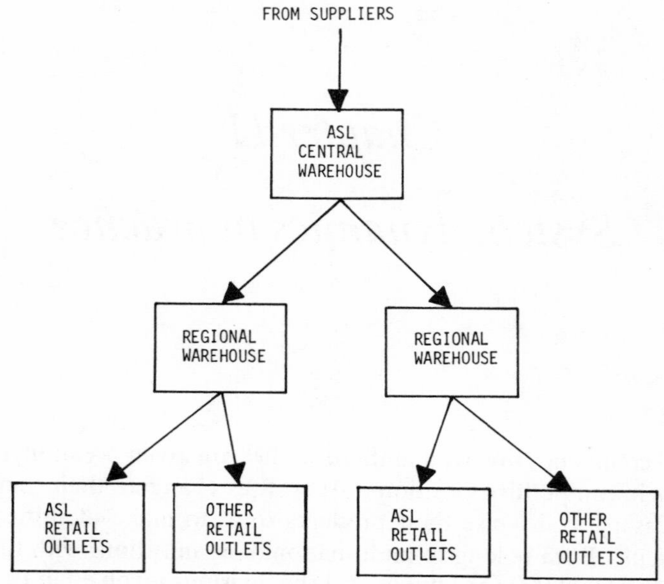

Figure 11.1 The ASL distribution system

11.1.2 The multi-echelon system

Investigation revealed that a multi-echelon distribution system existed. Figure 11.1 shows how it operated. The parts were made in a number of plants throughout the UK and were held in a central warehouse. The UK had been divided into discrete geographical areas each of which had its own regional warehouse. These received supplies from the central warehouse. Beneath the regional warehouses in the hierarchy were a large number of retail outlets, some of which were owned by ASL. Normally, the retail outlets ordered supplies from the nearest regional warehouse. In exceptional circumstances, urgent orders were despatched direct to the retail outlets from the central warehouse. ASL provided stock control advice for the retail outlets.

Thus there were large aggregate flows of material and information in a system which included many feedback loops. Management put a great deal of effort into controlling the operation and hence there were a great many decision rules. A further complication was the existence of delays due to forecasting, despatch lead times, batching of orders, etc. Previous knowledge of similar systems suggested that fluctuations of the type suggested by the general manager were indeed possible. Hence system dynamics models were constructed with the aim of studying these dynamic responses.

Four models were eventually built. Three of these were separate models for the retail branches, the regional warehouses and the central warehouse. The fourth model was a combination of the earlier three.

11.1.3 The retail branch model

Construction of this model began with a very simple view of the system as shown in Figure 11.2. Later this was enhanced so as to include the real-life complications, that is the analyst was consciously following the 'principle of parsimony'. Starting with this simple model, it was possible to introduce the client to the ideas of system dynamics and thus to gain his confidence. Via the influence diagrams, the analyst and client were able to discuss the obvious shortcomings of the simple model and successive improvements were made.

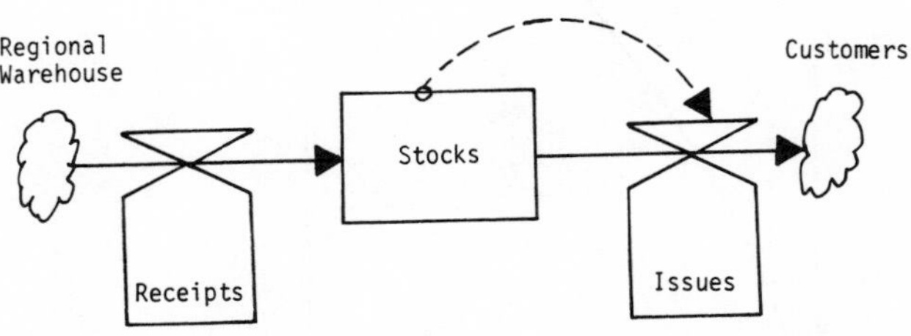

Figure 11.2 Simple retail branch model

All that the simple model of Figure 11.2 shows was that stock was created by the difference between receipts and issues in each branch. Obviously these processes of receipts and issues needed to be modelled. Figure 11.3 shows the first stage in this modelling. Receipts result from the orders placed on the regional warehouse followed by a substantial delay. Issues (sales) stem from customers' demands.

However, there was also the problem of the mix of products in stock to be considered. Figure 11.4 shows the relationship which was found to exist

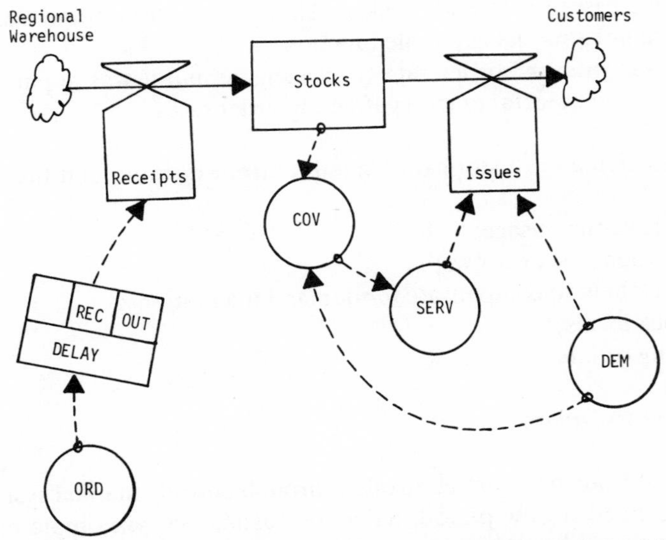

Figure 11.3 First revision to the simple retail branch model

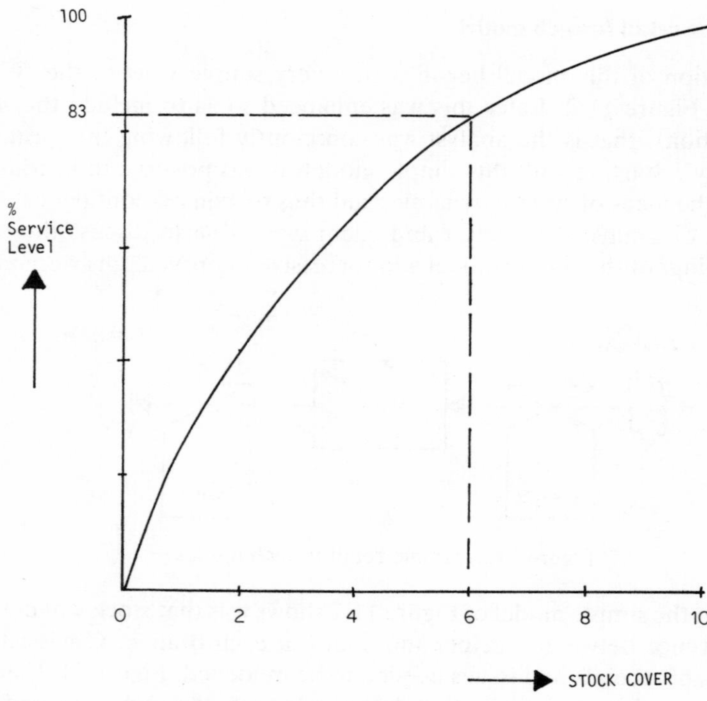

Figure 11.4 Stock cover

between stock cover and service levels. Stock cover was defined as the total weeks of stock divided by average weekly demand. Thus a stock equivalent to 6 weeks demand meant that 83% of customers could be satisfied from stock. The link between issue rate and stock levels was established and built into the system dynamics model as a table function.

There was then the order rate to investigate and it was apparent that the following were important factors affecting order rates.

Forecast demand (historical demand, current demand and the forecasting system);
expected lead-time usage;
usage between stock reviews;
buffer stock held to compensate for demand fluctuations;
actual stock levels;
outstanding orders;
lead times;
supplementary orders.

The retail branches were controlled through entirely manual systems which involved a fixed review period. Sales forecasting was via simple exponential smoothing. The smoothing process had the effect of damping out sharp fluctuations (which is good). But it also introduced a delay between changes in demand and their reflection in sales forecasts (which is bad).

The manual stock control system used the sales forecast, modified to allow for delivery lead times, safety stocks and the stock review period. This leads to a target stock level which was computed manually at intervals determined by the review periods. Expensive and fast moving items were reviewed more often than the rest. Thus for some products, this introduced a delay of several weeks before changes in sales led to revised target stock levels. The difference between free and target stocks leads to an order placed on the regional warehouse. The supplies however, were only received after a lead time delay of several weeks. In the retail branch model this lead time delay was held constant, using the average delay experienced. Figure 11.5 shows the final model of the retail branches.

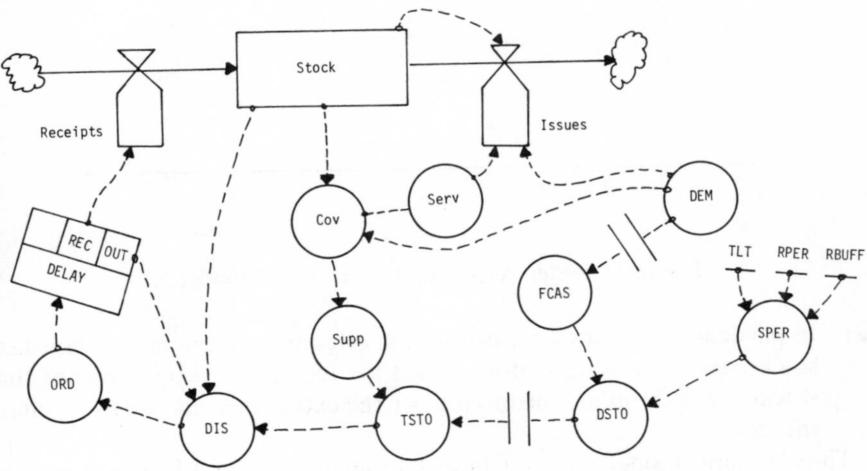

Figure 11.5 Final retail branch model

Figure 11.6 shows the effect of subjecting this retail branch model to a step increase of 5% on a previously steady demand rate. The immediate effect is a considerable decrease in stock levels caused by the sluggish response of the stock control system. The forecast of demand rises steadily until it reaches the new steady state after about 6 months. The orders placed on the regional warehouse display highly erratic behaviour. The order rate initially lags behind the sales rate and then overshoots after about 3 months. Eventually it falls to a new steady state level. Notice that for a period of about 4 months, the 5% increase in sales leads to an amplified response in the order rate to the regional warehouse.

Why should this happen? A number of reasons are apparent.

(1) The various delays lead to an immediate fall in stock levels. This in turn leads to higher orders being placed on the regional warehouse.

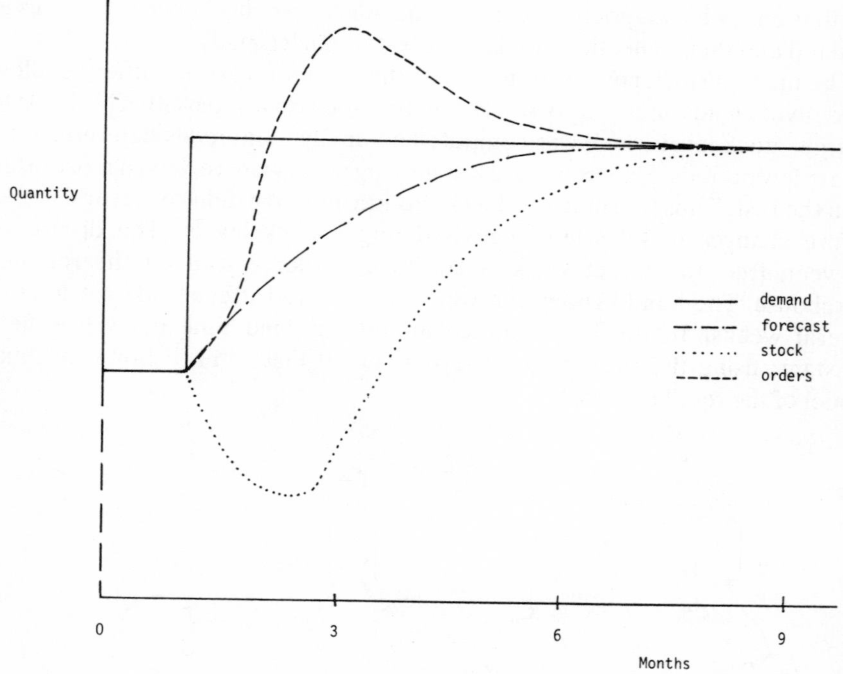

Figure 11.6 Step response of retail branch model

(2) In particular, the stock control system attempted to maintain a constant stock cover of n weeks' stock. Thus the increased demand means that stocks are built up, not just to replace the extra sales but also to maintain the stock.

Thus, a simple model of a retail branch brought considerable insight into the effect of demand fluctuations. The delays and the stock cover ratio led to amplification and the system took about 6 months to settle down. And this after only a 5% change in sales rates.

11.1.4 The regional warehouse model

At the regional warehouses, the systems were rather different from those in the regional branches. The stock control was achieved via a computer system which aimed to keep stocks between maximum and minimum levels. Thus the levels were continually monitored and replenishments were ordered as soon as the minimum level was reached. Back orders were also possible because unsatisfied orders from retail branches were held on a backlog file until supplies were received. The forecasting was based on a weighted moving average rather than exponential smoothing. Hence though the overall structure of the branch and regional models were similar, the details were completely different.

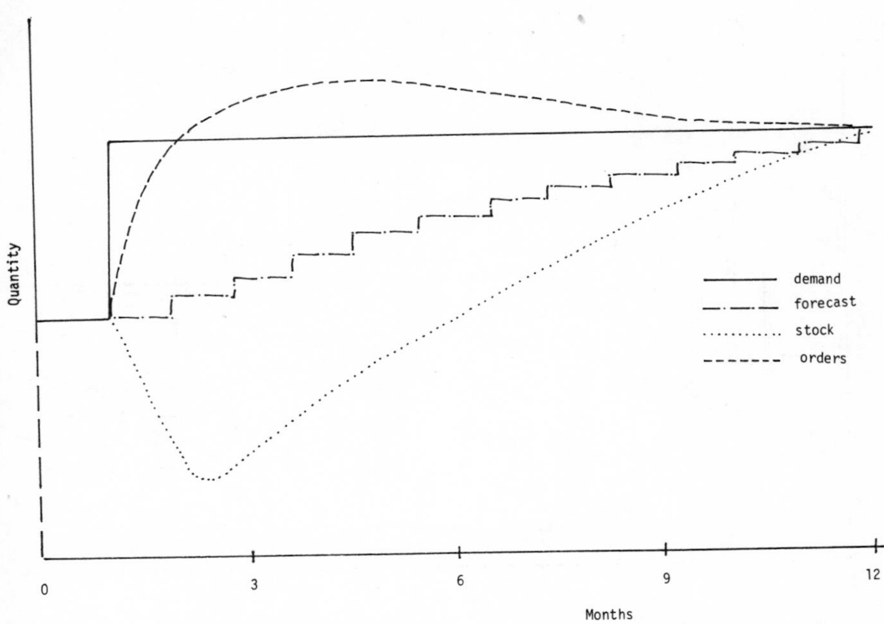

Figure 11.7 Step response of regional warehouse model

Figure 11.7 shows the output from the model when previously steady demand is increased by 5%. As at the branch level, stocks initially fall and the order rate overshoots the increased demand rate but the different forecasting system leads to stepped increases in forecasts. Overall, the regional warehouse responds in a way which is qualitatively similar to the retail branch. However, the system takes over 12 months to settle down. The retail branch took about 6 months to settle down.

11.1.5 The central warehouse model

The management systems at the central warehouse were computer controlled, though more sophisticated than in the regional. Orders from the regions were entered via data input terminals and interacted with the stock control systems to produce invoices, despatch notes and other paperwork. The demand forecasting used a double exponential smoothing system, allowed for seasonality in demand, identified outliers, etc. A full-scale production control and planning system placed orders on the factories as and when necessary. Overall, the systems were different from those employed at both branch and regional levels. Hence, the detail of the model differed from that of the earlier two.

Figure 11.8 shows the effect of increasing demand by 5% on the central warehouse after a previously constant demand. The demand forecast slowly rises to meet the new demand rate and it takes over 12 months to do this

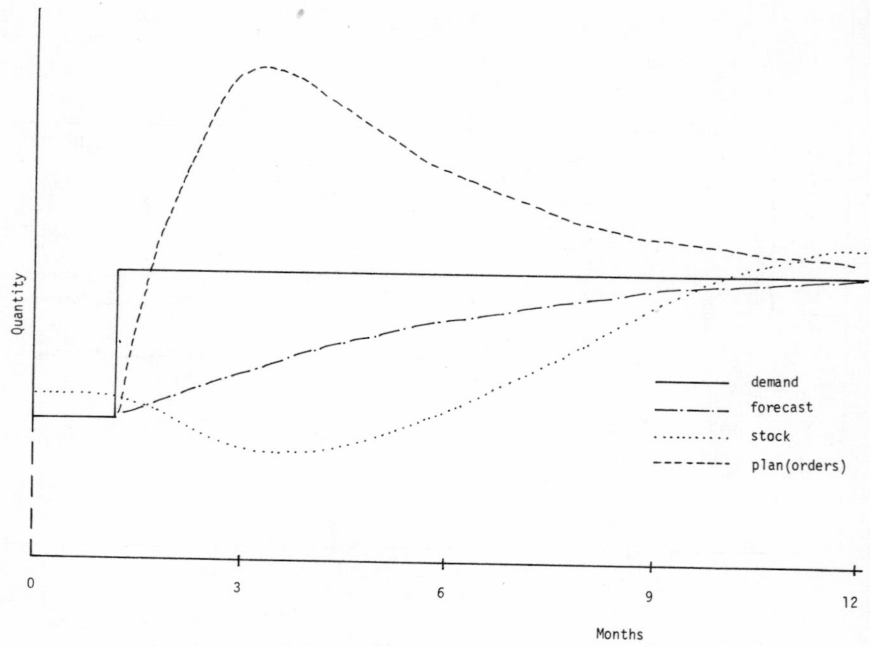

Figure 11.8 Step response of central warehouse model

because of the small constants used in the double exponential forecasting system. This forecasting system has been introduced to dampen out the effect of certain large customers placing orders only a few times each year. The rate at which orders were placed on the factories overshoots by a large amount. The stock levels have still not settled down after 12 months of simulated time. The general manager's suspicions were beginning to look correct.

11.1.6 The total system model

It was also important to model the interactions of these three systems. Though the retail branches may experience a 5% step change in sales, their demand on the next level of the system will be amplified and delayed. As well as this amplification, the phasing of the new rates may differ somewhat. Hence the already unsatisfactory state of affairs may look much worse after aggregating the three models. Figure 11.9 shows an outline influence diagram of this aggregrate model. To make the model more realistic, the lead times experienced by the retail branches were no longer assumed constant. Increased demand on the regional warehouse from several retail branches would lead to a lengthening of the lead times. Similarly service levels would change.

Figure 11.10 shows the result of subjecting the total system model to a step increase of 5% in sales at the retail branches. As might be expected from the three separate models, a familiar pattern emerges. The increase in customer sales leads to overshoot in the demands placed by the retail branches on the

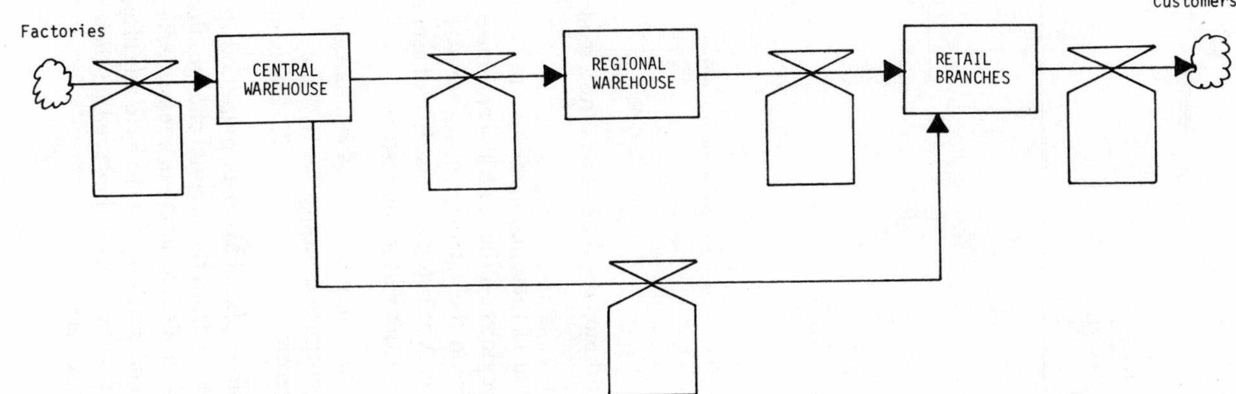

Figure 11.9 Outline of total ASL model

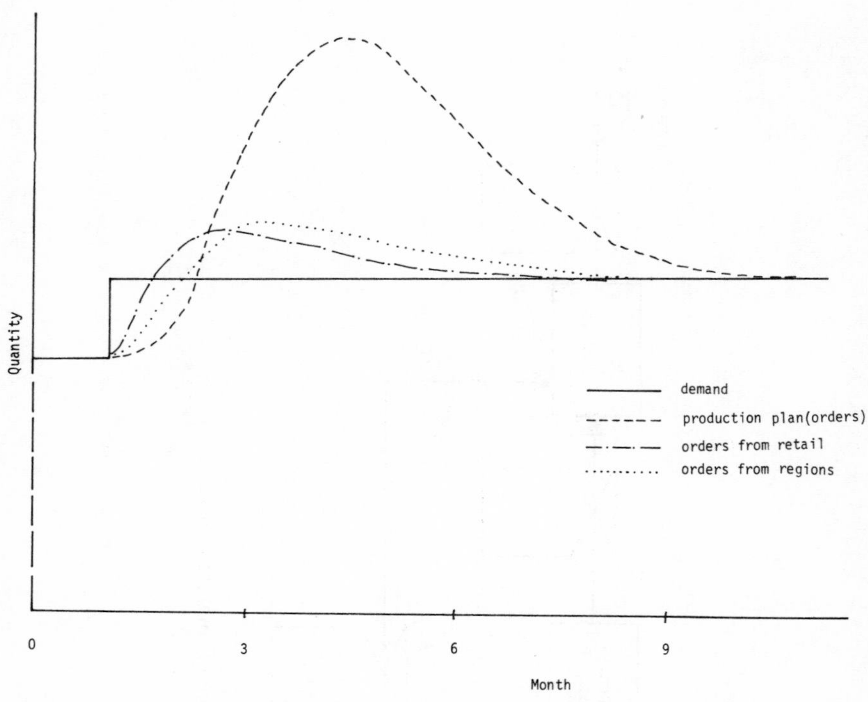

Figure 11.10 Step response of total ASL model

regional warehouses. In turn, these increases lead to greater overshoot in the orders placed from the regions on the central warehouse. Finally, the central warehouse places orders on the factories at a rate way above the 5% step increase in customer sales. A 5% step increase in end user demand leads to the following maximum order rates within the system.

Retail branch to regional warehouse	+8% maximum.
Regional warehouse to central warehouse	+10% maximum.
Central warehouse to factories	+23% maximum.

Thus changes in the market place have been amplified up to four times within the system. The further away from the original change, the greater the degree of amplification. The various delays make such massive fluctuations inevitable because corrective action takes a long time to have any effect. There is also the risk that management may over-react if they see that their attempts to control things bring no immediate effect.

11.1.7 Some conclusions

The intuition of the general manager was clearly correct and he needed no persuasion of this for two reasons. Firstly, most people love to be correct.

Secondly, the stage by stage modelling had allowed him to keep continual contact with the progress of the study.

How could the operation of the system be improved? Many of the problems were caused by the interaction of the different systems found in the three levels of the hierarchy. Each of these systems made sense at its own level; put together, the effect was unfortunate. The first point is that the managers of the three levels were able to learn how their different policies interacted. It was clearly impossible to optimize the behaviour of the entire system; however, each manager could now be made aware of the difficulties faced by others elsewhere in the system.

Give that the project was commissioned by the manager responsible for the central warehouse it is fair to ask what benefits he received. As mentioned earlier, his intuition was proved correct. Also, the models clearly showed the effects of the delays within the system and identified the important interactions. In this sense, the 6 months of part time work which went into the project could be viewed as problem structuring. The manager and the analyst were now aware of the weak points of the system and could now examine ways of improving its performance.

From the initial study, a further 18 months of part time work was commissioned. Detailed investigations of various possible improvements were carried out. These were as follows:

(1) operate without regional warehouses;
(2) cut down information delays so that central warehouse could monitor end-user demand rather than simply using demand data from the regional warehouses;
(3) modify the forecasting systems;
(4) operate a stock control system not based on stock cover ratios;
(5) change the parameters of the existing stock control systems.

Implementation of some of these followed.

11.1.8 A postscript

ASL hit a cash flow crisis shortly after the final meeting of this project and traditional remedies emerged from the directors' desks. One suggestion was that a 5% cut in stocks across the board would free the required cash. Thus a golden opportunity arose to use an existing model to see what would actually happen.

What the simulations showed was that a 5% cut in target stock levels implemented simultaneously at all three levels would result in the following changes in actual stocks.

a 6.7% drop at the central warehouse;
a 10.7% drop at the regional warehouses;
a 7.9% drop at the retail branches.

It would take the retail branches 4 months to reach this level whereas the central warehouse would take 6 months. For a substantial part of this 6 months, stocks would be rising at the central warehouse due to de-stocking lower in the system. This de-stocking would occur faster than schedules on suppliers could be cut.

Hence the directors were able to see that their notion of a 5% cut across the board would produce rather worse effects than anticipated. If stocks were to be rebuilt later, corresponding problems would arise. The 5% cut was not implemented.

11.2 DYNASTAT LTD.

11.2.1 An expansion programme

Dynastat make a range of electromechanical controllers for oil-fired heating systems. These devices use sophisticated electronics and are fitted to heating units for which Dynastat holds worldwide patents. Because of these controllers, the heaters use up to 15% less oil than competitive products. The rise in oil prices which occurred in the mid 1970s resulted in great increases in demand. At first this increase was managed by using sub-contractors to produce some units. But it became clear that Dynastat was stretched to its limits and large scale investment was necessary.

The board agreed an investment programme costing about $70 000 000 with the aim of doubling the output of the Dynastat factories. Whilst planning the programme it became obvious that a key problem would be the need for more skilled manpower. A particular difficulty was the Rockingham plant near London. In the past it had been difficult to recruit enough skilled workers, and it seemed as if this could be a severe brake on the expansion program.

11.2.2 The manpower problem

An analyst from the internal consulting group was asked to advise on this problem. At the first meeting, the personnel manager of the Rockingham plant said that he was convinced that the programme was impossible. His experience suggested that the skilled manpower targets were out of reach. As the meeting continued, it became clear that he had thoroughly analysed the recruitment potential — however, labour turnover seemed to have been forgotten. After a quick analysis of available figures, it became clear that the labour turnover for skilled workers was about 25% per annum, labour turnover being defined as the number leaving in a year divided by the average number of employees during the year. Later checks showed that 25% was typical for this type of industry.

In system dynamics terms, manpower can be regarded as a level fed by recruitment and depleted by labour turnover. Hence the simple model shown in Figure 11.11 was constructed. By using it, the recruitment rate to fill a

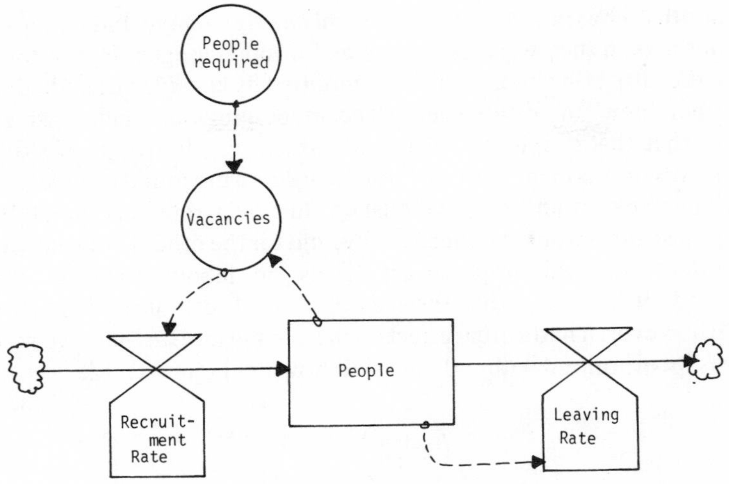

Figure 11.11 First simple Dynastat model

specified number of jobs can be calculated. Remarkable as it may seem, Dynastat had previously been unable to relate labour turnover and recruitment to the expansion program. But before this simple model could be used, appropriate functions for turnover and recruitment were required.

11.2.3 Recruitment

One fear was that the current high level of economic activity would make it even more difficult to recruit enough skilled workers. Analysis of available data showed that the numbers of skilled workers recruited in the past was positively correlated with the health of the economy. The apparently good relationship is rather misleading as it might suggest that recruitment is easier when the economy is booming. However, the reality is that more recruitment is necessary when the economy is booming and few recruits are needed when product demand is low. Hence some other way of modelling recruitment was needed.

A further complication is that Dynastat needed to model future recruitment rates and there was no guarantee that their economic cycles would coincide with that of the rest of the nation. Thus, the forecasts of hiring rates were produced by a combination of analysis and management judgement. To ensure consistency, the same forecasts of national economic activity produced for demand forecasting were used when predicting hiring rates and labour turnover. However, the forecasts were modified to allow for expected regional differences.

11.2.4 Turnover

Analysing historical leaving rates produced some interesting results. The leaving rate was very high immediately after joining Dynastat but was very low after 6 months. Thus new recruits were highly likely to leave, but if they survived for 6 months then they were likely to stay for much longer. Hence for further analysis, the 'attrition curve' could be simplified by considering skilled workers to be either 'new' or 'established'. The modelling was made easier by the discovery that this simple model would suffice for all groups of skilled and semi-skilled workers in the factory. 'New' workers were found to have a turnover of 170% per annum and the 'established' turnover rate was about 10% per annum. These rates would not necessarily hold for the other Dynastat factories.

The effect of local employment levels on labour turnover was also investigated. It appeared that the leaving rate of 'established' staff was not affected; however, it had a great effect on the leaving rate for 'new' workers. This effect was incorporated within the model shown in Figure 11.12.

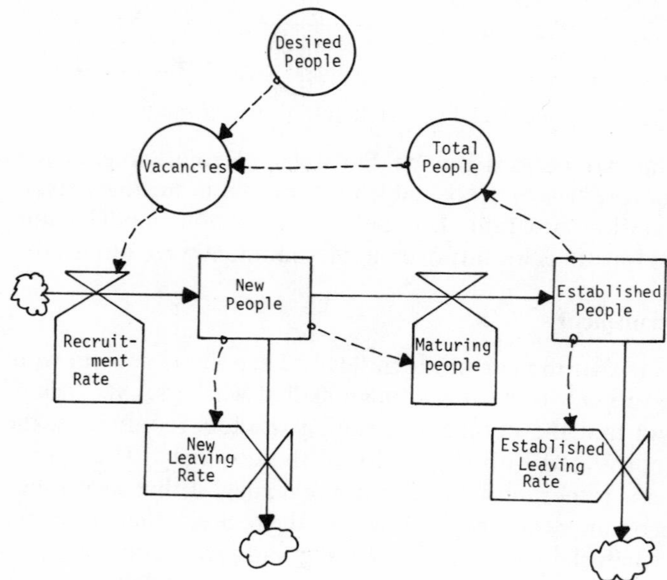

Figure 11.12 More complex Dynastat model

11.2.5 Some effects of this structure

If the model of Figure 11.12 is in a steady state, then the hiring rate must be positive, for the aim is to recruit enough workers to replace those who leave. However, there are delays in the system. As in most organizations, new workers were hired to fill existing vacancies — that is, no hiring action was taken until some workers had left. Hence, steady state is possible only if vacancies exist to drive the recruitment rate. This means that there would always be a shortage of workers in the factory if current policies were followed.

Without even simulating with the model, a further problem is apparent. The overall average turnover was 25% per annum, represented by 170% for 'new' workers and 10% for 'established' workers. Suppose that Dynastat wish to increase the workforce from 4000 to 6000 — a 50% increase. If the different rates are ignored, then the temptation is to recruit enough workers to fill the 25% overall turnover plus the 2000 extra. However, this is clearly wrong. There will be a turnover of 170% amongst the 'new' workers (if the economic conditions were unchanged) and thus the overall turnover will be much higher than 25% because the balance between 'new' and 'established' workers will have changed.

11.2.6 Validating the model

The principles of 'white box' validity (see Chapter 1) having been followed throughout model construction, a 'black box' check was now required. That is, could the model reproduce the past behaviour of the system? As the modelling occurred in 1977, the period 1971 to 1977 was chosen for this validation exercise. The results of initializing the model at January 1971 and running it until 1977 are shown in Figure 11.13. Statistical analysis confirmed that this adequately represented the actual system behaviour. Note, however, that this was not an entirely satisfactory check as the 1971 to 1977 data had been used to parameterize the model. However, some confidence was built up.

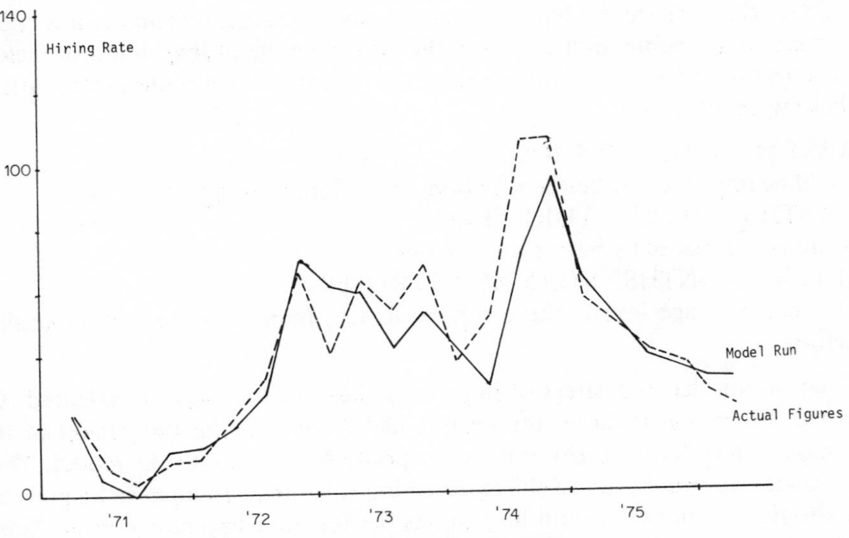

Figure 11.13 Dynastat initializing run

11.2.7 Simulation results

Figure 11.14 shows the results of the first run. It shows an enormous shortfall in available labour. This run assumed that previous policies were followed. The gap was so large that no conceivable increase in the hiring rate would close it. Hence attention was focussed on the leaving rates and it was clear that reducing the 170% leaving rate of 'new' workers was crucial.

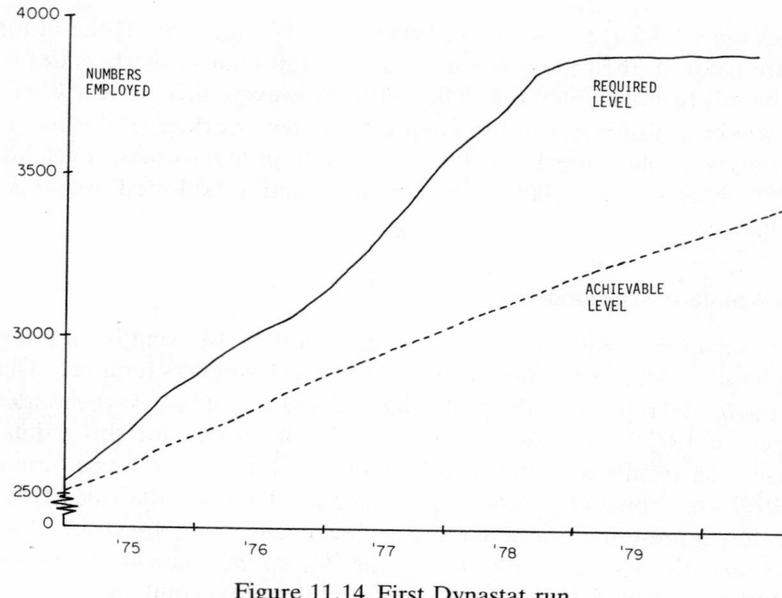

Figure 11.14 First Dynastat run

To do this, the model had to be made more detailed by subdividing 'new' workers. After some discussion and thought, it emerged that different factors caused workers to leave at various stages of their first few months at 'Dynastat'. These were as follows.

FIRST MONTH: 'JOB SHOCK'
Could be improved by better selection, induction, training, etc.
MONTHS 2 to 6: 'CULTURE SHOCK'
Could be improved by better supervision.
AFTER 6 MONTHS: 'NORMAL ATTRITION'
Affected by wage levels, the company image, motivation and other similar factors.

Using the model, the effect of improving these factors was investigated. Of course, for many of these, the analyst had to rely on the judgement of the managers in order to incorporate appropriate functions into the model. Thus the model was used to show the effect of improvements thought to be possible by the managers who would be responsible for their implementation. Some cross-checking of different opinions helped refine the process.

The complete model is shown in outline form in Figure 11.15 and the feedback links are obvious. Many factors were inter-related; for example, a high recruitment rate reduces the training available. This may affect the leaving rate of 'new' employees. A series of runs were used to investigate a range of actions which might reduce labour turnover. Examples were as follows.

Improved job descriptions;
improved selection procedures;

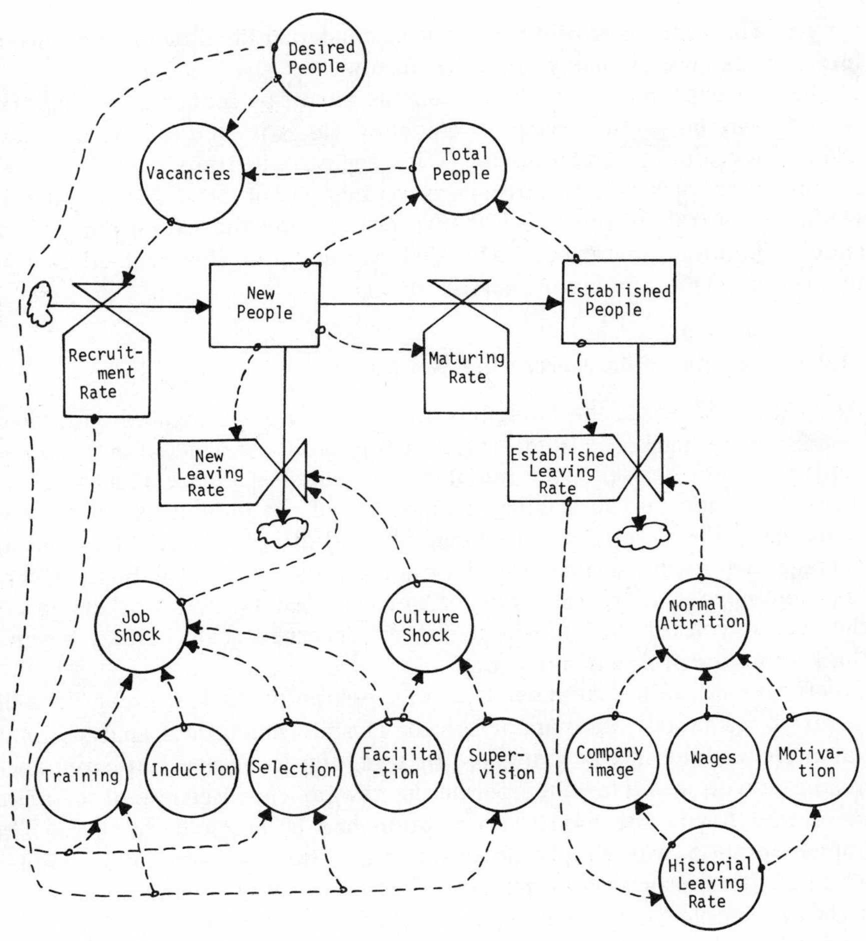

Figure 11.15 Complete Dynastat model

a more professional approach to recruitment;
better training;
closer supervision;
retraining current workers.

As a result of these simulations, albeit based partly on the estimates of the managers, it was clear that the expansion plan was feasible.

11.2.8 Predicting length of service

It seemed likely that some recruits might be classified as 'high risk'. To check this, the records of several hundred past employees were examined for obvious indicators. This showed that a simple system of weighting factors such as age, marital status and previous job history gave a good prediction of length of service. This prediction could easily be calculated at the time of a recruitment interview and used sensibly with other factors.

This was expected to produce a tangible payoff by reducing the 'high risk' recruits. An individual leaving the company was estimated to have cost about $800 in recruitment and training. With an overall turnover of 25% and a labour force of 4000, turnover was costing about $800 000 per annum. Reducing overall turnover to 20%, even ignoring the expansion program should therefore save about $160 000 per annum. This seemed a useful by-product of the simulation exercise.

11.2.9 The value of the exercise to Dynastat

As in the ASL case, the modelling was not very sophisticated and yet the benefits were high. The models were deliberately constructed in a parsimonious way. For example, the initial simple model of Figure 11.11 served to focus discussion on the leaving rates. This had not previously been a great concern to the company. Producing the results of Figure 11.14 led the management to give serious consideration to ways of reducing the turnover of 'new' employees. Indeed, the idea of 'new' and 'established' workers entered the everyday vocabulary of the managers concerned. That is, they began to think about the problem in new ways.

A further advantage stemmed from the apparently unscientific way in which much of the model was parameterized. Despite much data analysis, many parameters could only be estimated by using the judgements of experienced managers who would have to operate the new policies. Because of their close involvement with the model, no solution had to be 'sold' to them. Thus implementation was simply never at issue. Because simulation models, whether discrete or system dynamics, should be built in stages and can be shown as simple flow diagrams, this sort of commitment is possible. In this sense, simulation is not a last resort.

11.3 SYSTEM DYNAMICS IN PRACTICE

The ASL and Dynastat cases have been included for two reasons. Firstly, they were successful exercises which led to distinct improvements within the organizations. Secondly, they illustrate important features of the use of system dynamics and of other simulation methods. These features are discussed below.

11.3.1 Simple models

Simplicity is not a virtue in itself, for over-simplification can clearly be disastrous. However, most analysts are beset by the desire to build all-inclusive models which are over-complicated. All management science models are simplifications. If a model could incorporate the full richness of the system being modelled then the model would be an exact replica of the system. This means that it would be just as difficult to control and, possibly, just as expensive to operate. Simplification is not disastrous, it is inevitable. Indeed, given that most management systems are in a constant state of flux, then an analyst would be totally occupied in keeping a replica up to date.

The approximations that make up the model need to be appropriate to the task in hand. Hence, in the Dynastat case, it was possible to consider the skilled workforce as a single homogeneous body. This was clearly a simplification because not all the men and women would be equally skilled or equally productive. However, the model was not intended to reflect these individual differences, it was built to assess whether a sufficiently large labour force would be available to support an expansion plan. Given that the plan did not specify the precise set of skills required of the workforce and given that this was thought to be sensible, the model incorporated an appropriate level of complexity.

Chapter 2 has already discussed the 'principle of parsimony'. It suggests the development of models which are initially simple and include only the grosser, structural features of the system. Refinements are made as and when necessary, though the overall structure remains unchanged.

11.3.2 Communication

Given that most management scientists operate in consulting roles to managers, their methods need to be appropriate to that role. A consultant who maintains little or no contact with the client group is unlikely to make much impact. Discrete simulation and system dynamics offer great opportunities for the type of communication which leads to implementation. The secret lies in the use of flow diagrams, parsimonious models and graphical output.

Flow diagrams, whether activity cycles or influence diagrams, are simple to understand. Hence the management science model need not remain a completely black box to the client. By the sensible use of diagrams, the main structural features can be displayed enabling the client to agree to them before detailed programming occurs. As the models are successively enhanced, much of this can also be displayed on the diagram. The Dynastat case illustrates this very clearly. The personnel manager had not thought to focus much attention on the question of the rate at which new recruits left the company. The flow diagrams showed the importance of this point and led to its incorporation in the study.

A further refinement mentioned in Chapter 5 is to add animated graphical output on a TV or VDU as the programs run. This adds movement to the simplicity of the flow diagrams. Thus the client is able to gain a stronger impression of how the model shapes up to the real system.

11.3.3 New thinking

This follows from the good communication produced by a simple approach to modelling. As an example, consider Dynastat, who gained three new insights from the system dynamics study. The first, as mentioned in Section 11.3.2, was the realization that keeping workers at Dynastat was as important as recruiting them in the first place. With hindsight, this does seem rather obvious, but in the hectic time following the announcement of the expansion plan other aspects pre-occupied the managers concerned.

The second insight was the distinction drawn between new and established staff. The analysis of labour turnover figures clearly revealed the existence of these two groups of workers. Obviously, the consideration of only two groups was a simplification — yet it provided enough reality to enable the managers to control their system more effectively.

The third insight stemmed from the second. It was the realization, again after data analysis, that certain types of recruit were more likely than others to leave Dynastat not long after joining the company. This led to the development of a simple screening procedure which identified the 'at risk' applicants. This again changed the managers' thinking about their recruitment practices.

11.3.4 Evolutionary involvement

Sometimes the client group may be able to specify exactly what they require of the analyst. Occasionally they are correct. More often, the call for help stems from a feeling that some improvement must be possible. In these cases, the modelling can only be exploratory at first. A feature of such exploration is the asking of sensible questions, 'what if we try to …?' From the answers to these questions comes the development of issues which require detailed research. This exploration approach to problem structuring (Pidd and Woolley, 1980) is well illustrated in the ASL case. Here the successive development of different models for the various sectors of the company led to more detailed questions being asked. Thus system dynamics modelling led on to the detailed program of work described in Section 11.1.7

REFERENCE

Pidd, M., & Woolley, R. N. (1980) A pilot study of problem structuring. *Jnl Opl Res. Soc.*, **31**, 1063–1068.

Name Index

Subject Index